Interstate Conflicts and the International Civil Aviation Organization

This book investigates the International Civil Aviation Organization (ICAO) and politicized debates held there. The author explores how participants have employed depoliticization as a defensive diplomatic technique in a multilateral forum. Analyzing cases such as the ICAO membership/statehood of Spain, Taiwan, Cyprus, and South Africa; various instances of the Arab–Israeli conflict; shootdowns of the Korean aircraft by the USSR and Iranian aircraft by the United States; and the 21st century tensions between Russia and Western countries, the book focuses on how states under criticism defended themselves and used depoliticization rhetoric to weaken ICAO decisions. The book allows us to see how rivalries play out in a different environment to more investigated cases in the UN and INGOs such as the International Olympic Committee. This broad scope will appeal to scholars and students of international relations and political science, the Cold War, the Sino–Taiwanese conflict and the Arab–Israeli conflict. It will also appeal to practitioners working in civil aviation.

Michał M. Kobierecki is an associate professor of political science at the University of Lodz, Poland. He has over 50 scientific publications, including two books, one of which is published in English. He spent his whole research career working on international relations, with a specific emphasis on politics and sport.

Global Institutions

Edited by Thomas G. Weiss, *The CUNY Graduate Center, New York, USA* and Rorden Wilkinson, *University of New South Wales, Sydney, Australia*

About the series

The "Global Institutions Series" provides cutting-edge books about many aspects of what we know as "global governance." It emerges from our shared frustrations with the state of available knowledge—electronic and print-wise—for research and teaching. The series is designed as a resource for those interested in exploring issues of international organization and global governance. And since the first volumes appeared in 2005, we have taken significant strides toward filling many conceptual gaps.

The books in the series also provide a segue to the foundation volume that offers the most comprehensive textbook treatment available dealing with all the major issues, approaches, institutions, and actors in contemporary global governance. The second edition of our edited work *International Organization and Global Governance* (2018) contains essays by many of the authors in the series.

Understanding global governance—past, present, and future—is far from a finished journey. The books in this series nonetheless represent significant steps toward a better way of conceiving contemporary problems and issues as well as, hopefully, doing something to improve world order. We value the feedback from our readers and their role in helping shape the on-going development of the series.

A complete list of titles can be viewed online here: www.routledge.com/Global-Institutions/book-series/GI

United Nations Sanctions Regimes and Selective Security
Thomas Kruiper

Global Health Governance (2nd Edition)
Sophie Harman and Andres Papamichail

Interstate Conflicts and the International Civil Aviation Organization
Depoliticization in Multilateral Diplomacy
Michał M. Kobierecki

Interstate Conflicts and the International Civil Aviation Organization

Depoliticization in Multilateral Diplomacy

Michał M. Kobierecki

Routledge
Taylor & Francis Group
LONDON AND NEW YORK

First published 2025
by Routledge
4 Park Square, Milton Park, Abingdon, Oxon OX14 4RN

and by Routledge
605 Third Avenue, New York, NY 10158

Routledge is an imprint of the Taylor & Francis Group, an informa business

British Library Cataloguing-in-Publication Data
A catalogue record for this book is available from the British Library

ISBN: 9781032695365 (hbk)
ISBN: 9781032695389 (pbk)
ISBN: 9781032695402 (ebk)

DOI: 10.4324/9781032695402

Typeset in Times New Roman
by Newgen Publishing UK

Contents

Figures

Tables

Acknowledgments

The author would like to thank the authorities of the Faculty of International and Political Studies of the University of Lodz for the funding that allowed the realization of the research, in particular to prof. Ryszard Machnikowski, Faculty's Dean, and prof. Andrzej Dubicki, head of the Department of Political Theory and Thought. The research would not have been feasible without the invaluable assistance of the staff at the International Civil Aviation Organization. Despite their considerable workload, they generously accommodated the researcher at the ICAO headquarters in Montreal and facilitated access to essential documents. Special acknowledgment is extended to Mr. Krzysztof Kędzierski, International Cooperation Officer at the European Aviation Safety Agency, for his invaluable help, advice, and assistance in acquiring the most recent documents. The author would like to thank Piotr Strożek and Paweł Stępień for their valuable advice. Lastly, the author wishes to express gratitude to family: wife Anna, son Juliusz, daughter, Oliwia, and parents, Katarzyna and Bogdan, for their patience and for shouldering some of the family responsibilities during the work on the book. Anna deserves particular credit for being a supportive wife and a critical reviewer.

Acronyms

ACC	Area Control Centre
ANC	Air Navigation Commission
ATC	Air Transport Committee
ATS	Air Traffic Service
CORSIA	Carbon Offsetting and Reduction Scheme for International Aviation
EC	Executive Committee
EU	European Union
EUROCONTROL	European Organisation for the Safety of Air Navigation
FAO	Food and Agriculture Organization
FFIT	Fact-Finding Investigation Team
FIR	Flight Information Region
IAEA	International Atomic Energy Association
IATA	International Air Transport Association
ICAO	International Civil Aviation Organization
ICCAIA	International Coordinating Council of Aerospace Industries Associations
IFALPA	International Federation of Air Line Pilots' Associations
IGO	intergovernmental organization
ILO	International Labour Organization
IMF	International Monetary Fund
INGO	international non-governmental organization
IO	international organization
IOC	International Olympic Committee
IR	international relations
MLS	microwave landing systems
NATO	North Atlantic Treaty Organization
NGO	non-governmental organization
NOTAM	Notice to Airmen
PANS	Procedures for Air Navigation Services
PICAO	Provisional International Civil Aviation Organization

PLO	Palestine Liberation Organization
SARPs	Standards and Recommended Practices
UN	United Nations
UN GA	United Nations General Assembly
UN SC	United Nations Security Council
UNESCO	United Nations Educational, Scientific and Cultural Organization
US	United States
USAP	Universal Security Audit Programme
USSR	Union of Soviet Socialist Republics
WHO	World Health Organization

Introduction

Intergovernmental organizations (IGOs) are inherently embedded in the world of international politics. Established out of the need to create a permanent forum for interstate relations, from the beginning, they have served states as a place where they can realize their foreign policy goals.[1] The development of the multilateral system led to the growth of the number of international organizations (IOs) and the scope of their interest and specialization, which stemmed from the increased complexities of modern international relations (IR) and the increased interdependence. Political organizations prevailed but were supplemented with numerous specialized organizations focusing on a limited scope of international reality. Specialized IOs dealt with such areas as health, telecommunication, meteorology, or aviation, each of which went beyond a nation-state's boundaries and thus required some degree of international cooperation. On a declaratory level, their focus is thus on non-political, often technical issues. However, even non-political areas can easily fall victim to political tensions and power struggles, an assumption even more evident if bodies composed of nation-states with often contradictory interests are considered.

Most specialized IGOs attempt to distance themselves from politics. They try to focus on non-political aspects or at least pretend to do so. As Louis and Maertens observed, IGOs tend to 'do politics' while 'pretending to be outside or above the political realm.'[2] The assumption about the discrepancy between the declaratory non-political character of IGOs and their actual political character serves as the foundational assumption for this volume. If an IGO is supposed to be separated from politics, arguments about the political character of claims one opposes or about the non-political character of claims one attempts to introduce appear as a potentially convenient tool for pursuing foreign policy goals in a multilateral environment.

Politics may be understood in multiple ways. For the purpose of this study, we have employed Aaron Wildavsky's approach, which regards politics 'as conflict over whose preferences are to prevail in the determination of policy.'[3] Politics understood this way is perceived as a category of conflict, regarded as a contradiction of interests, both in the context of waging conflicts and attempting to solve them. Contradictory interests between states, unavoidable in an international forum, may thus inject politics into IOs easily, on multiple levels, and in regard

DOI: 10.4324/9781032695402-1

to multiple issues. State representatives, even when the specialized character of specific IGO requires expert knowledge in a respective field, are first and foremost diplomats with the primary goal of promoting national interests. At the same time, decisions and actions of IGOs may become subject to pressure from the outside.[4] Such a broad understanding of politics, however, may also be problematic, widening the scope of the study of the politicization of IOs. For this reason, while approving the conflictual approach to politics, we have followed the understanding of the politicization of IOs proposed by Lyons et al., who defined it as situations in which 'highly controversial issues not always relevant to the agencies' work are introduced by nations to further their political interests.'[5]

Politics is present in all sorts of specialized IOs. Some, such as the United Nations Educational, Scientific and Cultural Organization (UNESCO) and International Labour Organization (ILO), are believed to be more prone to politicization. Others, such as the International Monetary Fund (IMF) and International Atomic Energy Association (IAEA), are believed to be less politicized,[6] but virtually any, under certain circumstances, may become a forum for political tensions. This has also been true for the International Civil Aviation Organization (ICAO), one of the United Nations (UN) specialized agencies, which serves as a subject for the research presented in this volume. ICAO's key aims include developing the principles and techniques of international navigation and fostering the planning and development of aviation,[7] as well as achieving sustainable growth of global civil aviation and serving as a global forum of states for international civil aviation.[8] The profoundly technical character of international aviation, combined with the limited powers ICAO enjoys compared to other IOs, theoretically makes it a potentially less politicized IGO. Still, as demonstrated throughout the empirical chapters, politics often found its way to ICAO. Most often, deliberations with political overtones stemmed from international conflicts and estrangements that were waged in multiple areas and on multiple forums, including those that theoretically should not be politicized. Such deliberations, in principle, reflected other UN proceedings on sensitive matters of IR, though not always. In such instances, ICAO was becoming a venue for attacking political opponents, sometimes in reference to actual misconduct in the field of international aviation, sometimes because state representatives attempted to leverage any possible occasion to hit political adversaries.

Situations when political conflicts are waged on the forum of an IGO are usually connected to criticism of one side against another. Such attacks may be verbal and limited to critical rhetoric against another country or may be connected to actual decisions expected from the organization, such as expulsion or condemnation. Since any action leads to a reaction, an attack against a state or a group of states on the forum of an IO naturally leads to defense, performed either by representatives of the state being attacked or by representatives of states sympathetic toward the attacked ones. The playbook of multilateral diplomacy features multiple techniques and strategies. Defensively, state representatives might, for example, hit back by underlining the offenses committed by the attacking side (the party criticizing it on a given forum) or highlighting lack of evidence. On the forum of a declaratively technical organization, a frequent argument in such situations refers to the political character of an issue as unfit for the organization. Such defensive depoliticization as a diplomatic tactic, which focuses on direct argumentation that an issue should not be discussed, a decision should not be made, or a document should not be phrased in a certain way because of its political character, is the main subject of this book.

The book addresses international conflicts that resulted in diplomatic standoffs on the forum of ICAO, including such cases as the membership/statehood of Spain, Taiwan, Cyprus, and South Africa, various instances of the Arab–Israeli conflict (regarding difficulties in access to aviation services, attacks on airports or other targets, shootdowns and interceptions of civil aircraft, the status of Jerusalem airport, the observer status of the Palestine Liberation Organization), shootdowns of the Korean aircraft by the USSR and the Iranian aircraft by the United States, estrangements between Russia and Western countries resulting from forced landing of a civil aircraft in Minsk and the Russian invasion of Ukraine. It focuses on how states being verbally attacked in the multilateral environment defended themselves, although it also considers arguments used by those attacking their political adversaries and arguments used by representatives of states not directly engaged in respective conflicts. The key research question concerns the arguments used by the delegates (in the case of the ICAO Assembly) and representatives (in the case of the ICAO Council) engaged in political debates held in the ICAO. The main argument is that the participants in these debates have been employing depoliticization rhetoric to defend countries they represent from criticism or verbal attack, claiming that ICAO was a technical organization and political issues should not be debated there. Thus, implying the political character of the claims raised by their opponents was supposed to terminate the inconvenient deliberations, avoid the adoption of undesirable decisions, make the phrasing of certain documents less critical, or simply to respond to unfavorable remarks. Such a diplomatic tool for the purpose of this study has been termed 'defensive depoliticization.'

The research of politicized debates waged on the forum of ICAO allowed the study of defensive depoliticization as a diplomatic technique but also allowed a more in-depth analysis of this diplomatic tool. This connects to a more detailed hypothesis, according to which depoliticization is a relatively ineffective tool for avoiding undesirable decisions in a multilateral organization. Apart from that, the study sought to make generalizations regarding depoliticization as a defensive diplomatic tool and, more generally, regarding politicized disputes on the forum of specialized IOs. Among other things, defensive depoliticization has been considered a 'last resort' tool, particularly useful if more substantial arguments are unavailable or if it is used together with other tools. The study also focused on the perception of politics in IOs based on the statements of representatives, delegates, and members of the organization's bureaucracy. Thus, according to the second detailed hypothesis, a negative perception of politics served as a foundational assumption for the defensive use of depoliticization, which corresponds with the functional theory discussed below.

The most crucial theoretical notions the book builds on are the already mentioned politicization and depoliticization in IOs, though applied predominantly to study diplomatic conduct in multilateral environments. We have adopted an understanding of politicization of IOs as transferring political issues, such as inter-state conflicts, into the originally non-political forums as a result of the behavior of states seeking to further their political interests, particularly in the context of inter-state conflicts. In this sense, we have referred to the definition proposed by Lyons et al., who defined politicization of IOs as situations in which 'highly controversial issues not always relevant to the agencies' work are introduced by nations to further their political interests.'[9] As a result, controversial issues featuring mutual accusations and confrontational language on the ICAO forum, if connected with international political conflicts and estrangements, were considered adequate for the analysis.

The second crucial theoretical concept employed in the study is depoliticization, understood as a reversed process toward politicization. As Colin Hay put it, politicization and depoliticization are analogous, though in reversed directions.[10] Depoliticization is performed in IOs to 'silence the political character of IO action' in order to help IOs fulfill their tasks and conceal their engagement in politics.[11] There are various types of depoliticization of IOs. For example, Flinders and Buller distinguished institutional depoliticization, rule-based depoliticization, and depoliticization through preference-shaping and agenda-setting,[12] all focusing on different methods of putting politics away from the IO, although the focus here is more on protecting the organization and increasing its effectiveness.

Depoliticization of IOs, as described above, has been observed on many occasions within the empirical part of this research and is reflected in the dependent variable dedicated to neutral depoliticization meaning one employed to protect the organization from politicization rather than the criticized state from the criticism. However, to cover the use of depoliticization rhetoric for defensive purposes, we have proposed an additional notion of defensive depoliticization considered a diplomatic technique, understood here as argumentation that certain issues are political and should not be discussed on the forum of a technical organization such as ICAO, for the purpose of defending particular states from verbal attacks and ostracism, which are often though not always based on political rationale. Just as depoliticization in general terms, defensive depoliticization does not aim to move politics away. In fact, it often features political claims itself. As a diplomatic tool, besides for defensive purposes, depoliticization rhetoric can also be used in a neutral manner, and offensively, the last case exemplified by an argument that not condemning a state or behavior would mean favoring one of the sides of a political standoff. This implies that from a diplomatic context, in multilateral bodies we can speak of defensive, neutral, and offensive depoliticization. Although all three have been observed throughout the study, our focus is on defensive depoliticization. Out of the existing theoretical approaches to depoliticization, defensive depoliticization is most similar to discursive depoliticization, which focuses on the tools used to close down political debates. Instead of focusing on arenas, institutions, or actors, discursive depoliticization focuses on ideas and language,[13] although throughout the study, discursive depoliticization was also visible in some states' attempts to initiate political debates. Details on different types of depoliticization will be discussed in detail in Chapter 2.

The theoretical framework of the research is associated with the perception of IOs as forums for diplomatic processes. It connects with the distinction concerning the roles of IOs in IR, politics, and diplomacy. According to Karns and Mingst, IOs, and in particular international IGOs, have become major arenas for diplomacy and decision-making but also belong to diplomatic actors engaging in diplomatic activities.[14] Still, it needs to be underlined that it is not the only way of perceiving the roles of IOs. According to Archer, IOs' major roles include instrument, arena, and actor. In the first case, IOs are considered instruments used by their members for particular ends. Such goals usually concern realizing foreign policy objectives. The second role refers to the IO being an arena, or forum, within which action takes place, providing a meeting place for members. Finally, the third role refers to IOs as independent actors, although according to Archer, few fulfill the criterion of independence fully, arguing that we should speak of autonomous rather than independent IOs.[15] The roles of IOs have been somewhat similarly discussed by Hurd, according to whom IOs can operate as actors, forums, resources, or their combinations. That means each IO is capable of taking action in its own right (actor), is a location where actors such as states come to discuss, debate, and decide (forum), and is a kind of resource which states and other actors can use to advance their political agendas (resource).[16] It is fairly similar when IOs' activity in the area of diplomacy is considered. According to Pigman, from such a perspective, IOs can act as diplomatic venues, diplomatic actors, or both.[17]

Out of the three roles IOs play in IR, their role as forums is particularly crucial from the perspective of this study, although in many of the analyzed cases, we could also recognize attempts to use them as instruments or resource. According to Hurd, IOs are places in space and time, and part of their utility is to act as 'meeting places where states discuss interests and problems of mutual concern.'[18] IOs thus provide experienced logistical support for large international meetings. Most of them also have plenary bodies with representatives of all the members, with the purpose of general deliberations about the organization's work. Such plenary bodies have a legitimizing effect on the IO and can facilitate negotiations among members.[19]

The perception of IOs as forums for interstate diplomacy stems from the origins of IOs. The beginning of diplomacy in IOs can be attributed to its evolution since the 19th century. Groups of nation-states began to negotiate institutional arrangements in which they pooled elements of their sovereignty to achieve shared objectives, for example, concerning communication (establishment of the International Telegraph Union in 1865), trade (the Brussels Sugar Convention of 1902), security (the Versailles Treaty of 1919). These occurrences are connected to the development of the idea of international society, while the new institutions were becoming the venues allowing governments of nation-states to pursue diplomacy.[20] It is also connected to the fact that certain international problems had to be dealt with on a permanent basis.[21] Thus, IOs are commonly referred to as standing diplomatic conferences. Their advantages include permitting the initial breakthroughs to be consolidated, keeping the problems under constant surveillance, encouraging the accumulation of specialized knowledge, signaling commitment, and providing technical assistance to states, all without the problems typical for ad hoc conferences.[22]

The emergence of IOs as diplomatic forums is also connected to another trend in international diplomacy. Contemporary diplomacy no longer implies functional equality of nations, with smaller states, though formally equal, being unable to perform many diplomatic functions. This trend, however, has been mitigated by the rise of the role of IOs understood as venues for diplomacy. Smaller and poorer states devote their diplomatic resources to the activity with and through major international or regional organizations. Such venues serve as forums for diplomatic business and locations for the necessary bilateral diplomacy.[23] The fact that, on the forum of IOs, there is a place for both multilateral and bilateral diplomacy was also noted by Muldoon, who argued that acting on the forum of an IO is, in principle, about multilateral diplomacy, but bilateral diplomacy is also important. Much of the activity in the UN and other organizations is bilateral, with diplomats conducting bilateral discussions with certain countries before the multilateral meetings which are to consider, discuss, and negotiate such issues.[24] Perception of IOs as forums for pursuing IR and diplomacy by states and other actors makes IOs convenient places where IR and diplomatic actors may seek solutions to international problems. However, as argued throughout the book, they may also seek to hit political adversaries and ostracize them.

Several IR theories explicitly have been dealing with IOs in general and specifically with the diplomacy taking place on their forum. Providing arenas for solving practical problems has been argued by liberal institutionalism and functionalism.[25] The latter paradigm has been particularly influential in conceptualizing the IOs' need to stay away from politics, the central argument of depoliticization. Functionalism in IR, according to Mitrany, stems from the idea that a technical approach to international political problems could promote peace 'by neutralizing the politicization' and 'organizing interdependence.'[26] As Mitrany stated, 'co-operation for the common good is the task, both for the sake of peace and of a better life, and for that it is essential that certain interests and activities should be taken out of the mood of competition and worked together.'[27] According to Haas, functionalists 'believe in the possibility of specifying technical and "non-controversial" aspects of governmental conduct, and of weaving an ever-spreading web of international institutional relationships on the basis of meeting' human needs and desires. International institutional relationships are supposed to meet the needs existing outside of the political realm, while their function is an equivalent of an 'organizational task,' for example, the function of the Food and Agriculture Organization (FAO) is to increase the production of food and its supply.[28] The function of IOs is thus to realize their statutory objectives, such as improving the safety and development of international civil aviation in the case of ICAO.

The depoliticizing argument is consistent with the concept of functionalism, with clearly pejorative connotations of 'politicization.'[29] Deliberations in ICAO analyzed throughout this volume revealed multiple situations when politics was described in an unequivocally pejorative way, as something odd in the technical organization, which does nothing else than undermine its credibility and neutrality, impairing the effectiveness of realizing its functions. Such statements correspond with the functional approach, although they do not necessarily reflect the reality of the functioning of such organizations. This, in turn, corresponds with the criticism that the functionalist approach to IOs encountered. Critics claimed functional opposition between 'good' technicians and 'bad' politicians reflected wishful rather than scientific thinking.[30] That problem is also visible in this study, with its focus on depoliticization used as a diplomatic tool to defend oneself from criticism and ostracism on the forum of IOs. Within deliberations leading to such use of depoliticization, states have been attacking their political adversaries in essence to realize their interests. These were also state interests that led their representatives to defend their states, also with the use of depoliticization. The functional depoliticization argument thus appeared not to reflect a genuine will to protect ICAO from politicization but a selfish will to avoid criticism and ostracism. Situations when states utilize IOs to further their national interests are more typical for the realist paradigm, which perceives IOs as instruments of state policy.[31] It should be noted, though, that politicized deliberations in ICAO were not particularly common compared to the general scope of its activity and agenda, oriented predominantly at the realization of its statutory objectives or functions. However, instances of politicization, though relatively rare, still occur. Functionalism perceives the politicization of functional institutions, in principle, as an organizational defect. Proponents of such an approach perceive such politicization as the result of '"irresponsible states" (…) disturbing the purposes of a specialized agency by attempting to place inappropriate controversial items on the agenda,'[32] an expression surprisingly often used by those employing the depoliticization rhetoric on the forum of ICAO. Apart from that, politicization of IOs may be explained as an indicator of trends in the international system or a bargaining tactic.[33] Each of the three justifications has merit and resonates with the results of this study. Still, in accordance with the functional approach, we have assumed states' attempts to wage political conflicts with each other on the forum of specialized agency as an organizational defect, one that many neutral participants in the deliberations sought to correct, on which those defending their states sought to capitalize through the depoliticization argument. Still, it should not be forgotten that the politicized debates, to some extent, reflected the realist pursuit for the realization of foreign policy objectives by the states engaged in the conflicts waged on the forum of an IO.

Defensive depoliticization as a research subject has not been dedicated substantial interest by scholars representing such fields as IR, diplomatic studies, or political science, even though, as demonstrated by the example of ICAO throughout this volume, it has been employed by state representatives on many occasions. Most publications dealing with depoliticization consider it from a different perspective. Depoliticization as a research subject has been explored most intensively since the 2000s. In its first generation, depoliticization literature focused on depoliticization as a mode of statecraft, that is, the tools used by politicians to make certain areas appear non-political so that the governments would not be held responsible for the failures in these areas.[34] The most influential authors of this strand of literature include Burnham,[35] Flinders, and Buller.[36] In the late 2000s and 2010s, the scope of analysis of depoliticization was generally widened beyond the state and referred to rhetorical strategies employed by various social actors aiming to close down 'the appearance of an issue as being political,'[37] a strand represented, for example, by Wood and Flinders.[38] Although the majority of studies of depoliticization focused on the domestic dimension of the process, authors such as Petiteville,[39] Louis, and Maertens[40] undertook depoliticization in reference to IOs, although their focus was similar to the studies of domestic depoliticization, that is, as a tool of increasing the effectiveness of these organizations and the working of depoliticization in practice. In general, though, research on depoliticization from the perspective of IR remains limited.

This volume builds extensively on the findings of the authors mentioned above, but it stands out for its approach to depoliticization from a novel perspective, not as a form of improving the efficiency of an IGO through distancing it from politics but as a diplomatic tool. Such an approach places this volume in the literature strand dedicated to depoliticization but also as part of the diplomatic studies since defensive depoliticization is, first and foremost, a diplomatic tactic. Thus, the novelty of the book lies in its theoretical contribution. The issues of depoliticization and diplomacy in the multilateral environment have received substantial attention from scholars, but there were no studies dedicated to depoliticization as a diplomatic tactic. This book's ambition is to fill this void and open a scientific debate about the issue, as arguments derived from the research could further be studied in reference to other IGOs and non-governmental organizations.

Besides contributing to the scholarly literature on depoliticization and diplomacy, this book contributes to the literature on the history of the International Civil Aviation Organization through its subject and owing to extensive use of archival documents. Unlike many other UN agencies, ICAO has not been dedicated particular attention of scholars. Publications focusing on ICAO have been rare, whereas studies on processes occurring in various IGOs often overlook ICAO. Still, several books dedicated to ICAO have been published. The most crucial publications include Eugene Sochor's *The Politics of International Aviation*, which attempted to analyze its evolution as a political body,[41] and *ICAO: A History of the International Civil Aviation Organization* by David MacKenzie, which, among other things, focused on the organization as a forum for international disputes.[42] Although both books referred to international conflicts waged on the ICAO forum, neither focused on the diplomatic tactics the member state representatives employed during such debates. Other crucial monographs dedicated to ICAO include Alan Dobson's *A History of International Civil Aviation*, which focuses on the general history of civil aviation but not necessarily on the political aspects,[43] and Ludwig Weber's *International Civil Aviation Organization (ICAO)*, which analyzes the structure, competence, and management of the ICAO and is dedicated in principle to the students of international law.[44] Apart from that, political aspects of international civil aviation were also undertaken by Betsy Gidwitz in *The Politics of International Transport*, but ICAO was dealt with only marginally.[45] Out of these monographs, this volume is most similar in subject to Sochor's *The Politics of International Aviation.* Sochor argued that ICAO is a political body despite its founders' expectations and discussed issues such as the international aviation system, the technical evolution of air transport, problems connected to aviation in the developing world, terrorist threats, international conflicts, or air safety. This volume adopted Sochor's argument about the political nature of ICAO but focused on the strategies for waging political conflicts on the ICAO forum. In this case, ICAO provides a ground for studying depoliticization as a diplomatic tactic in a multilateral organization, arguing that state representatives used the organization's technical character to dismiss inconvenient debates. Besides that, the book refers to some developments in the history of ICAO not published elsewhere, such as the recent conflict between Russia and Western countries.

The research has been performed through qualitative content analysis of the ICAO archival documents, specifically using structuring content analysis since the criteria for the study have been determined in advance.[46] Individual statements of certain state representatives and complex debates were studied in search of references to politics and claims that the ICAO as a technical organization was not a proper forum for such issues. Particular attention was dedicated to the situations when international conflicts were more or less directly debated on the forum of ICAO, although depoliticization practices were also emerging from simple statements by the delegations' chairs. The content of ICAO documents was analyzed in search of the language of depoliticization used by delegates/representatives of particular countries. Such language was recognized based on references to 'politics' and 'political' in relation to issues under discussion or to 'technical' regarding the limitation of the jurisdiction of ICAO. In particular, we searched typical textual passages: formulations that questions under discussion were 'political,' not adequate for the technical ICAO or more adequate for other (political) forums, calls to focus on the technical/economic/aviation aspects of the discussed matters, formulations about ICAO's limited jurisdiction, accusations of bringing political issues before ICAO. Statements featuring such depoliticizing language were then coded based on their context, whether they had defensive character oriented at terminating the inconvenient discussion or softening the critical resolutions, or had a more genuine goal of keeping the ICAO focused on technical matters – the latter obviously were not considered defensive depoliticization but rather as expressions of depoliticization in general terms, although it has to be acknowledged that such potentially neutral statements could well have meant to defend, though in a more concealed way. The coding was based on the content and tone of statements.

The analysis allowed the identification of 46 politicized deliberations in ICAO which featured defensive depoliticization, relating to 15 controversies and 7 conflicts. The numbers differ because some conflicts led to politicized debates during a single ICAO meeting, while others were waged several times, and several conflicts concerned more than one controversy. In order to provide additional generalizations regarding defensive depoliticization, instances of political controversies were further investigated with regard to three independent and three dependent variables. Independent variables used in this part of the study included the political bloc of the defending country, the power status of the defending country, and whether the controversy was related to aviation-related misconduct. The introduction of the variable of the political bloc of the defending country was connected with the fact that it is usually easier to defend oneself if allies are willing to vote in one's favor. In the study, the following blocs were used: Western (Taiwan, Turkey, Israel, United States), Arab states (specifically Egypt and Lebanon but some criticism was more generally targeting the Arab countries), and Russian (Russia, Soviet Union, Belarus). The remaining countries defending themselves were coded as Other (in reference to Spain after World War II, South Africa, and Cyprus) and constitute a sort of a control group in regard to political blocs. Belonging to a particular political bloc was based on military and political alliances and other forms of close collaboration. Defending countries were further assigned based on their power status according to the Global Power Index (GPI) according to Frederick S. Pardee Center for International Futures calculation for the year of the controversy in ICAO. We followed the interpretation of Frederick S. Pardee Center for International Futures, according to which world powers have more than nine percent of global power, middle powers possess between two and nine percent of global power, while lesser powers have less than two percent of global power.[47] The variable concerning aviation-related misconduct differentiated situations when the defending state committed a civil aviation offense, such as illegal interception of an aircraft or a shootdown, or the controversy was not directly linked to civil aviation.

Independent variables were then equated with the measures for the three dependent variables: whether defending states were defended by other delegations, whether neutral depoliticization was used, and whether the defense was successful. The variable regarding being defended by other delegations refers to situations when the defending state received or did not receive support from other delegations that spoke in its favor, which presumably should be connected to the political bloc it belonged to and the gravity of the offense since some of them are difficult to be defended by others. The variable regarding neutral depoliticization considers the eventual occurrence of situations when other delegations or representatives argued the need not to engage in political considerations but not with the purpose of defending the attacked state. The last dependent variable concerns the effectiveness of defense, measured based on reaching defensive goals such as avoiding an undesirable decision.

Data necessary for the study were collected through the query of archival documents of the International Civil Aviation Organization. Documents were consulted in several ways. A lot of them are available online on the ICAO's website which was the first channel of accessing them. Unfortunately, many of the documents crucial for the study have not been made public online, making additional forms of data collection necessary. The author consulted some documents during a research visit to the ICAO headquarters in Montreal in July/August 2022. Third, some of the necessary documents not available on ICAO's website have been obtained digitally at request.

The study covered several types of documents. The organizational structure of ICAO required the study of documents of two of its bodies – the Assembly and the Council. Accordingly, the documents produced by these two bodies were investigated, in particular minutes of the plenary sessions of the Assembly and minutes of the Council meetings, supplemented by the minutes of the meetings of the Executive Committee of the Assembly, annual reports of the Council, occasionally working papers and other documents. Minutes of the plenary meetings of the Assembly and reports of the Council served as the primary source of data. If evidence of defensive depoliticization was detected, further documents relating to the issue were consulted. The study concerned documents from the entire history of ICAO, between 1944 and 2023 (the last document available to the author). However, the cases discussed in the empirical chapters do not cover the entire period as they only reflect situations of depoliticization used as a defensive diplomatic tool.

It is important to note that not all instances of politicization of the ICAO proceedings led to the use of depoliticization. The conflicts and estrangements discussed in this book are only a fraction of the conflicts and estrangements that occurred in the analyzed period. Even though not all of them were raised in ICAO, many have been. Besides those included in the study, the analysis of documents allowed the identification of such political controversies as the bombing of PLO headquarters in Tunisia by Israel in 1986, the shooting down of Libyan Boeing 727 over Sinai by Israel in 1973, the war in Yugoslavia, the Iraq–Iran war, the Iraqi invasion of Kuwait, Cuba–US tensions. Controversies such as these are not dealt with in the book because they were either not deliberated in ICAO excessively enough to gather necessary data or did not feature defensive depoliticization.

It is necessary to explain the terminology used in the book. The description of the representatives of the ICAO member states corresponds with the original materials – state representatives in the Assembly were called 'delegates,' while in the Council 'representatives' or 'observers,' according to their actual status. To avoid unnecessary wording, alternate representatives or chief delegates were described simply as representatives/delegates. In the majority of cases, names of the speakers were not mentioned, with references only to specific countries' representatives, observers, delegates, etc. Minutes also featured lists of participants, but only in some cases they would allow explicit identification of the speaker since, on many occasions, there was more than one person occupying similar positions within a delegation. Thus, for the sake of clarity, we use the positions as cited in the sources, while when speaking more generally, we refer to representatives.

The collection of data was subject to several limitations. Firstly, the exact form of certain documents has been changing over the years. For example, some minutes of the Assembly's Plenary meetings included the exact transcripts of statements made by various delegation chairs, while others did not. Furthermore, the format of some documents, Executive Committee minutes in particular, did not allow for a detailed tracing of the deliberations, for example, it did not feature the statements of particular delegations. The availability of digitalized documents varied in different periods. Some of the most valuable documents from the perspective of this research – the Minutes of the Council's meetings – to a large extent are not available online, whereas ICAO currently does not have a dedicated unit dealing with archival documents, making the amount of material that could be obtained on-site limited. All this led to the situation that even though the study concerned the entire history of ICAO, not all periods and meetings have been investigated at the same level of detail. Still, with the research not being focused on the level of politicization or depoliticization but on the attempts to depoliticize as a diplomatic tactic, these limitations did not decisively impact the study, making it possible to realize the research objectives.

Careful readers should note the inconsistent notation of some of the cited documents' titles. It is caused by the inconsistency in how they were titled originally. Generally, we sought to avoid amending the titles of the documents, with the exception of some minutes of the plenary meetings, which in the original notation referred to minutes of a specific meeting without reference to 'plenary,' which was referred to in a subtitle. To avoid unnecessary wording, 'plenary' was added to the title of the document, while the subtitle was ignored.

One of the challenges faced during the study featured coding some statements of state representatives. In particular, this concerned depoliticizing statements of speakers not directly involved in a particular conflict. In some situations, it was difficult to distinguish neutral depoliticization, that is, one seeking to protect the organization from politicization, and defensive depoliticization. After all, the purpose of defensive depoliticization is to utilize the functionalist argument about no place for political conflict on the forum of specialized organizations. Thus, even though in most cases it was clear that such arguments were used simply to defend, based on other arguments or the party (attacked state and its allies), occasionally it was not possible to unequivocally tell whether a statement featured neutral and defensive depoliticization. Moreover, for comparative analysis, it was necessary to simplify some of the observations. For example, when Belarus was subject to criticism after the forced landing of Ryanair Flight 4978, the Russian representatives assumed the defense of its ally, largely because most of the deliberations took place in the Council, where Belarus could only send an observer. Based on this and on the political proximity between the two countries, the controversy was assumed to represent the Russia–West conflict. Similarly, the Soviet Union has been coded as Russia, and the Cold War East–West rivalry as the Russia–West conflict.

The book is composed of six chapters. The first two constitute the theoretical part. Chapter 1, entitled *The ICAO: History, structure, and functioning*, has an explicitly introductory character and aims to familiarize the reader with the organization that serves as the subject of the entire study. Chapter 1 features information about the origins and creation of ICAO, a short description of its structure and functioning, and a section dedicated to its relevance, for example, in reference to its apparent success in improving the safety of international aviation. In turn, Chapter 2 entitled *Politics, politicization, and depoliticization in international organizations* is predominantly theoretical and deals with crucial theoretical concepts the research is built on. The chapter focuses on the interrelated concepts of politicization and depoliticization. In both cases, the chapter features a review of the general understanding of these terms and then moves to the discussion of their relevance to the functioning of IOs. The chapter concludes with a conceptualization of depoliticization as a diplomatic technique.

Chapters 3–6 constitute the empirical part of the book. They deal with several international conflicts and estrangements that resonated in the ICAO. For the sake of clarity of reasoning, empirical chapters have been arranged in a problem-oriented way, although several controversies could have well been assigned to other chapters. Accordingly, Chapters 3 and 5 deal with specific types of controversies: membership issues and shootdowns of civil aircraft, respectively, whereas Chapters 4 and 6 deal with specific international conflicts, that is the Arab–Israeli conflict and the 21st-century Russia–West conflict. Chapter 3, entitled *Conflicts over ICAO membership and members' statehood*, is dedicated to situations when state representatives in ICAO questioned the statehood or membership of other states or demanded their expulsion from ICAO based on their international status or their political offenses. The chapter features four specific controversies. The first one refers to the early Spanish membership in ICAO. Even though Spain was a founding member of ICAO, when the organization was entering into a relationship with the United Nations, it was required to expel Spain as one of the Axis allies. The deliberations were not particularly confrontational but still featured depoliticization rhetoric used to defend Spain from expulsion. The second case concerns Taiwanese membership in ICAO and the verbal argument raised by some representatives that it should be the People's Republic of China, not Taiwan, to be present in ICAO. The third controversy relates to the ICAO membership of South Africa and an attempt by African states to isolate it internationally in response to the apartheid policy. The final controversy of Chapter 4 is dedicated to the conflict between Turkey and Cyprus. This particular case could also be included elsewhere in the book since it encompassed several different critical arguments used by representatives of both countries. Still, since these ICAO deliberations also featured questioning the membership of Cyprus, which according to Turkish delegates, only represented the Greek Cypriot community, thematically, it also fitted to the chapter.

Chapter 4, *The Arab–Israeli conflict in the ICAO*, as suggested in its title, is dedicated to various instances of the conflict between Israel and the Arab states, considered one of the most problematic for the functioning of post-World War II IOs. Six instances of the conflict have been mentioned in the chapter. Firstly, it dealt with Israeli complaints about the aviation-related difficulties caused by its Arab neighbors in the 1950s and the way the representatives of Arab states were responding. The second case under study concerned the Israeli attack on Beirut International Airport in 1968, this time with the Israeli representatives being forced to defend their country, also using defensive depoliticization. The third case concerned the interception of a Lebanese civil aircraft by the Israeli air force in 1973, again forcing Israeli diplomats to defend their country. The fourth case is connected to the airport in Jerusalem, which, according to Arab states, Israel had no right to use because it was located in the occupied Arab territories. Within the fifth case, slightly different from the previous ones, Israel was employing depoliticization rhetoric in an attempt to prevent the Palestine Liberation Organization from receiving the right to participate in ICAO meetings as an observer. The final case is dedicated to the interception of Libyan civil aircraft by Israel in 1986. Apparently, the majority of the cases were about Israel employing defensive depoliticization, usually in reference to actual aviation-related misconduct, but the first case shows that both sides of this political conflict actually used the tool.

Chapter 5, entitled *The political context of shootdowns of civil aircraft*, is the second of the chapters dedicated not to a particular conflict but to a particular controversy, this time the shootdown of civil aircraft. Such occurrences have not been uncommon in civil aviation history, but two such cases sparked particularly heated and politicized deliberations in ICAO, both considered in Chapter 5. The first controversy, at the same time one of the most famous, concerned the shootdown of the Korean Airlines aircraft en route from New York to Seoul in 1983, which fitted within the Cold War East–West rivalry. The tragedy brought a lot of confrontational language to the ICAO, resulting in defensive depoliticization from the Soviet Union and its Communist allies. The second controversy also concerned the United States, but this time as the guilty side, which defended itself using depoliticization after its navy shot down Iranian civil aircraft in 1988, a tragedy which, although occurred under the circumstances of the Iraq–Iran war, was waged in the ICAO within the wider US–Iranian estrangement.

The final Chapter 6, entitled *Tensions between Russia and the West on the forum of ICAO*, is the most up-to-date. Even though the tensions between Russia and Western countries started growing in the 2010s and increased after the annexation of Crimea by Russia in 2014, they only led to politicized debates in the ICAO in the 2020s, in the context of two events, both analyzed in the chapter. Firstly, in 2021, a Ryanair flight was forced to land in Minsk, after which a Belarusian oppositionist and his girlfriend were detained. The second event concerned the Russian invasion of Ukraine with the support of Belarus in February 2022. Even though in the first case Belarus was responsible for the occurrence, those were predominantly the Russian delegates and representatives who defended Belarus. Thus, in both cases, Russia has been assumed to be the main actor employing defensive depoliticization, and both controversies have been interpreted as a manifestation of the Russia–West conflict transformed into the forum of ICAO.

The contribution of the book is twofold. Firstly, its subject has not been dedicated particular attention in the IR scholarship. Few books are devoted to the International Civil Aviation Organization, one of the United Nations agencies, and even fewer consider it from a political perspective. This volume attempts to fill this gap. Secondly and more importantly, the contribution of this book lies in theoretical input. The issues of depoliticization and diplomacy in the multilateral environment have received substantial attention from scholars, but there were no studies dedicated to depoliticization as a diplomatic tactic. Furthermore, the book introduces the notion of defensive depoliticization, a technique in the diplomatic playbook used by state representatives on the forum of functional organizations when being attacked, criticized, or ostracized. We hope the book will initiate a scientific debate concerning the use of depoliticization rhetoric in IOs, with other specialized agencies and influential non-governmental organizations constituting a potential subject for further studies of the arguments presented throughout this volume.

The book is intended primarily for scholars and students of IR and political science. It discusses the history of the ICAO, one of the UN-specialized bodies, which has received relatively little attention from political scientists. As a result, the book is intended to interest IR scholars and students who are interested in IOs. Secondly, the book addresses the issue of depoliticization, which political scientists should find interesting. The book's approach to depoliticization differs slightly from most common perceptions, yet it still fits into the broader meaning of the term. Furthermore, it features cases stemming from important international conflicts. For this reason, the book should be of interest to students of the Cold War, the Sino–Taiwanese conflict, the Arab–Israeli conflict, the US–Iran conflict, or the recent conflict between Russia and Western countries, all leading to heated political debates on the technical forum of the ICAO. Results of the research reported in this volume should allow them to learn about another forum for these rivalries, alongside the most investigated bilateral relations and struggles on the forum of the UN and some INGOs such as the International Olympic Committee. For these reasons, despite the apparent focus on the politics on the ICAO forum, the scope of the book is broad. Naturally, it should be of interest not just to academics and students but also to members of the general public interested in politics, IR, and civil aviation, as well as to the practitioners of diplomacy.

Notes

1 Randall W. Stone, *Controlling Institutions: International Organizations and the Global Economy* (Cambridge: Cambridge University Press, 2011), 2–3.
2 Marieke Louis and Lucile Maertens, *Why International Organizations Hate Politics: Depoliticizing the World* (London: Routledge, 2021), 184.
3 Aaron B. Wildavsky, "Budgeting as a Political Process," in *The International Encyclopedia of the Social Sciences*, ed. David L. Sills (New York: Crowell, Collier, and Macmillan, 1968), 192.
4 See: Franck Petiteville, "International organizations beyond depoliticized governance," *Globalizations* 15, no. 3 (2018): 301–313, https://doi.org/10.1080/14747731.2017.1370850.
5 Gene M. Lyons, David A. Baldwin, and Donald W. McNemar, "The "Politicization" Issue in the UN Specialized Agencies," *Proceedings of the Academy of Political Science* 32, no. 4 (1977): 81.
6 Ibid., 88–89.
7 "Convention on International Civil Aviation." Signed at Chicago on 7 December 1944: 20.
8 "Vision and Mission," *ICAO*, accessed November 20, 2023, https://www.icao.int/about-icao/Council/Pages/vision-and-mission.aspx
9 Lyons, Baldwin, and McNemar, "The "Politicization" Issue," 81.
10 Colin Hay, *Why We Hate Politics* (Cambridge: Polity, 2007), 78–81.
11 Louis and Maertens, *Why International Organizations*, 185.
12 Matthew Flinders and Jim Buller, "Depoliticisation: Principles, Tactics and Tools," *British Politics* 1 (2006): 299, https://doi.org/10.1057/palgrave.bp.4200016

13 See: Matt Wood, and Matthew Flinders, "Rethinking Depoliticisation: Beyond the Governmental," *Policy & Politics* 42 no. 2 (2014): 152, https://doi.org/10.1332/030557312X655909; Matthew Flinders, and Matt Wood, "Discursive Depoliticization and Political Disengagement," in *The Routledge Handbook of Language and Politics*, ed. Ruth Wodak and Bernhard Forchtner (London: Routledge, 2017), 603–617.
14 Margaret P. Karns, and Karen A. Mingst, "International Organizations and Diplomacy," in *The Oxford Handbook of Modern Diplomacy*, ed. Andrew F. Cooper, Jorge Heine, and Ramesh Thakur (Oxford: Oxford University Press, 2013), 142.
15 Clive Archer, *International Organizations* (London: Routledge, 2001), 68–69, 73, 79.
16 Ian Hurd, *International Organizations: Politics, Law, Practice* (Cambridge: Cambridge University Press, 2013), 28.
17 Geoffrey Allen Pigman, *Contemporary Diplomacy: Representation and Communication in a Globalized World* (Cambridge: Polity, 2011), 29.
18 Hurd, *International Organizations*, 30.
19 Ibid., 31.
20 Pigman, *Contemporary Diplomacy*, 22.
21 Juergen Kleiner, "The Inertia of Diplomacy," *Diplomacy and Statecraft* 19, no. 2 (2008): 333, https://doi.org/10.1080/09592290802096380
22 G. R. Berridge, *Diplomacy: Theory and practice* (Basingstoke: Palgrave Macmillan, 2010), 145–147.
23 Pigman, *Contemporary Diplomacy*, 23–24.
24 James P. Muldoon Jr., "Introduction," in *Multilateral diplomacy and the United Nations Today*, ed. James P. Muldoon Jr., Joann Fagot Aviel, Richard Reitano and Earl Sullivan (Routledge: New York, 2005), 7.
25 Karns and Mingst, "International Organizations and Diplomacy," 146.
26 Louis and Maertens, *Why International Organizations*, 6.
27 David Mitrany, *A Working Peace System: An Argument for the Functional Development of International Organization* (Chicago: Quadrangle Book, 1966): 55.
28 Ernst Haas, *Beyond the Nation State. Functionalism and International Organization* (Stanford: Stanford University Press, 1964): 6.
29 Lyons, Baldwin, and McNemar, "The "Politicization" Issue," 85.
30 Louis and Maertens, *Why International Organizations*, 7.
31 Archer, *International Organizations*, 123.
32 Lyons, Baldwin, and McNemar, "The "Politicization" Issue," 86.
33 Ibid., 86–88.
34 Matthew Wood, "Politicisation, depoliticisation and anti-politics: Towards a multilevel research agenda," *Political Studies Review* 14, no. 4 (2016): 522–523, https://doi.org/10.1111/1478-9302.12074
35 Peter Burnham, "New Labour and the Politics of Depoliticisation," *British Journal of Politics and International Relations* 3, no. 2 (2001): 127–149, https://doi.org/10.1111/1467-856X.00054
36 Matthew Flinders and Jim Buller, "Depoliticisation: Principles, Tactics and Tools," *British Politics* 1 (2006): 295–296, https://doi.org/10.1057/palgrave.bp.4200016
37 Wood, "Politicisation, depoliticisation," 524.
38 Wood and Flinders, "Rethinking depoliticization," 152.
39 Petiteville, "International organizations beyond," 302.
40 Louis and Maertens, *Why International Organizations*.
41 Eugene Sochor, *The Politics of International Aviation* (Basingstoke: Macmillan, 1991).

42 David MacKenzie, *ICAO: A History of the International Civil Aviation Organization* (Toronto: University of Toronto Press, 2010).
43 Alan Dobson, *A History of International Aviation: From its Origins through Transformative Evolution* (London: Routledge, 2017).
44 Ludwig Weber, *International Civil Aviation Organization (ICAO)* (Alphen aan den Rijn: Wolters Kluwer, 2023).
45 Betsy Gidwitz, *The Politics of International Air Transport* (Lexington: Lexington Books, 1980).
46 See: Philipp Mayring, "Qualitative Content Analysis," in *A Companion to Qualitative Research*, ed. Uew Flick, Ernst von Kardorff and Ines Steinke (Sage: London, 2004), 269.
47 Jonathan D. Moyer, Alanna Markle, Collin J. Meisel, and Adam Szymanski-Burgos, "Relative National Power Codebook." Diplometrics. Denver, CO: Frederick S. Pardee Institute for International Futures, Josef Korbel School of International Studies, University of Denver, 2024.

1 The ICAO

History, structure, and functioning

International Civil Aviation Organization (ICAO) is one of the United Nations specialized agencies, established alongside many others within the general creation of the post-World War II international order. This introductory chapter aims to introduce the organization, including its history and circumstances behind its foundation, a review of its objectives, organizational structure and decision-making processes, and its predominantly technical character. In this chapter, we will also refer to ICAO's position in the international environment, its relevance regarding international civil aviation, and the organizational and functional reasons for its politicization. The chapter seeks to provide background information that should allow readers to understand better the developments and processes analyzed in the subsequent empirical chapters of the book. The chapter will also attempt to place ICAO within the typology of international organizations and discuss its relevance in international relations (IR), development, and security.

The origins

Aviation is a relatively new invention, yet very rapidly managed to develop on an unprecedented scale and became one of the most crucial means of transport. With its inherently transnational character, the need for international regulation appeared since hot–air balloons first began to cross international borders. This need became even more pressing when aircraft appeared. As a result, the first diplomatic conference to deal with civil aviation was held in Paris in 1910. The main area of debate concerned the dissonance between freedom in the air and national sovereignty over the airspace. Among the main standpoints, Germany and France favored the concept of greater freedom of air travel, while on the other side, the British opted for the concept of state sovereignty over the airspace, arguing that aviation 'could never be divorced from political implications.'[1] The Paris Conference adjourned without having signed a convention, even though delegates agreed on many crucial issues, such as aircraft nationality, aircraft certificates, crew licenses, and the possibility of establishing zones.[2] These early multilateral developments imply the specific character of civil aviation, which is inherently transnational and thus requires

DOI: 10.4324/9781032695402-2

international arrangements, visible even at the stage of the early 20th century when air travel was only in its infancy.

After the end of World War I, the international community once again addressed the issue of regulating international civil aviation. During the Paris Conference of 1919, the so-called Paris Agreement was drafted, proclaiming states' sovereignty over their airspace. Together with the Havana Convention of 1928, which anticipated the concept of freedom in the air, both documents governed international aviation in the mid-war period.[3] The Paris Conference also established the first international organization to deal with civil aviation – the International Commission for Air Navigation (ICAN), a permanent body with headquarters and Secretariat in Paris. ICAN was mandated to oversee, implement, and modify the Paris Convention, settle disputes between members, and collect information and statistics concerning aviation.[4] ICAN was to function under the auspices of the League of Nations, but it was largely autonomous in practice. In principle, it was to cope with the technical matters concerning civil aviation.[5] Importantly, ICAN is believed not to have reached its goals, for instance, because of the lack of universal membership, thus paving the ground for a new post-war aviation organization as most states began to recognize the need for some kind of institutionalization of aviation, although at the time they were not ready to give away control over civil aviation.[6]

The outbreak of World War II not only halted the growth of civil aviation but also led to a reconfiguration of the world power, creating the need to rearrange the international aviation system. Already during the war, international aviation became one of the subjects of post-war planning, with several scenarios being considered concerning the regulation of the system, ranging from resuming the pre-war system based on sovereignty over air space, through the opening of the skies via first and second air freedoms,[7] to the ideas to combine the second option with the bilateral exchange of commercial flights, multilateral commercial agreement, or the creation of an internationally owned airline which would monopolize international services.[8] The primary focus of consideration revolved around the economic aspect of the expanding civil aviation sector. The principal point of contention laid in the contrast between a heightened emphasis on state sovereignty over airspace and a more internationalist approach advocating for the liberalization of airspaces, thus continuing the very first deliberations from the early 20th century.

Multilateral negotiations on international aviation were most intense during the post-war system's establishment. The key role should be associated with the Chicago Conference of 1944. The concept of organizing the aviation conference was connected to the belief shared by the Americans, British, and Canadians that the war would end with a victory and that civil aviation would play an important role in the post-war restoration. However, besides this common belief and the wartime alliance, all these countries had their own, sometimes contradictory interests.[9] The discussions between the three countries, as well as internal debates in each of them, were held throughout 1944, although the key deliberations were conducted by the Americans and the British, with the first opting for 'freedom in the air,' the latter preferring 'order in the air.' The consensus stipulated organizing an international conference.[10]

The US government undertook the final initiative to organize an aviation conference, seeking to remove the obstacles in the international aviation system stemming from American companies' interests, political and security issues.[11] Accordingly, the American government issued invitations to the conference to 55 states, of which 54 sent delegations.[12] Like in the case of other post-war conferences and organizations, Germany and Japan were not invited. Of those invited, only Saudi Arabia and the Soviet Union did not send their representatives.[13] Saudi Arabia did not accept the invitation at all, whereas the Soviet Union accepted it and sent a delegation but refused to attend at the last moment because of the participation of Switzerland, Portugal, and Spain, which have presented a policy hostile to the Soviet Union.[14] During the conference, delegates were to discuss the economic reality of post-war civil aviation and establish a new international organization that would oversee civil aviation.

Chicago Conference was one of the largest international conferences held until then, with 955 participants, including 185 delegates, 156 advisors, and 306 members of the conference Secretariat.[15] Before it began, it was clear it would be shaped by the 'classic power struggle,' with the US capitalizing on its dominant position in civil aviation, while the British – on having overseas connecting – points in the colonies and in the Commonwealth.[16] The deliberations centered around the differences of interests, which were visible before the conference even started. In principle, the Americans opted for state sovereignty over airspace and the right for innocent passage for the members, while commercial rights were to be negotiated bilaterally. According to the American position, the international organization was to have limited power and focus on administrative functions. In most areas, the American standpoint was backed by Latin American states, though they opposed the idea that major powers should dominate the executive of future organization. The British idea for post-war aviation was different. They argued that it should prevent the blocking of transit rights, fierce competition, and heavy subsidization of national airlines. Britain called for a powerful organization to be established to manage civil aviation, enable the exchange of the first four freedoms, and set frequencies and rates.[17] Other ideas for post-war aviation included one proposed by the delegate from New Zealand, who opted to create a global airline instead of allowing national or commercial rivalries. Such an airline should be owned and controlled internationally by a body attached to the United Nations. This position was backed by Australia.[18] Both countries agreed upon a joint proposition in Canberra already before the conference, even though they were aware it was unacceptable to some countries. The fourth main proposal, presented by Canada, is perceived as an attempt to compromise the British and the Americans. It assumed strong international organization, the exchange of four freedoms, dividing flight frequencies based on traffic embarked, as wished by the British, and a transitional period with an 'escalator clause' which allowed airlines to increase their frequency of service, according to the American expectations. The divergence between the British and the Americans originated from their goals of dominating civil aviation and was the result of differences in their assets, such as the availability of aircraft, possessions of colonies, location, and size of respective countries.[19]

The conference was based on plenary sessions, works of numerous committees, and informal behind-the-scene negotiations. The committees worked effectively on technical matters and the creation of an international organization. The more problematic economic issues were more often discussed privately and only progressed if the Americans and the British could agree.[20] The private consultations called the ABC-talks (an acronym for the Americans, British, and Canadians) did not bring any agreement.[21] The only thing that all three agreed upon was the need to establish an international organization to oversee the development of air transport. However, when it came to the details, there were also differences. According to the Americans, the future organization should receive advisory powers, while the British opted to equip it with regulatory powers.[22] Such deliberations were mixing with those regarding the economic organization of post-war aviation, particularly regarding the fifth freedom. The main problem was that the British feared this would allow Americans to enter their local market.[23] In order to overcome the impasse, the US President Franklin D. Roosevelt and the British Prime Minister Winston Churchill engaged directly in discussions on the issue. In one of the letters, Roosevelt even threatened that Congress might not accept the Lend-Lease help for Britain if an agreement on aviation was not reached, but it did not make Churchill change his mind. In the end, the British and Americans agreed that the commercial issues should be settled later by the new international aviation organization, while in Chicago, they should focus on other areas.[24]

Despite a lack of consensus on some of the most crucial issues, on December 7, 1944, the delegates signed several agreements, including the Convention on International Civil Aviation, a Final Act with a standard form for future air agreements and technical annexes, an Interim Agreement on International Civil Aviation with the size, shape, and powers of the Provisional International Civil Aviation Organization (PICAO), the International Air Services Transit Agreement which granted first two freedoms to all signatories, and the International Air Transport Agreement with the five freedoms. The last two agreements were only signed by 26 and 16 states, respectively, whereas most delegations accepted the Final Act, Convention and the Interim agreement.[25] From the perspective of this research, the most crucial was the Convention on International Civil Aviation, often referred to as the Chicago Convention, which became the statutory document for the future ICAO.

Chicago Convention recognized every state's complete and exclusive sovereignty over its airspace and assumed its applicability only to civil aircraft, putting state aircraft beyond its jurisdiction.[26] Part II of the Convention, dedicated to the ICAO, is particularly important for this study. The Convention formed the ICAO, with its objectives and aims outlined in Article 44 and assuming the promotion of the development of civil aviation and encouragement of 'the arts of aircraft design and operation for peaceful purposes.'[27]

The Chicago conference was important in setting out the basic principles for the safety and order of civil aviation. It has contributed to the standardization of air travel but failed to make further contributions to liberalizing commercial services, which still had to be negotiated. The conference confirmed states' sovereignty over the airspace above their territories and thus had many parallels to the Paris Convention. Concerning standardization, the Convention provided basic rules on such issues as airport charges, registration, disease control, accident investigation, licensing and certificates, cargo restrictions, standards for radio and meteorological services, codes, and signals.[28] The problem with the negotiations was that each participating country, particularly the US and UK, sought to secure their commercial interests. In the final settlements, the conference opened the sky but, at the same time, left space for bilateral negotiations.

The signing of the Chicago Convention did not mean the automatic establishment of ICAO because of the necessary ratification process. Envisaging the interim period, the Chicago Conference also adopted the Interim Agreement on International Civil Aviation, which established a 'provisional international organization of a technical and advisory nature,' the PICAO, with the declared goal of collaboration in international civil aviation.[29] PICAO was formed on June 6, 1945, in Montreal.[30] Like ICAO, it had an Assembly, which, similarly to the Chicago conference, became a forum for economic negotiations of a multilateral agreement. Already during the opening session of the PICAO Assembly, the American delegate said that he had hoped PICAO could repeat its success in the technical field in the economic area, expressing his hope that a multilateral agreement on commercial rights could be reached.[31] These goals were not fulfilled, but PICAO effectively prepared the ground for the permanent organization. After the necessary 26 states ratified the Convention on April 4, 1947, PICAO turned into ICAO.[32]

The establishment of ICAO, initiated in the late years of World War II, was part of the general process occurring in IR during the wartime period and directly afterward, aiming to create a new, post-war order. Wartime enemies were not participating in this process, whereas the Soviet Union chose not to participate in establishing the aviation order. Even though the debates, in principle, were held among the allies, the Chicago conference did not manage to reach all of its goals. Its main success referred to establishing an international organization to oversee the development of safe international aviation, which was declaratively to serve the purpose of world peace. The powers of the new organizations were limited, though, reflecting the divergent positions of key aviation powers participating in the conference.

General information and organizational structure

ICAO is an intergovernmental organization established by the Chicago Convention in 1944. It operated since 1945 as PICAO and since 1947 as ICAO. Currently, it has 193 member states and belongs to the United Nations system as one of the UN specialized agencies.[33] Among the objectives of ICAO, the Chicago Convention features the development of 'the principles and techniques of international air navigation' and fosters 'the planning and development of international air transport.'[34] Additionally, according to its website, ICAO seeks to achieve sustainable growth of global civil aviation through its mission to serve as a global forum of states for international civil aviation.[35] According to Weber, these objectives emphasize ICAO's predominantly technical nature.[36]

Like most international organizations, ICAO has a formal structure composed of several bodies, similar to that of other UN organizations. The Assembly and the Council are the most crucial bodies directly mentioned in the Convention. The Assembly is, in principle, a gathering of all the member states. According to the Chicago Convention, it shall be convened by the Council at least once every three years, whereas extraordinary Assemblies may be called by the Council or by the request of one-fifth of the contracting states. All contracting states have equal rights in the Assembly and one vote each. The Assembly shall, among other things, elect the Council, vote annual budgets, delegate its powers to the Council when necessary, and deal with any matter unspecified in the Convention.[37] Details on the functioning of the Assembly have been changing over the years. The first ICAO Assembly opened in Montreal on May 6, 1947.[38] At the time, it was decided that the next session would be held in Geneva. It then became an agreed practice that every third session shall be held elsewhere than in Montreal, where ICAO has its headquarters. During the next Assembly in Geneva, it was decided that full Assemblies shall be organized every three years, while in other years, limited Assemblies dealing with administrative and technical matters shall be held. Since 1973, as a result of the growth of the organization, all sessions have been held in Montreal.[39] So far, there have been nine extraordinary sessions of the Assembly – in 1961, 1970, 1971, two in 1973, 1984, 1990, 1993, and 2003[40] – convened to fill vacancies in the Council urgently or to amend the Convention concerning such issues as terrorism or shootdown of civil aircraft.[41]

During its session, the Assembly establishes subsidiary bodies: Executive Committee (EC), Technical, Economic, Legal and Administrative Commissions. The EC coordinates the work of all subsidiary bodies and prepares the main policy decisions for the plenary.[42] Its importance is highlighted by the fact that it is composed of Presidents of the Council and Assembly and delegates from all contracting states, often represented by chief delegates. The EC thus serves as a kind of 'steering committee' of the Assembly.[43] For this reason, many crucial politicized debates in the ICAO Assembly have been held not only at the plenary meetings but also, or sometimes even more intensively, in the EC, with the plenary sessions often only confirming the EC's decisions.

While the ICAO Assembly is considered its 'main policy-setting body,'[44] it also functions as 'a major diplomatic event.'[45] This dual role led to choosing its deliberations as one of the main focuses of this study. According to ICAO's website, the Assembly 'pursues diplomatic and technical consensus on current priorities, policies, and targets for international civil aviation.'[46] Its diplomatic significance is marked by the fact that chief delegates often hold the position of Cabinet Ministers, Directors of Civil Aviation, or Ambassadors.[47] Thus, besides technical skills, they are supposed to have diplomatic skills. Together with the democratic character of the Assembly, with all member states represented and each having one vote, these circumstances made the Assembly vulnerable to incidents of politicization.

According to the Chicago Convention, the Council is a permanent body responsible to the Assembly[48] which also selects the states represented there. Currently, it comprises 36 member states elected by the Assembly for a three-year term. The election to the Council is specific and takes place in three categories: states of chief importance in air transport (1), states with the largest contribution to the provision of facilities for international civil air navigation (2), and states whose designation will ensure representation of major geographic areas (3).[49] The Convention, however, does not imply how to determine chief importance or making the largest contribution. Concerning group 3, some regions established rotation schemes over time to ensure their representation. One of the first such schemes was introduced by Scandinavian states[50] which were then followed by other regions, such as Central America,[51] East Africa,[52] Austria–Benelux–Switzerland Group.[53] Group 1, in principle, has been occupied by world powers.

The number of states in the Council has been changing over the years. Originally, it was 21, but the Council membership grew together with the organization's growing membership. According to Milde, enlargements were driven by '"ad hoc" pragmatic political considerations rather than any long-term planning,' for example, after the Soviet Union joined ICAO in 1970 and aspired to Council membership while previous members desired to keep their seats, or similarly when the People's Republic of China became a member.[54] The election of Council members also has not been immune to politicization. For example, according to MacKenzie, Canada has backed particular candidates based on political merits.[55] One of the most severe examples of politicization of Council elections took place after the Russian invasion of Ukraine in 2022, discussed in Chapter 6.

There are a number of functions realized by the Council. Its responsibilities include convening the Assembly, submitting annual reports to the Assembly, carrying out the Assembly's directions, discharging duties and obligations according to the Chicago Convention, and administering the ICAO finances. The Council appoints the Air Transport Committee (ATC), Committee on Joint Support of Air Navigation Services, Finance Committee, Committee on Unlawful Interference, Technical Co-operation Committee, and the Human Resources Committee, members of the Air Navigation Commission (ANC), Secretary General. Other crucial functions include adopting Standards and Recommended Practices (SARPs) and generally giving directions to the work of ICAO. It oversees the work of the Secretariat and is responsible for diplomatic and technical decision-making, while the Assembly is not in session.[56] Council decisions need to be approved by the majority of its members.[57]

Adopting SARPs is believed to be the most important function of the Council connected to law-making. It stems from the need for international standardization of aviation practices and procedures and is the distinctive feature of ICAO in the UN system. SARPs are applicable worldwide under specific conditions, except for the rules of the air over the high seas, which are mandatory for all states. After being adopted by the Council, usually by unanimity, SARPs come into force unless disapproved by a majority of contracting states, which has never occurred. Regarding standards in general, states are not obliged to comply. However, they should 'collaborate in the highest practicable degree of uniformity,' whereas if they find it impossible to comply, they are obliged to notify differences between their practice and the standard. All this would suggest SARPs are legally weak, but states are motivated to implement them since non-compliance could eliminate them from meaningful international air transport.[58]

The Council also has judicial responsibilities connected to the settlement of differences between contracting states. They include adjudication of disputes on the interpretation and application of the Convention under articles 84 and 54(b) and relating to the International Air Service Transit Agreement.[59] Additionally, under Article 54(n), the Council is obliged to consider any matter brought by a contracting state but does not have to take a decision. Historically, most such cases stemmed from complaints against another state or a pending dispute, such as the United Kingdom's complaint against the Spanish declaration of a prohibited area near Gibraltar, Nigeria's against Portugal's alleged unlawful flights and support for Biafra rebels, Lebanon's against Israel regarding an attack against Beirut airport, or Iranian against the United States after the shootdown of its civil aircraft.[60] The last two of these controversies will considered in Chapters 4 and 5.

As demonstrated above, besides typical administrative and management functions, the Council also holds functions of a 'law-making nature' and in settlement of differences, which, according to Milde, is unique in the entire UN system.[61] The Council's juridical function is sometimes criticized. Rose argued that the ICAO Council is a 'political body with mainly nonlawyer members who represent their states' and thus may not be well-positioned in dealing with interstate disputes.[62] Either way, the Council has been granted considerable power within ICAO. According to Sochor, it has a primary rather than a secondary source of authority compared to the Assembly.[63] Tourtellot called the Council 'the most powerful body of the organization, closely resembling the United Nations Security Council.'[64] Its power contributed to politicization attempts. Council member states have been acting according to their national interests.[65] As a result, despite ICAO's technical character, the Council has also been becoming a place of politicized debates, with state interests prevailing in the discussions. Therefore, the Council constituted the second main subject of the study.

The Secretariat is the next main body of the ICAO, although unlike the Assembly and the Council, it was not mentioned in the Convention. It is responsible for administrative and expert bureaucracy, supporting diplomatic interactions and research.[66] The Secretariat should not be attached with particular political or diplomatic significance. According to Sochor, unlike most UN agencies where people working in the Secretariat are vulnerable to political pressure, the ICAO Secretariat has been insulated from such pressure since the staff needs to be composed of highly trained specialists and few administrators.[67] Additionally, unlike in other UN agencies, the head of the Secretariat is not the first person in the organization, a specificity which shall be discussed below.

Apart from the most crucial bodies mentioned earlier, the Chicago Convention also established two subsidiary bodies, i.e. the ATC and the ANC. Duties of the ATC were not determined in the Chicago Convention and were to be defined by the Council.[68] In principle, it is to settle economic issues regarding aviation.[69] The ANC is appointed by the Council and consists of people with qualifications and experience in the science and practice of aeronautics, with the mission to provide technical expertise for the organization.[70] It is composed of 19 members, nominated by member states but not representing the interest of any state or region. One of its main functions is to consider and recommend SARPs and Procedures for Air Navigation Services (PANS) to be considered and adopted by the Council and to manage the technical work of the organizations.[71] The tasks and composition of the ANC should make it a body least prone to politicization. However, according to Sochor, on a few occasions, it also became a forum for political bargaining. For example, in the 1970s, the ANC was considering the adoption of one of the microwave landing systems (MLS) as standard equipment. Competing systems were developed by the United Kingdom, France, West Germany, and a joint US-Australian team. Each government was backing its own system. After years of deliberations, the ANC eventually recommended the US-Australian system in a secret ballot. The decision by many is viewed as political concerning the fact that, according to many experts, the British system was more advanced and easier to implement. The technical decisions were also subject to lobbying by aviation subjects such as aircraft manufacturers, like in the case of allowing the use of twin-engine aircraft on longer routes, lobbied in particular by Boeing.[72] Such political bargaining, however, does not correspond directly with the politicization understood as bringing political conflicts to the forum of ICAO. The explicitly technical character of the ANC generally spared it most of the political deliberations that the Assembly and Council dealt with.

ICAO, in principle, has a general structure. Like other international organizations in the UN system, it comprises the Assembly, the Council, and the Secretariat. A more unique feature of ICAO is its leadership, which is composed of two persons, the President of the Council and the Secretary General. The President of the Council is elected by the Council for a three-year term and can be re-elected but has no voting rights. President's missions include convening meetings of the Council and other bodies, representing the Council, and carrying out the functions assigned by the Council.[73] According to ICAO, the President of the Council 'serves chiefly as a consensus builder during diplomatic engagements among the 36 voting Council States.'[74] According to Sochor, the President of the Council is the most influential position in the ICAO.[75] MacKenzie enumerated his roles as administrator, arbitrator, ambassador, conciliator, civil servant, international aviation diplomat, and part-time referee. Speaking of the diplomatic functions of the President, their growth is believed to be the most visible during the term of Walter Binaghi – the second President, in office between 1957 and 1976, who, according to MacKenzie, from being a technical expert, has become an international diplomat and executive. A strong diplomatic position is also associated with the subsequent President Assad Kotaite, in office between 1976 and 2006. According to MacKenzie, Kotaite 'embraced his role as international aviation diplomat and added a personal touch,' a good negotiator in several aviation disputes.[76] Secretary General is second person in the

ICAO, the head of the Secretariat responsible for the administration. Secretary General is the chief executive officer, provides leadership to the ICAO staff, and is responsible to the Council.[77] Unlike the President, the Secretary General is appointed and not elected, which indicates administrative functions, although the appointment, as argued by Milde, involves political decisions and concerns geographic rotation.[78]

Having two top-ranking civil servants is a characteristic feature of the ICAO compared to other UN agencies.[79] Interestingly, no clear delimitation of their jurisdiction would justify such a duality.[80] Both positions are mentioned in the Convention, but their powers have been defined very narrowly there. As a result, the boundaries between the President of the Council and the Secretary General have been established evolutionarily.[81] Their responsibilities were initially delineated already by the Interim Council, with the Secretary General being the chief executive and administrative officer, while the President of the Council was to conduct external relations with states and other international organizations, represent the Council, and conduct special liaison missions, particularly in relations with the UN.[82] Over the years, the powers of the President were permitted to grow.[83] According to Sochor, the personalities of incumbents played an important role in this process.[84]

The duality of ICAO leadership and the existence of an independent President raise the issue of whether such a person can be an intermediary when there is a technical or political conflict. Generally, the Council's President is believed to have a very important role in this manner. Assad Kotaite is a particularly good example. He has rendered good offices in negotiations and contributed to solving problems at an early stage, for example, in issues connected to the Arab–Israeli or Iran–Iraq conflicts.[85] Shortly after taking office, Kotaite was asked to provide good offices in a Senegal-Cape Verde dispute over flight information services between Dakar and North America. This led to a compromise splitting the disputed area.[86] Kotaite was praised numerous times for his diplomatic efforts to ease the conflicts. In one of the statements, the chief delegate of South Africa called him 'a truly great diplomat.'[87] This, in turn, marks a significant change from his behavior before he became the President. As the representative of Lebanon to the Council, he was strongly engaged in attacking Israel after its helicopter raid on Lebanon in 1968.[88] This potentially makes the President of the Council another actor engaged in conflicts waged in ICAO, apart from the state representatives. On the other hand, the Secretary General's role appears to be more technical and thus less engaged in political disputes.

Another crucial consequence of ICAO's organizational structure, this time regarding the possibility for politicization, stems from the power distribution in the organization. In the case of the Assembly, it is similar to other international organizations. With the one country, one vote principle, it is relatively easy for states to bring political matters and sometimes to achieve expected decisions even against the interests of world powers. More crucial differences concern the Council. In the UN, the status of world powers, at least for the post-war reality, has been reflected in the UN Security Council (UN SC), with five permanent members enjoying veto power. ICAO does not reflect the global power distribution that directly. Strong aviation nations have a dedicated Council election group and usually have been elected, but their seat is not guaranteed. Chapter 6 will discuss an example of such an exceptional situation when Russia, a state normally occupying a seat in the Council, was not elected. Moreover, group 1 Council members do not enjoy veto power and occupy only 11 out of 36 seats. It does not mean powerful states do not play a leading role in the organization, but their privileges are somehow limited. Such a situation, combined with member states' right to bring issues under the Council's consideration and the decisions being made by a majority of Council members, makes it potentially easier than, for example, in the UN, to achieve desirable decisions such as condemning or isolating political adversaries, despite ICAO's generally limited powers. Such a situation sets the stage for the potential politicization of ICAO deliberations and highlights its characteristics as a forum organization.

ICAO and the international environment

The organizational structure and patterns of functioning of ICAO make it a potential forum for politicized deliberations despite the organization's technical focus. The second area of ICAO's potential political engagement stems from its standing as an international organization and its relations with the international environment. ICAO belongs to the United Nations system and maintains relationships with a number of IR actors, such as states, international organizations, and non-governmental organizations. Relationships with states are most evident. As an intergovernmental organization, ICAO deals with states on multiple levels, such as communication regarding the adoption of SARPs and states' right to notify differences or reporting the general statistical information to ICAO. This kind of relationship was problematic in some periods, with states failing to report information,[89] but it still reveals intensive relations between ICAO and states. Another crucial area of the ICAO–states relationship refers to the ICAO's role in settling disputes between states, with governments being able to seek ICAO's assistance in conflict resolution under Chapter XVIII of the Chicago Convention or under Article 54.

Besides states, ICAO has been maintaining relationships with other IR actors. Most importantly, that concerns the UN. As mentioned above, ICAO is a UN agency. At the time of the Chicago conference, negotiations on the replacement of the League of Nations were already underway but were not concluded until after the signing of the Chicago Convention.[90] ICAO was therefore established before the UN system began to exist, although the Chicago Convention assumed that ICAO might enter into appropriate arrangements with any general organization set up to preserve peace. The draft agreement with the UN was negotiated already by PICAO, while ICAO, at its first meeting, approved the Agreement and authorized the President to sign it with an appropriate UN official.[91] Negotiations regarding entering into the relationship with the UN were delayed by the expectation that Franco's Spain would be expelled, an issue discussed in Chapter 3. Eventually, on October 1, 1947, the President of the Council signed a protocol with the UN Secretary-General to bring the agreement into force.[92]

Becoming a UN agency meant the vast development of mutual contacts, for example, through participation in UN meetings concerning aviation issues.[93] According to Sochor, this relationship means that ICAO became an 'executive organ' or 'executive arm' of the UN in the field of aviation. ICAO is also subject to UN recommendations, which on some occasions also brought political controversies to ICAO, for example, regarding dealing with the apartheid, the rights of Palestinians, and cooperation with the Organization of Islamic Conference,[94] some of which were studied in subsequent chapters. ICAO has also been engaged in the distribution of the UN development assistance through numerous programs throughout the years, such as the Technical Assistance Programme, Expanded Programme of Technical Assistance for Economic Development,[95] Trust Funds, and Associate Experts Programme.[96] Apart from that, ICAO has been providing more specific services to the UN. For example, the UN Secretary General requested that personnel be supplied to man the Congo airports under UN control and to train Congolese personnel.[97] The 21st century brought UN–ICAO collaboration in such areas as the protection of the environment and mitigating climate change, with ICAO acting as the UN's arm in this field in reference to aviation.[98]

Being part of the UN system, ICAO collaborates with other UN agencies. International Telecommunications Union, International Atomic Energy Agency, International Labour Organization, International Maritime Organization, Universal Postal Union, World Meteorological Organization, World Health Organization, and World Tourism Organization belong to the most natural partners for ICAO,[99] although this list only denotes the most crucial partnerships. When it comes to organizations from beyond the UN system, ICAO has been cooperating, for example, with the Council of Europe.[100] The current list of international organizations that may be invited to attend appropriate ICAO meetings, though without the observer status, includes 10 UN programs, 5 UN regional commissions, 14 UN specialized agencies, and 25 other intergovernmental organizations.[101] In this sense, ICAO is similar to other intergovernmental organizations. Its engagement with them, among other things, stems from the fact that there are a number of global problems at the interface between their jurisdiction, for example communicable disease may spread more rapidly owing to global air transport, justifying ICAO's cooperation with the World Health Organization. Apart from that, ICAO has maintained relations with international non-governmental organizations (INGOs), with a special place occupied by the International Air Transport Association (IATA).[102] ICAO held regular meetings with IATA, whose representatives are invited to most ANC meetings and the ATC meetings. Other INGOs that ICAO has been intensively collaborating with include the International Federation of Airline Pilots' Associations (IFALPA).[103] The current list of INGOs that may be invited to ICAO meetings features 47 organizations.[104]

The various types of actors ICAO collaborates with stem from the complex and multidimensional situations it sometimes has to deal with. International crises disturbing civil aviation serve as a good example. For instance, in 2011, during the armed conflict in Libya, ICAO worked with the North Atlantic Treaty Organization (NATO), European Organisation for the Safety of Air Navigation (EUROCONTROL), Malta, Egypt, IATA, and the Libyan authorities to ensure the safety of operations in the region.[105] Besides that, on various occasions, ICAO has also collaborated with airlines. For example, in the early years of its existence, ICAO established weather stations and rescue teams in the North Atlantic area, financed by the airlines that have been using these facilities.[106] All these examples serve as evidence for ICAO's close connections with external actors. It also shows that besides technical expertise, it does realize some of the functions typical for service organizations. Considering the wealth of international interactions in which it is engaged, the multistakeholder diplomacy model[107] could be applied to explain its position, referring to the need for broader cooperation and engagement of various stakeholders as a result of the complexity of processes connected with pursuing politics. These considerations picture ICAO as an IR and diplomatic actor, which, in order to realize its goals, needs to engage in various networks. ICAO's relationships with other IR actors have sometimes been leading to its politicization, both directly and indirectly. For example, its relationship with the UN on several occasions made ICAO engage in sensitive issues with political overtones, such as regarding apartheid in South Africa.

ICAO's relevance

Despite a generally limited mandate compared to some other international organizations, ICAO has been relevant in contributing to the development of safe air travel. The general goal of establishing ICAO was to promote the safety and orderly development of civil aviation,[108] while for ICAO itself, the main goal from the beginning of its existence was to set the basic international standard – SARPs, which have been contained in the annexes to the Chicago Convention. They have been designed by the drafters of the Convention as separated from its body so that they could be adopted by the Council and come into force without the ratification process, contrary to the amendments to the Convention which are adopted by the Assembly and need to be ratified.[109] SARPs are considered ICAO's most important contribution to civil aviation, including requirements necessary for air navigation (standards) and the desirable practices (recommended practices),[110] although, besides the high seas, states might notify that they would not apply them. This situation exemplifies the restricted character of the authority of ICAO as an intergovernmental regulatory agency, with its decisions relying on the goodwill of states.[111] Still, the number of differences filed by states has been relatively low, although at some point, a negative trend appeared, with states failing to notify that they were not able to implement the standards. For many years, ICAO tolerated that situation, according to Milde, for political purposes, but in the 1990s it admitted it could not determine the state of implementation of its regulations. In 1992, the United States took unilateral action to ensure that foreign carriers operating to and from the United States adhere to ICAO SARPs. Unilateral steps to blacklist airlines were also made by the European Union. Only after that, in 1995, did the ICAO initiate safety oversight. After subsequent changes, it began auditing aviation in member states, which sought to observe SARPs to avoid their shortcomings and failures to be revealed.[112] The balance sheet when it comes to technical standard-setting by ICAO thus appears to be positive despite its limited authority. It is also worth noting that monitoring compliance with norms or treaties is considered one of the sources of authority of international organizations,[113] understood as a potential source of their politicization.

The situation is entirely different with regard to the economic issues, discussed already during the Chicago Conference. At the time, the Americans sought liberalization of air travel, but other states feared the dominant position of the United States. The United States did not get its preferred freedom of the skies solution and eventually opted for bilateral negotiations regarding the economic dimension of air navigation, with the subsequent US–UK Bermuda Agreement as a role model. The agreement assumed strict control over entry and marketplace capacity, whereas the fare-setting authority was delegated to IATA.[114] On a multilateral level, delegates at the Chicago conference failed to reach a compromise on a multilateral settlement, but further negotiations were to be held on the forum of the newly established ICAO.

Despite not being given authority over economic regulations as a result of the American position,[115] particularly in the first years of its existence, ICAO became a forum for economic negotiations. These problems were first handled by the ATC established by the Interim Council in 1945. ATC prepared a draft of a multilateral agreement in April 1946, which linked the development of civil aviation with world peace, to be achieved through the exchange of five freedoms. The problem, however, was that the Americans wanted to secure the fifth freedom through the multilateral agreement and to leave the details, such as the route selection, to bilateral negotiations, in which they could use their advantage.[116] For some time, the issue of the economic agreement remained one of the key points of interest within ICAO. Often it was included in the agenda of the Assembly sessions. However, with the passing of years, there was no advancement concerning the multilateral agreement. According to the ICAO Council Report from 1954, 'the Council reached the conclusion that there was no immediate prospect of progress towards universal multilateral agreement,'[117] leading ICAO to focus on other aspects of its activity.

Certain attempts to return to the issue were made in the 1970s and 1980s after the United States began changing its international aviation policy. The new approach assumed the reduction of restrictions in capacity, frequencies, route selection, multiple designation of air carriers, and removing the restrictions on charter air services. This led many governments to consider searching for a multilateral agreement in ICAO, which in response staged air transport conferences in 1977, 1980, and 1985. However, many states opposed liberalization, particularly those with state-owned airlines, for which free competition would have been more challenging. In contrast, their governments could not allow such airlines to go bankrupt for reasons such as national prestige, state security, or sovereignty.[118] In the 1990s, many governments were more favorable toward open skies agreements. ICAO used the momentum sponsoring the World Wide Air Transport Colloquium in 1992 and the World Wide

Air Transport Conference in 1994. However, differences between states proved to be too deep, and the US soon became isolated in its aim to achieve liberalization.[119] Even though the exchange of economic rights still remains one of ICAO's main goals, it has adopted an advisory role in this area, providing states guidance in bilateral negotiations.[120] Interestingly, even though ICAO is still attempting to facilitate diplomatic efforts to reach a compromise on the multilateral economic agreement on civil aviation, such issues were only being directly debated on its forum in the first years of the organization's history.

Other crucial aspects regarding ICAO's relevance refer to its engagement in tackling the terrorist threat and, more recently, dealing with the environmental impact of aviation. In the first case, ICAO successfully negotiated international instruments to enhance the safety of air travel. Its achievements in this field include Conventions from Tokyo, Hague, and Montreal.[121] These accomplishments, however, were put into question by the 9/11 attacks, which led to ICAO's further engagement. For example, it organized a ministerial conference in Montreal in February 2002, which approved the Council's proposals concerning security, leading, among other things, to the establishment of the Universal Security Audit Programme (USAP) to perform audits and evaluate aviation security in all contracting states.[122]

The environmental problem is another of the global threats and challenges ICAO has been dealing with. Relevant debates have been held on its forum since the 1970s, partly due to the noise pollution problem connected to Concorde flights.[123] Nowadays, environmental protection belongs to ICAO's global priorities. The key areas ICAO member states have agreed to concentrate on include climate change and aviation emissions, aircraft noise, and local air quality, while the main way of pursuing these goals is through developing new global aviation standards.[124] ICAO has also engaged in developing a global market-based measurement system for emissions, leading to the issuing of adequate SARPs.[125] The Carbon Offsetting and Reduction Scheme for International Aviation (CORSIA) is believed to be a fairly important step, although generally, ICAO is considered ineffective in addressing climate change so far.[126]

Despite limited regulatory capabilities, ICAO has proven to be an efficient machinery for international cooperation in the air, dealing with issues such as safety, the latest techniques, regular services. The permanently decreasing number of aviation fatalities per million passengers[127] may serve as the best justification for this argument, although naturally, it is not only ICAO that contributes to the increased safety. Still, ICAO has not been successful in every area of its activity. For example, it has not managed to adopt multilateral economic regulations for civil aviation. As a result of states sticking to the sovereignty of their airspace, most economic regulation of civil aviation takes place through bilateral aviation agreements. This implies that a lot of the aviation-related diplomacy is held beyond ICAO, particularly with regard to economic issues. All these circumstances, particularly regarding a relatively limited authority of the organization, have some implications for the issue of politicization in ICAO. In such an organization, waging political conflicts and attacking political adversaries has a highly symbolic character, with confined possibilities of injuring adversaries other than through verbal criticism or condemnation.

Conclusions

ICAO is an international organization preoccupied with technical matters of civil aviation, focusing on its safety and development. Such were the intentions of the ICAO founders, and most of its activities are oriented on technical matters. Still, despite an inherently technical character compared to other intergovernmental organizations, ICAO was never fully able to distance itself from political issues. According to MacKenzie, although the most important part of the activity of ICAO as an international organization is the technical operations, in particular in the pursuit of technical standardization of international civil aviation, these issues are often overshadowed by the public face of the organization, which connects to international politics.[128] In a similar spirit, Dobson mentioned a number of difficult situations with political overtones that ICAO had to deal with, mentioning the ostracism of Spain after the war for its ties with the Axis, the Cold War friction, the Arab–Israeli conflict, the apartheid in South Africa, Portugal's colonialism, and India–Pakistan conflict as the most glaring examples. Regarding ICAO's efficiency, Dobson concluded that it was more effective when non-political issues were settled, whereas when the politics collided, its role was becoming less constructive.[129] Although much of the crucial aviation negotiations are held beyond ICAO, the possibility of bringing political issues before ICAO has been incentivized by its organizational shape, with a relatively less privileged position of world powers.

Collisions between politics and aviation stemmed from political conflicts between states, which sought to hit their political opponents on the forum of ICAO. This partly relates to the preamble of the Chicago Convention, which states that international civil aviation can 'help to create and preserve friendship and understanding' among nations, while its abuse 'can become a threat to the general security.'[130] Politicized deliberations on the forum of ICAO usually had a contradictory character, although it has to be admitted that during many of them, delegates and representatives referred to the provision of the Convention's preamble, often to justify bringing an issue to the forum. The collisions between international aviation and politics led to the need for diplomatic engagement of various stakeholders on the forum of ICAO, predominantly state representatives. Such situations were turning a theoretically non-forum organization into a political forum, which constitutes one of the key pillars of the analysis presented in this book.

The explicitly technical character of ICAO, combined with its limited authority, theoretically should make it relatively immune to political interference. As demonstrated in the empirical chapters of the book, politics still made it to the forum of ICAO. To some extent, a review of ICAO's structure and functioning explains this phenomenon. Firstly, with its relatively democratic character and a relatively limited influence of world powers, ICAO is a convenient forum where states might seek to realize their foreign policy objectives and hit political opponents without the risk of having their motions vetoed by world powers.

Secondly, despite a non-political statutory focus, as a part of the UN system, ICAO inevitably has been embroiled in more general political controversies, such as the Arab–Israeli conflict. The low authority has limited the outcomes of many of such conflicts to merely symbolic. However, it does not mean that the attacked parties did not attempt to defend themselves, paving the ground for the employment of defensive depoliticization.

Notes

1 Eugene Sochor, *The Politics of International Aviation* (Basingstoke: Macmillan, 1991), 1.
2 John Cobb Cooper, "The International Air Navigation Conference, Paris 1910," *The Journal of Air Law and Commerce* 19, no. 2 (1952): 127.
3 Sochor, *The Politics of International Aviation*, 2–3.
4 David MacKenzie, *ICAO: A History of the International Civil Aviation Organization* (Toronto: University of Toronto Press, 2010), 15.
5 Alan Dobson, *A History of International Aviation: From Its Origins through Transformative Evolution* (London: Routledge, 2017), 12.
6 MacKenzie, *ICAO*, 20–22.
7 Five Freedoms of the air include: (1) Innocent passage or over-flight; (2) Technical stop for repairs or refueling; (3) The right to pick up passengers from an airline's country of origin and disembark them in territory of the other contracting party; (4) The right to pick up passengers in the other contracting country and disembark them in the airline's country of origin; (5) The right to pick up passengers from the other contracting party and carry them forward to a third-party destination. Dobson, *A History of International Aviation*, 37.
8 Dobson, *A History of International Aviation*, 39–40.
9 Jeffrey N. Shane, "Diplomacy and Drama: The Making of the Chicago Convention," *The Air and Space Lawyer* 32, no. 4 (special issue) (2019): 16.
10 MacKenzie, *ICAO*, 25.
11 Dobson, *A History of International Aviation*, 43.
12 "The History of ICAO and the Chicago Convention," ICAO, accessed September 10, 2020, www.icao.int/about-icao/History/Pages/default.aspx
13 Shane, *Diplomacy and Drama*, 17.
14 MacKenzie, *ICAO*, 25; Sochor, *The Politics of International Aviation*, 7.
15 MacKenzie, *ICAO*, 27.
16 Sochor, *The Politics of International Aviation*, 6.
17 MacKenzie, *ICAO*, 35–38.
18 Shane, *Diplomacy and Drama* 19.
19 MacKenzie, *ICAO*, 33–35, 39.
20 Ibid., 32.
21 Shane, *Diplomacy and Drama*, 20.
22 MacKenzie, *ICAO*, 13, 41.
23 Dobson, *A History of International Aviation*, 44.
24 MacKenzie, *ICAO*, 45–46.
25 Ibid., 51.
26 "Convention on International Civil Aviation." Signed at Chicago on 7 December 1944: 2.

27 Ibid., 20–21.
28 MacKenzie, *ICAO*, 52.
29 "United Nations Interim Agreement on International Civil Aviation." Effective June 6, 1945, *The American Journal of International Law* 40, no. 2 (April, 1946), Supplement: Official Documents (April, 1946): 63.
30 Elfita Agustini, Yaya Kareng, and Ong Argo Victoria, "The Role of ICAO (International Civil Aviation Organization) in Implementing International Flight Safety Standards," *IWPOSPA* (2020): 107, https://doi.org/10.18502/kss.v5i1.8273
31 Minutes of the First Plenary Meeting, Interim Assembly – Plenary Meetings, May 21, 1946, 26, A/29 21/5/46, DOC 1686, ICAO Archival Documents.
32 "Convention on International Civil Aviation."
33 "About ICAO," ICAO, accessed November 20, 2023, www.icao.int/about-icao/Pages/default.aspx
34 "Convention on International Civil Aviation": 20.
35 "Vision and Mission," ICAO, accessed November 20, 2023, www.icao.int/about-icao/Council/Pages/vision-and-mission.aspx
36 Ludwig Weber, *International Civil Aviation Organization (ICAO)* (Alphen aan den Rijn: Wolters Kluwer, 2023), 6.
37 "Convention on International Civil Aviation": 22–24.
38 MacKenzie, *ICAO*, 81.
39 Ibid., 147–148.
40 "All Assembly Sessions," ICAO, accessed October 20, 2023, www.icao.int/publications/Pages/assembly-archive.aspx
41 Michael Milde, *International Air Law and ICAO* (Utrecht: Eleven International Publishing, 2008), 131.
42 Weber, *International Civil Aviation Organization*, 20.
43 MacKenzie, *ICAO*, 53.
44 Weber, *International Civil Aviation Organization*, 19.
45 "The ICAO Assembly," ICAO, accessed November 20, 2023, www.icao.int/about-icao/assembly/Pages/default.aspx
46 "The ICAO Council," ICAO, accessed November 20, 2023, www.icao.int/about-icao/Council/Pages/Council.aspx
47 Milde, *International Air Law*, 132.
48 "Convention on International Civil Aviation": 24.
49 Ibid., 24–25.
50 See: Minutes of the Second Plenary Meeting, Assembly – Fifteenth Session, June 23, 1965, 42, A15-P/5, DOC 8516, ICAO Archival Documents.
51 See: Minutes of the Second Plenary Meeting, Assembly – Fourteenth Session, August 22, 1962, 39, A14-P/21, DOC 8269, ICAO Archival Documents.
52 See: Minutes of the Second Plenary Meeting, Assembly – Eighteenth Session, June 15, 1971, 22–23, A18 Min. P/2, DOC 8963, ICAO Archival Documents.
53 See: Minutes of the Second Plenary Meeting, Assembly 24th Session, September 20, 1983, 23, A24-Min. P/2, DOC 9415, ICAO Archival Documents.
54 Milde, *International Air Law*, 139–140.
55 MacKenzie, *ICAO*, 154.
56 "The ICAO Council," ICAO, accessed November 20, 2023, www.icao.int/about-icao/Council/Pages/council.aspx
57 "Convention on International Civil Aviation": 25.
58 Milde, *International Air Law*, 153–161.

59 Weber, *International Civil Aviation Organization*, 22.
60 Milde, *International Air Law*, 154.
61 Ibid., 139.
62 Cecily Rose, "Appeal Relating to the Jurisdiction of the ICAO Council," *American Journal of International Law* 115, no. 2 (2021): 308.
63 Sochor, *The Politics of International Aviation*, 57–58.
64 Christopher T. Tourtellot, "Membership Criteria for the ICAO Council: A Proposal for Reform," *Denver Journal of International Law and Policy* 11 (1981): 52.
65 MacKenzie, *ICAO*, 54.
66 ICAO, "About ICAO."
67 Sochor, *The Politics of International Aviation*, 66.
68 "Convention on International Civil Aviation": 25.
69 ICAO, "About ICAO."
70 "Convention on International Civil Aviation": 28.
71 "Air Navigation Commission," ICAO, accessed November 20, 2023, www.icao.int/about-icao/AirNavigationCommission/Pages/default.aspx
72 Sochor, *The Politics of International Aviation*, 60–71.
73 "Convention on International Civil Aviation": 25.
74 "Council President," ICAO, accessed November 20, 2023, www.icao.int/about-icao/Council/Pages/President.aspx
75 Sochor, *The Politics of International Aviation*, 62.
76 MacKenzie, *ICAO*, 287.
77 "Secretary General," ICAO, accessed November 20, 2023, www.icao.int/secretariat/SecretaryGeneral/Pages/default.aspx
78 Milde, *International Air Law*, 151.
79 Sochor, *The Politics of International Aviation*, 62.
80 Milde, *International Air Law*, 146.
81 Sochor, *The Politics of International Aviation*, 63.
82 MacKenzie, *ICAO*, 67.
83 Milde, *International Air Law*, 147.
84 Sochor, *The Politics of International Aviation*, 63.
85 Ibid., 63.
86 Ibid., 112–113.
87 Minutes of the Third Plenary Meeting, Assembly – 31st Session, September 20, 1995, 3–4, DRAFT A31-Min. P/3, ICAO Archival Documents.
88 Minutes of the First Meeting, Council – Extraordinary Session, January 20, 1969, 8, C/982-1 C-Min. EXTRAORDINARY/1, DOC 8793-1, ICAO Archival Documents.
89 See for example: Minutes of the Second Plenary Meeting, Third Assembly, June 8, 1949, 24, A3-P/26, 22/6/49, DOC 6457, ICAO Archival Documents.
90 Milde, *International Air Law*, 127.
91 Ibid., 127–128.
92 Report of the Council to the Assembly on the Activities of the Organization, June 1, 1947-March 1, 1948, 8, A2-P/5 19/3/48, DOC 5221, ICAO Archival Documents.
93 MacKenzie, *ICAO*, 92.
94 Sochor, *The Politics of International Aviation*, 51–52.
95 See: Report of the Council to the Assembly on the Activities of the Organization in 1949, Supporting Documentation for the 4th Session of the Assembly, March 23, 1950, 64–65, A4-P/1, DOC 6969, ICAO Archival Documents; Annual Report of the Council to the Assembly for 1957, Supporting Documentation for the Eleventh Session of the Assembly, May 1958, 35, A11-P/3, DOC 7866, ICAO Archival Documents.

96 Annual Report of the Council – 1984, Documentation for the Session of the Assembly in 1986, 83, 87, DOC 9451, ICAO Archival Documents.
97 Annual Report of the Council to the Assembly for 1960, Supporting Documentation for the Fourteenth Session of the Assembly, April 15, 1961, 49, A14-P/3, DOC 8140, ICAO Archival Documents.
98 Annual Report of the Council, 2007, 42, DOC 9898, ICAO Archival Documents.
99 "ICAO and the United Nations," ICAO, accessed November 1, 2021, www.icao.int/about-icao/History/Pages/icao-and-the-united-nations.aspx
100 Report of the Council to the Assembly on the Activities of the Organization in 1951, Supporting Documentation for the 6th Session of the Assembly, May 1952, 12–13, A6-P/1, DOC 7270, ICAO Archival Documents.
101 "Organizations able to be invited to ICAO Meetings," ICAO, accessed November 2, 2021, www.icao.int/about-icao/pages/invited-organizations.aspx
102 Report of the Council to the Assembly, vol. I, Supporting Documentation for the 3rd Assembly, June 1949, 6, DOC 6433, ICAO Archival Documents.
103 MacKenzie, *ICAO*, 180–181.
104 ICAO, "Organizations able to be invited to ICAO Meetings."
105 Annual Report of the Council: 2011, Documentation for the Session of the Assembly in 2013, 17, DOC 9975, ICAO Archival Documents.
106 Sochor, *The Politics of International Aviation*, 23–24.
107 See: Brian Hocking, Jan Melissen, Shaun Riordan, and Paul Sharp, *Futures for Diplomacy: Integrative Diplomacy in the 21st Century, Report No. 1* (The Hague: Clingendael, 2012), 11.
108 Dobson, *A History of International Aviation*, 48.
109 Sochor, *The Politics of International Aviation*, 23.
110 MacKenzie, *ICAO*, 52–53.
111 Sochor, *The Politics of International Aviation*, 222.
112 Milde, *International Air Law*, 165–167, 169.
113 Michael Zürn, *A Theory of Global Governance: Authority, Legitimacy, and Contestation* (Oxford: Oxford University Press, 2018), 156.
114 John E. Richards, "Toward a Positive Theory of International Institutions: Regulating International Aviation Markets," *International Organization* 53, no. 1 (Winter 1999): 17.
115 Dobson, *A History of International Aviation*, 58.
116 MacKenzie, *ICAO*, 107–108, 118–120.
117 Report of the Council to the Assembly on the Activities of the Organization in 1953, Supporting Documentation for the 8th Session of the Assembly, June 1954, 31, A8-P/2, DOC 7456, ICAO Archival Documents.
118 MacKenzie, *ICAO*, 349–352.
119 Ibid., 355–358.
120 Sochor, *The Politics of International Aviation*, 17.
121 Dobson, *A History of International Aviation*, 61.
122 MacKenzie, *ICAO*, 388.
123 Dobson, *A History of International Aviation*, 62.
124 "Environmental Protection," ICAO, accessed December 17, 2021, www.icao.int/environmental-protection/Pages/default.aspx
125 Karlheinz Haag, "International Action and the Role of ICAO," in *Aviation and Climate Change*, ed. Frank Fichert, Peter Forsyth, and Hans-Martin Niemeier (Abingdon: Routledge, 2020), 115.

126 Dinar Dewi Kania et al., "Does ICAO's Climate Change Mitigation Policy Based on International Agreements Reflect Global Environmental Justice?," *International Environmental Agreements: Politics, Law and Economics* 23, no. 4 (2023): 451, https://doi.org/ 10.1007/s10784-023-09619-5

127 "Global Aviation Fatalities per Million Passengers, 2023," Our World in Data, accessed December 20, 2023, https://ourworldindata.org/grapher/aviation-fatalities-per-million-passengers

128 MacKenzie *ICAO*, 173.

129 Dobson, *A History of International Aviation*, 60.

130 "Convention on International Civil Aviation": 1.

2 Politics, politicization, and depoliticization in international organizations

International organizations (IOs) are inherently embedded in the world of politics, while at the same time, most of them, particularly the technical ones, attempt to distance themselves from politics. As Louis and Maertens observed, IOs tend to 'do politics,' while 'pretending to be outside or above the political realm.'[1] This theoretical chapter is dedicated to the most crucial concepts of this book: politicization and depoliticization. Both notions will be discussed first in general, then more specifically in regard to IOs. The chapter concludes with an interpretation of depoliticization as a diplomatic technique on the forum of multilateral organizations and an introduction of the concept of defensive depoliticization. The purpose of the chapter is to provide a theoretical framework for the research and to discuss the theoretical foundation on which the empirical research of depoliticization as a diplomatic technique, by the example of International Civil Aviation Organization (ICAO), has been built.

Politicization

Politics may be understood in multiple ways, in the contexts of the struggle for power, the art of ruling the country, etc. For the purpose of this study, we have employed Aaron Wildavsky's approach, which regards politics 'as conflict over whose preferences are to prevail in the determination of policy.'[2] Politics understood this way is perceived as a category of conflict regarded as a contradiction of interests, both in the context of waging conflicts and attempting to solve them. Adopting this definition allows focusing on the problem of politics in the IOs, with an emphasis on state interests rather than on the domestic pursuit of power. When politics in IOs is considered, it may occur on many levels. IOs constitute sites of contradiction between states, provide the framework for mobilizing non-state actors, and engage in shaping global problems and the governance system in dealing with them.[3] It is, therefore, natural to look at intergovernmental organizations from the political perspective even if, as argued below, they attempt to distance themselves from politics.

The presence of politics in IOs connects with the two crucial categories from the perspective of this study: politicization and depoliticization. Both terms proved

DOI: 10.4324/9781032695402-3

useful for the study of the diplomacy occurring on the forum of ICAO, even though their predominant application concerned other specific issue areas, particularly domestic politics, European integration, and to a lesser extent in the study of IOs, although usually from a different perspective than the one presented in this volume.

There are a number of ways of defining politicization. It has been described as 'opening of something as political,' marking a phenomenon as political,[4] or making issues part of politics.[5] De Wilde and Zürn defined politicization as the 'demand for, or the act of, transporting an issue or an institution into the sphere of politics – making previously apolitical matters political.'[6] Other approaches assume politicization as situations when a social issue becomes 'subject of collective mobilization, debate, polarization, cleavages, controversies, and potential conflicts,'[7] or as moving something 'into the realm of public choice,' which is connected to the possibility of making collectively binding decisions on a particular matter.[8] Some scholars focus on the political conflict perspective on politicization. For example, according to Broekema, an issue is politicized 'when it has become subject to increased political conflict.'[9] Similarly, some authors underlined polarization as a crucial factor for politicization. According to Kriesi, literature on politicization generally distinguishes three conceptual dimensions of the term: issue salience (visibility), actor expansion (range), and actor polarization (intensity and direction), with fully politicized issues being politicized in all three dimensions.[10] De Wilde, in a study of the politicization of the European Union (EU) from the process-oriented perspective, argued that politicization as a process has multiple manifestations and functions, defining politicization as an 'increase in polarization of opinions, interests or values and the extent to which they are publicly advanced towards the process of policy formulation within the EU.'[11] Apart from that, there are approaches that connect politicization with the increase of controversiality of joint decision-making, or with the fact that a political party has picked an issue up regardless of its intrinsic importance.[12]

When considering IOs, there is a widespread agreement that they function within the political realm.[13] Politics is present in IOs, according to Petiteville, for two main reasons. Firstly, state representatives are first and foremost diplomats, with the main goal of promoting national interests. Bodies of IOs that are considered the most glaring forums for political debates include the UN General Assembly and the UN Human Rights Council, but even IOs theoretically less prone to politicization are not isolated from politics. Secondly, IOs' decisions and actions may become subject to pressure from the outside, for example, from governments and civil societies.[14] All this leads to the situation in which IOs become forums for political struggles.

Different types of IOs are associated with politics and diplomacy in different ways. Among several classifications, one of the most important divides IOs into forum and service organizations, although the division is not entirely sharp, and all IGOs, at least to some degree, serve as arenas for diplomatic exchange. In principle, forum organizations provide arenas for multilateral diplomacy, including agenda-setting, coalition-building, norm creation, delegate socialization, and bilateral diplomacy.[15] In other words, they are forums for member states to discuss important issues in the area of interest of a particular organization. In turn, in non-forum organizations, member state representatives and Secretariat staff have specialized or technical training and are less likely to be delegated from foreign ministries. Non-forum IGOs are categorized as service, regulatory, or technical organizations. Service organizations are authorized by states to provide certain services, as in the case of technical assistance programs pursued by UN agencies. Regulatory organizations are empowered to create binding rules and regulations. The diplomacy surrounding the creation of such regulations involves experts from the IGO, member states, other IGOs, and NGOs. Technical organizations are more oriented toward technical expertise, with their existence stemming from the fact that in contemporary global governance, specialized knowledge and expertise have become crucial. Thus, their Secretariats tend to be made up of experts. This type is typical for UN specialized agencies. Such IOs tend to be more independent since highly technical issues require specialized vocabulary and a shared framework. They are characterized by the significant involvement of Secretariat experts, while traditional diplomats from member states are involved when there is a need to negotiate treaty text.[16]

ICAO should be described as a non-forum, technical organization. Similarly to International Labour Organization (ILO) and Food and Agriculture Organization (FAO), it is believed to belong to the organizations that play vital roles in technical issue areas.[17] This does not mean ICAO does not have the qualities of other types of organizations. In fact, the qualities of forum organizations embodied by ICAO are closely connected to main assumptions and arguments of this research. Also, ICAO reveals some qualities of other types of non-forum organizations. It provides certain services like audits or recommendations regarding safety, which are typical for service organizations and contributes to setting rules that connect with regulatory organizations.[18] Still, the technical character of ICAO seems to be prevailing and is reflected already in ICAO's constitutional documents, as well as in its structure and operation.

The division into forum and service organizations is not very clear, and many IOs fall into both categories.[19] According to Karns and Mingst, the nature of diplomacy in different types of IGOs varies, with forum organizations being viewed more as agents of their member states, but the distinctions are not always apparent.[20] Diplomacy in non-forum organizations is more technical, and member state delegations, besides diplomats, include experts in certain areas.[21] The situation is similar regarding the politics in IOs. Intergovernmental bodies (forums) are believed to be more prone to engage in politics, whereas international bureaucracies (actors) tend to focus more on non-political technical expertise and neutralized discourses. However, according to Petiteville, the issue is more complicated, and there are examples of both types behaving otherwise.[22] According to Lyons et al., who studied several of the UN Specialized Agencies, UNESCO and ILO were to be the most politicized. The World Health Organization (WHO), FAO, and World Bank were placed in the middle of their 'Politicization Continuum,' while the IMF and IAEA were considered the least politicized, based on the readiness that the United States would withhold its funding. The difference is that IOs such as UNESCO have a broad and pluralistic mandate, whereas the IAEA has very technical and task-oriented functions. Politics in the IOs may also stem from the size and composition of the membership, from different perceptions of members regarding the potential benefits of their participation,[23] or the media visibility and the general public awareness of an institution.[24] Still, the argument about the technical character of less politicized IOs appears to be the most widespread, although also criticized. As Louis and Maertens argued, such distinctions reproduce functionalist classifications of IOs, limiting the understanding of multilateral processes.[25] As indicated in the book's empirical part, the technical nature of ICAO often served as an argument against discussing sensitive political issues, which at least partly validates the view about the less political character of technical organizations.

Politicization of IOs as a research subject has been gaining growing attention among scholars in recent years, particularly in connection to the authority transfer hypothesis, which assumes that politicization of international and transnational institutions has been growing as they exercise more authority and are becoming more intrusive. It is thus assumed that as the 'relative importance of different political levels changes, political attention changes accordingly.'[26] Other crucial hypotheses for this branch of research include the strategic competition hypothesis, according to which politicization is largely driven by strategically competing party officials; the cleavage transformation hypothesis, which states that party competition is constrained by ideology; as well as two hypotheses studied specifically in reference to the EU: the institutional misfit hypothesis, which assumes the greater discrepancy between the national interests and the EU system, the higher the potential for politicization; the proxy hypothesis, according to which EU citizens use other criteria of assessment to form their opinions about the EU.[27] In this book, politicization of IOs is not a direct research object and only provides circumstances for the actual object of analysis. Thus, we do not intend to test any of these hypotheses, although the strategic competition hypothesis and institutional misfit hypothesis contribute to the understanding of the reasons for increased political tension on the forum of ICAO.

Scholars have extensively studied the concept of the politicization of IOs from a theoretical perspective, but there is no universally accepted definition. As de Wilde et al. observed in reference to the scientific literature on politicization, its 'empirical understanding depends on the empirical focus of study.'[28] According to the apparently most widespread approach, politicization of IOs is defined as 'public awareness and activism directed at IOs.'[29] Politicization understood this way is a multi-dimensional concept that can be observed in such areas as 'the public visibility and awareness of international authority, the polarization of corresponding opinions and positions, as well as the mobilization of a broadened set of societal actors.'[30] As Parizek and Stephen argued, IOs, which are highly visible, typically have larger budgets, staffs, and political significance, thus becoming objects of particularly strong pressure from the under-represented states and the broader public.[31] In a similar manner, Zürn et al. connected politicization of IOs with their authority, with the rise of the latter leading to the politicization. We can speak of

IOs as having authority when the 'addressees of their policies recognize that these institutions can make competent judgments and binding decisions.'[32] According to Zürn, the authority of IOs can stem from their capability to set rules, monitor their implementation, interpret norms, and enforce decisions. This framework allows explaining politicization of various IOs. For example, the World Bank, the UN Security Council, and the World Trade Organization have been criticized for insufficient representation in decision-making regarding rule-making. In terms of monitoring, the International Atomic Energy Agency became subject to criticism for downplaying the negative effects of certain occurrences, whereas the UN Secretary-General, the UN Office of the High Commissioner of Human Rights, the World Food Programme, and the UN Commission on Human Rights for applying double standards in alerting the world regarding crises. International courts have been criticized for focusing on the crimes of the loser's side in reference to norm interpretation, whereas regarding enforcement of decisions, bodies such as UN SC have been criticized for non-action in certain cases.[33] Even though the understanding of politicization used by Zürn in this review is somehow different from the one employed in this volume, it demonstrates the widespread character of politicization of IOs regardless of their type, although the level of politicization varies across different organizations.

Approaches to politicization that focus on IOs as subjects to the pressure exerted by external actors as a result of their authority do not fully apply to ICAO, which has far less authority compared to many other organizations in the UN system. At the same time, its exceptionally technical orientation appears to make it of less interest to external actors. Since this study is neither focused on politicization nor on depoliticization per se, a more adequate understanding of politicization would be the one employed by Lyons et al. In their analysis of politicization of UN Specialized Agencies, Lyons et al. defined politicization as situations in which 'highly controversial issues not always relevant to the agencies' work are introduced by nations to further their political interests.'[34] We have adopted a similar understanding of politicization, combined with a strong reference to conflict as one of the crucial factors for politicization. Accordingly, states may use the forums of IOs, even the technical ones, to wage political conflicts in an attempt to realize their national interests. Such an understanding connects to one of the techniques of multilateralism according to Claude – mobilizing collective condemnation of a state that behaves below international standards, with states involved in disputes often attempting to use multilateral forums to enlist support for their positions.[35] That is exactly what was happening in most of the cases analyzed throughout the book, leading to backlash based on the concept of depoliticization.

As mentioned earlier, ICAO, an organization serving as the main subject for this research, should be classified as a non-forum, technical organization with limited authority. Thus, it should be expected to be more immune to political controversies and pressures. Admittedly, the lion's share of its work has been dedicated to technical-related issues such as the safety of civil aviation or its development. However, politics has also made its way to the ICAO. According to MacKenzie, the organization's political character increased in the 1960s. The influx of new members and the expansion of the Council to 27 seats (at the time) meant that powerful aviation states were less dominating. At the same time, within the Council, there were regional, linguistic, and financial fault lines, while the discussions in the Assembly and the Council increasingly reflected national interests.[36] In principle, these processes occurred simultaneously in other IOs. According to Lyons et al, politicization of UN agencies became a more serious problem since the 1970s as a result of the oil crisis, heightened tensions in the Middle East, and the Third World calling for a new international economic order,[37] whereas Zürn argued that that anti-apartheid and the Third World movements of the 1970s preceded the current politicization of international institutions,[38] and that politicization of international and transnational organizations grew since the 1990s as they were exercising more authority and were becoming more intrusive, in accordance with the authority transfer hypothesis.[39] Also, Karns and Mingst observed the problem of the growing politicization of the UN agencies, resulting in the US decisions in the 1980s to withhold parts of its dues.[40] It was also in the 1980s when the politicization of the EU became more apparent.[41] Interestingly, there is evidence that the increasing politicization of IOs has been occurring rather as 'a patchwork of politicizing moments.'[42] Either way, we may assume that it was the 1980s when politicization was fully introduced to IOs, even though in our study, we have found evidence for the politicization of ICAO even earlier, already in the first years of its existence. As discussed in detail in Chapters 3–6, on multiple occasions, international political controversies associated with political conflicts between states were leading to politicized debates, leading to the occurrence of the second key notion of this book – depoliticization.

Depoliticization

Politicization and depoliticization are strongly interconnected. As described by Hay, they are analogous, though with reversed direction.[43] Just like in the case of politicization, there are multiple definitions of depoliticization. It can be defined as a set of processes, including varied tactics, strategies, and tools, that remove or displace the potential for choice, collective agency, and deliberation around a particular political issue.[44] On a domestic level, depoliticization reflects the desire for greater expertise and technical planning to develop long-term solutions to societal problems, aiming to insulate decision-makers from political temptations, media storms, public protests, party politics, etc.[45] Depoliticization can also be defined as a process of making something non-political or putting it beyond the range of political debate and contestation, usually referring to a particular subject or organization.[46] It is important to mention that regardless of its aim to distance from politics, depoliticization in its domestic variant is believed to be highly political. For example, state managers may retain arms-length control over particular issues but at the same time benefit from the impression of depoliticization.[47] As we argue in the subsequent chapters, depoliticization in an international institution may have a similar character, and describing an institution as non-political does not necessarily imply that it is disconnected from politics.

Wood identified two generations of depoliticization literature and two generations of definitions of depoliticization. The first one appeared in the early 2000s and perceived depoliticization as the process of removing the political character of decision-making. The approach assumes depoliticization as a mode of statecraft and strategy of governing that concerns institutional arrangements aimed to avoid criticism for policy failure.[48] Within this generation, several specific definitions can be cited. Flinders and Buller defined depoliticization as

> the range of tools, mechanisms and institutions through which politicians can attempt to move to an indirect governing relationship and/or seek to persuade the demos that they can no longer be reasonably held responsible for a certain issue, policy field or specific decision.[49]

They proposed three tactics for such depoliticization in the context of domestic politics: institutional, rule-based, and preference-shaping depoliticization. Institutional depoliticization occurs through establishing a formal principal–agent relationship in which elected politicians set policy parameters, whereas the agent, such as an appointed administrator or governing board, enjoys some managerial and specialist freedom. The goal is to release the agent from short-term political considerations. In practice, it is often held through transferring powers and responsibilities to new institutions, for example, immediately after World War II national industries were created in Britain. Rule-based depoliticization involves adopting a policy that builds explicit rules into decision-making in order to constrain the need for political discretion. In other words, through tying their hands, politicians are insulated from societal pressure. Such rules should be neutral and universal, and should not discriminate any group to avoid protests. This kind of depoliticization typically has been implemented in the area of monetary policy. Finally, preference- shaping depoliticization is about recoursing to ideological, discursive, or rhetorical claims used to justify the position that a certain issue or function lies beyond the scope of politics or state control. Unlike to previous tactics, it does not require investing structural or legal capital and is centered around justifying the refusal to intervene or regulate certain issues. For example, EU policies may be framed by their drafters as neutral expert opinion, whereas on the domestic level, British Labour government used arguments concerning globalization to justify certain decisions and non-decisions. The challenge associated with preference-shaping depoliticization is that its maintenance may consume political capital as politicians may be forced to justify their positions.[50] Depoliticization perceived this way is supposed to bring a government certain benefits, such as shielding it from the consequences of unpopular decisions.[51]

The second generation of depoliticization literature emerged in the late 2000s and early 2010s alongside the desire to widen the analysis beyond the state. It refers to rhetorical strategies employed by various social actors aiming to close down 'the appearance of an issue as being political.'[52] Loosening the concept of depoliticization from the state and recognition of its other processes, for example, was advocated by Bates et al.[53] Within the second generation, we might refer to the approach presented by Wood and Flinders, who, besides depoliticization as a mode of statecraft, distinguished societal and discursive depoliticization. Societal depoliticization relates to the role played by various actors, such as media or interest groups, in shifting issues off the agenda of public deliberation. Within this approach, social deliberations surrounding an issue gradually erode until the existence of choices concerning it is no longer debated. Such political apathy is fueled by pressure groups, media, social movements, religious groups, business associations, as well as traditionally engaged politicians and political institutions. In turn, discursive depoliticization refers to '"speech acts" of individuals in the private and public arena that make certain issues appear to be "normal" or "natural."'[54] Discursive depoliticization is fairly similar to societal depoliticization and can be initiated both within and outside the state, but it focuses on the tools of closing down debates concerning political choice and contingency. Such depoliticization occurs 'when the debate surrounding an issue becomes technocratic, managerial, or disciplined towards a single goal, and hence changed in content,' and it is an interactive process between speaker and audience. Unlike societal depoliticization, discursive depoliticization is focused not on institutions, arenas, or actors but on ideas and language. A typical way of employing discursive depoliticization would involve promotion of an issue 'alongside a single interpretation and the denial of choice.'[55] This approach was used, for example, by Pepermans and Maeseele, who, in their study of climate change discourse, distinguished depoliticizing communication strategies such as technocratic, social marketing, green republican, and deliberative dialogue approaches, all aiming to foster social consensus and public engagement.[56] Such perception of depoliticization connects closely with the subject of this book, with actors (representatives and delegates of member states) seeking ICAO debates to focus on technical, thus less inconvenient aspects of specific issues, or to resign from discussing them at all. Still, in some cases, arguments typical for discursive depoliticization were also employed by the delegates and representatives while bringing political issues before the ICAO forum. Since discursive depoliticization is largely about linguistic or rhetorical denial of politics,[57] claims that an issue they were bringing was not political linked such statements to this form of depoliticization. In many cases, they referred to political issues connected to interstate estrangements and conflicts, but to make them appear appropriate for ICAO, they often anchored them on an aviation-related issue, which fulfills the definitional criteria of discursive depoliticization. Apart from that, on numerous occasions, representatives of states not engaged in particular conflict sought to limit the deliberations to technical matters, also exercising discursive depoliticization. All of them are the subject of the analysis of this book. However, its main focus is also placed in what we call defensive depoliticization, which focuses on direct argumentation that an issue should not be discussed because of its political character in order to escape from criticism or ostracism in such a multilateral forum.

Besides generations of defining or researching depoliticization, scholars have also been referring to dimensions of depoliticization. Feindt et al. distinguished three of them: process, strategy, and outcome. Depoliticization as a process denotes mechanisms through which an issue area is constituted as a less public or political affair, particularly regarding being subject to intensified public or political debate. Depoliticization as a strategy aims at 'removing an issue area from processes of political decision-making or even from the realm of public policy,' whereas depoliticization as an outcome denotes the degree to which an issue area has been established as a domain of public policy and the closeness of its links to political mechanisms of governance.[58] This book predominantly focuses on depoliticization as a strategy, though not on the core fact of removing politics, but on using this argument to pursue more particular state goals.

The second generation of definitions of depoliticization has also been employed in the studies of international institutions. According to Petiteville, depoliticization occurs when debates surrounding an issue become focused on technical or managerial issues or are disciplined toward a single goal.[59] Louis and Maertens understood depoliticization as a process of considering a situation, an actor, or an issue as something outside of politics and framed as apolitical, or a process of 'minimizing concealing, even eliminating politics within IOs.'[60] Employing arguments that an issue under discussion is political and thus beyond the scope of the organization roughly falls within this way of understanding depoliticization, although as mentioned earlier, other activities discussed in this book, such as bringing before ICAO political conflicts concealed behind aviation-related matters, or calling to focus the deliberations on technical matters also account for depoliticization.

As long as most IOs are at least to some extent subject to politicization, most of them, particularly the technical ones, attempt to distance themselves from politics in a manner similar to the so-called ideology of depoliticization that exists, for instance, in engineering. The ideology of depoliticization assumes that a specific space is purely technical, thus political and cultural concerns should be removed from it.[61] On a declarative level, such an approach has been very clear in many of the specialized UN agencies, including ICAO, with a close link to the functional approach to IOs discussed in the introduction.

The apolitical claims made by the people engaged in the IOs stem from a dilemma. IOs deal with political issues, but politics is seen as an obstacle to achieving their goals, making staff and members prefer technical debates rather than political ones. Additionally, to fulfill the goal of international cooperation, IOs are 'likely to distance themselves from the "dirty business" of politics.' All this makes them conceal their choices and biases, with the paradox of trying to get away with politics while being embedded in politics.[62] All such depoliticization, in principle, is done to 'silence the political character of IO action,' helping IOs to fulfill their tasks and conceal their engagement in politics, which could generate tensions. Such an approach to the studies of depoliticization of IOs focuses on what is being done in and by an IO, predominantly by its bureaucracy, to avoid or distance the organization from politics. It is exercised, according to Louis and Maertens, through a number of practices. They include producing expert and seemingly neutral reports or endless postponing of decision-making.[63] Lyons et al. mentioned such methods as negotiating and establishing committees responsible for drafting controversial resolutions before the general discussion, adopting proposals of working groups by consensus rather than through voting, compatible memberships in committees, for example, to separate Israel from Arab states, and separating political resolutions from programmatic actions.[64] Importantly, such an approach to depoliticization is only partially connected to depoliticization rhetoric as a diplomatic technique used by member states. The cases discussed in the book cover depoliticization understood this way. However, our focus is to analyze it from the perspective of debates between states on the forum of an IO.

Stone distinguished three types of depoliticization occurring in IOs, which reflect the domestic depoliticization tactics according to Flinders and Buller discussed earlier, with all three types connecting to certain methods. Institutional depoliticization is often used in the environment of IOs through innovations of indirect governance such as global public–private partnerships, transnational networks, or informal IOs such as G20, all providing some operational flexibility. Rule-based depoliticization is about neutral and universal rules being built into decision-making, often through soft law such as voluntary standards or best practices, to avoid rules that discriminate in favor or against particular states. Lastly, depoliticization through preference-shaping and agenda-setting assumes establishing a 'dominant rationality' and non-decision-making dynamics in order to delete certain issues or problems from the debate or consideration.[65] Here, we can see a link between the depoliticization of IOs and methods of multilateral diplomacy, where agenda-setting is one of key methods. Agenda-setting in IOs is basically about what is going to be on the agenda. It is normally considered from the perspective of introducing new agenda topics,[66] but it may be about removing the odd ones as well. Many of the cases analyzed in this book bear the hallmarks of the last type according to Stone, with diplomats attempting to start deliberations on political matters but claiming they are either not political or that they only referred to their technical or economic aspects.

Depoliticization as a diplomatic technique

The available literature contributed massively to the understanding of depoliticization in IOs. However, the purpose of this book is slightly different. It does not focus on the general depoliticization of IOs by the example of the ICAO, although such processes certainly occur and can be observed throughout the book. Rather, it is interested in the tools or techniques used by state representatives on its forum which build on the argument that it is a technical organization, thus politically neutral which should not engage in politicized deliberations. Such techniques use the depoliticization rhetoric, or argument, for either defensive, neutral, or offensive purposes. The focus of this book is specifically on defensive depoliticization, or in other words, depoliticization considered a diplomatic technique with the purpose of defending a state that is criticized or attacked on the forum of the organization. The conceptualization of such an approach to depoliticization requires reference to diplomatic techniques. That is challenging, however, with no accepted classification and different authors providing different examples of diplomatic techniques. For example, Rhodes wrote about such diplomatic techniques as patience, perseverance, and persuasion.[67] Young et al. distinguished preventive and quiet diplomacy techniques such as mediation, shuttle diplomacy, incentives, arbitration, and techniques of outside pressure: media campaign, lobbying, legislation, sanctions, international treaties.[68] A more concrete approach was offered by Kulski, who in a study of diplomatic techniques used by the Soviet Union wrote about simultaneously raising issues in various parts of the world, seizing the initiative to fix the framework of future negotiations, adopting an attitude of an injured party which has the right to redress, trying to place on top of the agenda matters regarding which they have the biggest assets, artificially inflating initial position, using propaganda to soften opponents by the pressure of public opinion, using force against weaker opponents, attempting to split a common block through separate bilateral approaches, manipulating semantics (for example referring to peaceful co-existence instead of Cold War).[69] Karns and Mingst, specifically in reference to diplomacy in IOs, wrote about techniques borrowed from parliaments, with member states seeking to build consensus or to put together a voting majority, which requires such skills as leadership, small, formal negotiating groups, using economic or military resources, ability to serve as a broker, informal contacts, various personal attributes.[70] Arguing that an issue is political and thus beyond the scope of discussion, a claim that directly builds on the concept of depoliticization discussed above or even on the ideology of depoliticization, directly fits among these techniques. Thus, according to the main argument of this book, depoliticization rhetoric should be considered one of the diplomatic techniques used in IOs.

Perception of depoliticization rhetoric as a diplomatic technique is based on the use of language. Conceptually, it borrows from the securitization theory debate. According to Buzan et al., securitization can be seen as a more extreme version of politicization, and any public issue can be located 'on the spectrum ranging from nonpoliticized (…) through politicized (…) to securitized.'[71] Importantly for this study, Buzan et al. distinguished a securitizing move from the actual securitization, which means that presenting something as an existential threat does not create securitization, which occurs only after the audience accepts it as such. Within the securitizing move, an issue is 'dramatized and presented as an issue of supreme priority,' thus labeled as security. The task of an analyst is to understand the process of constructing such a shared understanding of what is to be considered a threat rather than to assess the objective threats. Such a process of securitization in the language theory is called a speech act,[72] which, according to Searle, includes making statements, giving commands, asking questions, making promises, etc.[73] The situation with depoliticization as a diplomatic defensive technique is analogical. Paraphrasing the securitization debate, we are interested in the 'depoliticizing moves' or 'acts of depoliticization.'[74] In the framework of depoliticization theory, this connects to the already mentioned notion of discursive depoliticization, which focuses on the tools used to close down political debates. Instead of focusing on arenas, institutions, or actors, discursive depoliticization focuses on ideas and language.[75] Similarly as in the aforementioned securitizing moves, actors make speech acts claiming an issue is not subject to politics, although this does not mean its political nature vanishes. Such speech acts attempt to shift politics away from an issue, while their success depends on the reception of the audience. In their conceptualization of depoliticization, Flinders and Wood used the language studies concept of denial, linking depoliticization with denial strategies and focusing on denying the political nature of particular issues.[76] Indirectly, we have also built on this approach, but rather than on denial of the political nature of discussed issues, we analyzed arguments about the political nature of issues discussed within the ICAO and the reluctance to acknowledge the space for such debates within the organization. However, the debates analyzed in this volume also concern more general discursive depoliticization, with speakers introducing issues connected to politics but arguing their non-political character in order to initiate a specific deliberation.

Conclusions

The study presented in this book considers depoliticization from a novel perspective. It builds on conceptualizations of politicization and depoliticization with a particular focus on these processes occurring in IOs. We have adopted an understanding of politicization of IOs as transferring political issues, such as interstate conflicts, into the originally non-political forums. This occurs when states pursue their political interests, especially within the context of ongoing conflicts. The analysis covers attempts to move politics away from ICAO's forum or to frame certain issues as not political, although we focus on depoliticization perceived in a reversed way, on what we call defensive depoliticization, which alongside offensive and neutral depoliticization is perceived as a diplomatic tool. Defensive depoliticization, or in other words, depoliticization rhetoric as a defensive diplomatic technique, specifically features argumentation that certain issues are political and should not be discussed on the forum of a technical organization such as ICAO, or that specific decisions should not be made, for the purpose of defending particular states. Such depoliticizing moves, as argued throughout this volume, are considered a diplomatic technique, which implies that their intent is not to distance politics from the organization, but rather to leverage the negative connotations associated with politics to bolster their arguments while being criticized on its forum.

Notes

1 Marieke Louis and Lucile Maertens, *Why International Organizations Hate Politics: Depoliticizing the World* (London: Routledge, 2021), 184.
2 Aaron B. Wildavsky, "Budgeting as a Political Process," in *The International Encyclopedia of the Social Sciences*, ed. David L. Sills (New York: Crowell, Collier, and Macmillan, 1968), 192.
3 Louis and Maertens, *Why International Organizations*, 1.
4 Kari Palonen, "Four Times of Politics: Policy, Polity, Politicking, and Politicization," *Alternatives* 28 (2003): 171, 182.
5 Jeffrey T. Checkel and Peter J. Katzenstein, "The Politicization of European Identities," in *European identity*, ed. Jeffrey T. Checkel and Peter J. Katzenstein (Cambridge: Cambridge University Press, 2012), 2.

6 Pieter De Wilde and Michael Zürn, "Can the Politicization of European Integration be Reversed?," *Journal of Common Market Studies* 50, no. 1 (2012): 139, https://doi.org/10.1111/j.1468-5965.2011.02232.x
7 Franck Petiteville, "International Organizations beyond Depoliticized Governance," *Globalizations* 15, no. 3 (2018): 302, https://doi.org/10.1080/14747731.2017.1370850
8 Michael Zürn, "Politicization Compared: At National, European, and Global Levels," *Journal of European Public Policy* 26, no. 7 (2019): 978, https://doi.org/10.1080/13501763.2019.1619188
9 Wout Broekema, "Crisis-induced Learning and Issue Politicization in the EU: The Braer, Sea Empress, Erika, and Prestige Oli Spill Disasters," *Public Administration* 94, no. 2 (2016): 384, https://doi.org/10.1111/padm.12170
10 Hanspeter Kriesi, "The Politicization of European Integration," *Journal of Common Market Studies* 54 (2016): 33, https://doi.org/10.1111/jcms.12406
11 Pieter De Wilde, "No Polity for Old Politics? A Framework for Analyzing the Politicization of European Integration," *Journal of European Integration* 33, no. 5 (2011): 559–575, p. 572, https://doi.org/10.1080/07036337.2010.546849
12 Hooghe and Marks, "Politicization," 840, 844.
13 See: Michael N. Barnett and Martha Finnemore, "The Politics, Power, and Pathologies of International Organizations," *International Organization* 53, no. 4 (1999): 699–732; Lawrence B. Krause and Joseph S. Nye, "Refections on the Economics and Politics of International Economic Organizations," *International Organization* 29 (1975): 323–342, https://doi.org/10.1017/S0020818300017975; Michal Parizek, "Control, Soft Information, and the Politics of International Organizations Staffing," *The Review of International Organizations* 12 (2017): 559–583, https://doi.org/10.1007/s11558-016-9252-1; Louis and Maertens, *Why International Organizations*; Kenneth W. Abbott and Duncan Snidal, "Why States Act through Formal International Organizations," in *The Politics of Global Governance: International Organizations in an Interdependent World*, ed. Paul F. Diehl (Boulder: Lynne Rienner Publishers, 2001), 9–43; etc.
14 Petiteville, "International Organizations Beyond," 307–309.
15 Margaret P. Karns and Karen A. Mingst, "International Organizations and Diplomacy," in *The Oxford Handbook of Modern Diplomacy*, ed. Andrew F. Cooper, Jorge Heine and Ramesh Thakur, (Oxford: Oxford University Press, 2013), 146–147.
16 Ibid., 150–152.
17 Abbott and Snidal, "Why States Act," 10.
18 See: Karns and Mingst, "International Organizations and Diplomacy," 150–152.
19 James P. Muldoon Jr., "Multilateralism's New Mix: Implications for Diplomacy, International Organizations, and Global Governance," in *The New Dynamics of Multilateralism. Diplomacy, International Organizations, and Global Governance*, ed. James Muldoon, Jr., JoAnn Fagot Aviel, Richard Reitano, and Earl Sullivan, 333–343 (Boulder: Westview, 2011), 337.
20 Karns and Mingst, "International Organizations and Diplomacy," 152.
21 Beata Surmacz, *Ewolucja Współczesnej Dyplomacji: Aktorzy, Struktury, Funkcje* (Lublin: Wydawnictwo UMCS, 2015), 279.
22 Petiteville, "International Organizations Beyond," 303.
23 Gene M. Lyons, David A. Baldwin, and Donald W. McNemar, "The "Politicization" Issue in the UN Specialized Agencies," *Proceedings of the Academy of Political Science* 32, no. 4 (1977): 88–89.
24 Michal Parizek and Matthew D. Stephen, "The Increasing Representativeness of International Organizations' Secretariats: Evidence from the United Nations System, 1997–2015," *International Studies Quarterly* 65, no. 1 (March 2021): 201.

25 Louis and Maertens, *Why International Organizations*, 4.
26 Zürn, "Politicization Compared," 985.
27 Pieter de Wilde, Anna Leupold, and Henning Schmidtke, "Introduction: The Differentiated Politicisation of European Governance," *West European Politics* 39, no. 1 (2016): 11–12, https://doi.org/10.1080/01402382.2015.1081505
28 Ibid., 4.
29 Matthias Ecker-Ehrhardt, "Self-Legitimation in the Face of Politicization: Why International Organizations Centralized Public Communication," *The Review of International Organizations* 13, no. 4 (2018): 521, https://doi.org/10.1007/s11558-017-9287-y
30 Christian Rauh and Michael Zürn, "Authority, Politicization, and Alternative Justifications: Endogenous Legitimation Dynamics in Global Economic Governance," *Review of International Political Economy* 27, no. 3 (2020): 594, https://doi.org/10.1080/09692290.2019.1650796
31 Parizek and Stephen, "The Increasing Representativeness," 201.
32 Michael Zürn, Martin Binder, and Matthias Ecker-Ehrhardt, "International Authority and Its Politicization," *International Theory* 4, no. 1 (2012): 70, https://doi.org/10.1017/S1752971912000012
33 Zürn, *A Theory of Global Governance*, 155–159.
34 Lyons, Baldwin, and McNemar, "The "Politicization" Issue," 81.
35 Inis L. Claude Jr., "Multilateralism – Diplomatic and Otherwise," in *Diplomacy*, vol. I, ed. Christer Jönsson and Richard Langhorne (London: SAGE, 2004), 368–370.
36 David MacKenzie, *ICAO: A History of the International Civil Aviation Organization* (Toronto: University of Toronto Press, 2010), 169.
37 Lyons, Baldwin, and McNemar, "The "Politicization" Issue," 81.
38 Michael Zürn, "The Politicization of World Politics and Its Effects: Eight Propositions," *European Political Science Review* 6, no. 1 (2014): 51–52, https://doi.org/10.1017/S1755773912000276
39 Zürn, "Politicization Compared," 985.
40 Margaret P. Karns and Karen A. Mingst, *International Organizations: The Politics and Processes of Global Governance* (Boulder: Lynne Rienner Publishers, 2010), 140.
41 Hartmut Kaelble, "Identification with Europe and Politicization of the EU Since the 1980s," in *European Identity*, ed. Jeffrey T. Checkel and Peter J. Katzenstein (Cambridge: Cambridge University Press, 2012), 193–197.
42 Swen Hutter and Hanspeter Kriesi, "Politicizing Europe in Times of Crisis," *Journal of European Public Policy* 26, no. 7 (2019): 997, https://doi.org/10.1080/13501763.2019.1619801
43 Colin Hay, *Why We Hate Politics* (Cambridge: Polity, 2007), 78–81.
44 Paul Fawcett et al., "Anti-Politics, Depoliticization, and Governance," in *Anti-Politics, Depoliticization, & Governance*, ed. Paul Fawcett, Matthew Flinders, Colin Hay, and Matthew Wood (Oxford: Oxford University Press, 2017), 5.
45 Matthew Flinders and Matt Wood, "When Politics Fails: Hyper-Democracy and Hyper-Depoliticization," *New Political Science* 37, no. 3 (2015): 364, 374, https://doi.org/10.1080/07393148.2015.1056431
46 Alasdair Roberts, *The Logic of Discipline: Global Capitalism and the Architecture of Government* (Oxford: Oxford University Press, 2010), 140–141.
47 Peter Burnham, "Globalization, Depoliticization and 'Modern' Economic Management," in *The Politics of Change*, ed. Werner Bonefeld and Kosmas Psychopedis (London: Palgrave Macmillan, 2002), 22, https://doi.org/10.1057/9780333993798_2

48 Matthew Wood, "Politicisation, Depoliticisation and Anti-Politics: Towards a Multilevel Research Agenda," *Political Studies Review* 14, no. 4 (2016): 522–523, https://doi.org/10.1111/1478-9302.12074
49 Matthew Flinders and Jim Buller, "Depoliticisation: Principles, Tactics and Tools," *British Politics* 1 (2006): 295–296, https://doi.org/10.1057/palgrave.bp.4200016
50 Ibid., 298–309.
51 Peter Burnham, "New Labour and the Politics of Depoliticisation," *British Journal of Politics and International Relations* 3, no. 2 (2001): 129, https://doi.org/10.1111/1467-856X.00054
52 Wood, "Politicisation, Depoliticisation," 524.
53 Stephen Bates, Laura Jenkins, and Fran Amery, "(De)politicisation and the Father's Clause Parliamentary Debates," *Policy & Politics* 42, no. 2 (2014): 245, https://doi.org/10.1332/030557312X656007
54 Matt Wood and Matthew Flinders, "Rethinking Depoliticisation: Beyond the Governmental," *Policy & Politics* 42 no. 2 (2014): 152, 158–159, https://doi.org/10.1332/030557312X655909
55 Ibid., 161, 164.
56 Yves Pepermans and Pieter Maeseele, "The Politicization of Climate Change: Problem or Solution?," *WIREs Climate Change* 7 (July/August 2016): 478–479, https://doi.org/10.1002/wcc.405
57 Matthew Flinders and Matt Wood, "Discursive Depoliticization and Political Disengagement," in *The Routledge Handbook of Language and Politics*, ed. Ruth Wodak and Bernhard Forchtner (London: Routledge, 2017), 603.
58 Peter H. Feindt, Sandra Schwindenhammer, and Jale Tosun, "Politicization, Depoliticization and Policy Change: A Comparative Theoretical Perspective on Agri-food Policy," *Journal of Comparative Policy Analysis: Research and Practice* (2020): 512–513, https://doi.org/10.1080/13876988.2020.1785875
59 Petiteville, "International Organizations Beyond," 302.
60 Louis and Maertens, *Why International Organizations*, 3.
61 Erin A. Cech and Heidi M. Sherick, "Depoliticization and the Structure of Engineering Education," in *International Perspectives on Engineering Education. Philosophy of Engineering and Technology*, vol 20, ed. Steen Hyldgaard Christensen, Christelle Didier, Andrew Jamison, Martin Meganck, Carl Mitcham, Byron Newberry (Cham: Springer, 2015), 9. https://doi.org/10.1007/978-3 319-16169-3_10
62 Louis and Maertens, *Why International Organizations*, 3.
63 Ibid., 185.
64 Lyons, Baldwin, and McNemar, "The "Politicization" Issue," 89–90.
65 Diane Stone, "Global Governance Depoliticized: Knowledge Networks, Scientization, and Anti-Policy," in *Anti-Politics, Depoliticization, & Governance*, ed. Paul Fawcett, Matthew Flinders, Colin Hay, and Matthew Wood (Oxford: Oxford University Press, 2017), 93–94.
66 Karns and Mingst, "International Organizations and Diplomacy," 147.
67 R.A.W. Rhodes, "From Marketisation To Diplomacy: It's the Mix that Matters," *Australian Journal of Public Administration* 56, no. 2 (1997): 40–53, https://doi.org/10.1111/j.1467-8500.1997.tb01545.x
68 Juliette Claire Young, John Robertson Young, and Béatrice Agathe Aubert, "Insights from Diplomacy for the Prevention and Resolution of Conservation Conflicts," *Conservation Letters* 15, no. 5 (2022): 1–9, https://doi.org/10.1111/conl.12891

69 W. W. Kulski, "Soviet Diplomatic Techniques," *The Russian Review* 19, no. 3 (1960): 221–224.
70 Karns and Mingst, "International Organizations and Diplomacy," 145.
71 Barry Buzan, Ole Wæver, and Jaap de Wilde, *Security: A New Framework for Analysis* (Boulder: Lynne Rienner Publishers, 1998), 23.
72 Ibid., 26.
73 See: John R. Searle, *Speech Acts: An Essay in the Philosophy of Language* (Cambridge: Cambridge University Press, 1969).
74 See: Laura Jenkins, "The Difference Genealogy Makes: Makes: Strategies for Politicisation or How to Extend Capacities for Autonomy," *Political Studies* 59, no. 1 (2011): 156–174, https://doi.org/10.1111/j.1467-9248.2010.00844.x.
75 Wood and Flinders, "Rethinking Depoliticization," 152.
76 Matthew Flinders and Matt Wood, "Discursive Depoliticization and Political Disengagement," in *The Routledge Handbook of Language and Politics*, ed. Ruth Wodak and Bernhard Forchtner (London: Routledge, 2017), 603–617.

3 Conflicts over ICAO membership and members' statehood

A group of conflicts that was turning International Civil Aviation Organization (ICAO) into a forum of politically motivated debates is linked to an issue of membership in the organization, with certain states questioning others' right to be members. These disputes sometimes stemmed from the issues of statehood and international recognition, with one party attempting to deny the statehood of another, but there were also other reasons – historical matters, domestic policy matters, or international conflicts, sometimes overlapping with each other. Four such conflicts will be discussed in this chapter, that is an issue of Spain's ICAO membership concerning its support for the Axis during World War II, the membership of the People's Republic of China and Republic of China, the problem of South African membership in the context of international isolation imposed on the country in response to the apartheid, and questioning the right of Cyprus to be ICAO member state as a consequence of the conflict between Cyprus and Turkey.

Spain's ICAO membership

The problem of Spain's membership in ICAO differs from most other cases analyzed in this book as it did not result from direct political tensions. Rather, it was a legal matter connected to general international sanctions and ICAO's entering into a relationship with the UN. Still, despite its not directly political character, it has led to the use of depoliticization rhetoric as a defensive tool.

Under General Franco's rule, Spain did not participate directly in World War II. After its outbreak, Spain declared neutrality and non-belligerency, but it supported the Axis countries. For example, it joined the Steel Pact.[1] Despite these shades on the history of Spain, it entered the post-war period in international aviation as an engaged and active country. Spain was a founding member of ICAO, participated in the Chicago conference, and ratified the Chicago Convention.[2] However, its situation in other international organizations (IOs) was not the same. The San Francisco conference, gathered to establish the United Nations, accepted the Mexican proposition that no state whose regime was established with the help of the Axis, if it was still in power, could be admitted to the UN.[3] Initially, it was not a problem in ICAO, which was established independently from the UN, but the situation changed as

DOI: 10.4324/9781032695402-4

the partnership between the two organizations was being established since the UN expected its agencies to follow the same policy regarding former Axis allies.

ICAO dealt with the issue during the First Assembly in 1947. The UN expected ICAO's compliance with the UN General Assembly resolution from December 12, 1946, which recommended debarring Franco Spain from membership of UN agencies.[4] The issue was first debated in Commission I, which was responsible for constitutional and general policy questions. The Portuguese delegate spoke about the importance of universal membership of ICAO and that political interests should not disrupt the organization because of the technical consequences. This view was supported by the delegate from Argentina, who claimed that ICAO was 'a technical organization whose efficiency should not be impaired by adherence to recommendations of a purely political character.'[5] The American delegation, joined by the delegates from the United Kingdom and Venezuela, argued for the necessity of approving the agreement with the UN, presenting a dissenting viewpoint.[6]

Other delegates also joined the discussion, either supporting Spain's continued membership or favoring entering into the relationship with the UN. The delegate from the Union of South Africa said his government did not support the Franco regime in Spain but criticized the way the Interim Council dealt with the issue. He said he believed ICAO was a non-political body, while the proposal to suspend or expel Spain was based only on political grounds. He continued that to achieve its goals, ICAO needs worldwide membership, while Spain was situated on the international air routes. Concluding, the South African delegate expressed his hope to find a solution without resorting to expelling a member state. The Chinese delegate expressed his understanding of the arguments raised by those against expelling Spain but claimed they had no other choice and thus supported the US standpoint. The Spanish delegate, on the other hand, said that 'Spain was surprised to learn that non-technical and non-economic influences were impairing the technical autonomy of ICAO' and questioned the advantages of entering into relations with the UN.[7] After that, the delegate from Peru said he was against expulsion of Spain, referring to the non-political character of ICAO, although he was not against entering into relations with the UN. On the other hand, there were also voices of support for expulsion. The American position was also supported by the delegates from Czechoslovakia, Belgium, Australia, France, and Canada, although the latter two did this as a result of the belief in the importance of the agreement with the UN.[8] Presenting a contrary opinion, the Irish delegate said that 'his government felt that the function of the Organization is to look on matters coming before it, not from a political angle, but from the point of view of the interests of international aviation' and that there was no reason why Spain should be expelled.[9] In the end, the Commission unanimously adopted the draft agreement and then voted in favor of expelling Spain, with 18 votes in favor, 3 against, and 4 abstentions.[10] As we can see, in this very first ICAO debate with political overtones, a number of delegations have already employed depoliticization rhetoric. This was naturally the case for Spain, but many other delegations used similar arguments even if the vote results did not fully reflect this. Since we could not identify any political pattern for defending Spain, it should be assumed that at least some of the speakers arguing politics should be kept away from ICAO did this because of genuine will to protect the organization from politicization. Still, besides Spain which certainly used depoliticization argument in defense, some other delegations might also have sought to defend it, though without revealing a clear political stance it is impossible to determine whether their interventions were in fact neutral, or rather defensive but in a concealed way. This situation demonstrates one of the methodological difficulties of this research since the fact that defensive character of depoliticization used by third actors was not evident in their interventions does not mean their purpose was not to defend such state. However, such apparently unbiased statements calling for not engaging in politics will be interpreted as neutral depoliticization, although defensive intentions could sometimes be figured from the context, for example, when Communist states argued in favor of states belonging to the same bloc.

The discussions then moved to the plenary meetings of the First Assembly. The expulsion of Spain was advocated by the delegates from the United States and the United Kingdom, the latter arguing that agreements and understandings with the UN and other organizations 'testify to the international prestige of PICAO.'[11] The delegates from France[12] and Canada also argued that it was necessary to affiliate ICAO with the UN.[13] The draft resolution ultimately passed with a 27-3 vote. Ireland, Portugal, and Switzerland voted against the expulsion, while Argentina and the Union of South Africa abstained. The Dominican Republic and Spain were absent. The Swiss delegate explained his position, stating that Switzerland was not a UN member state and did not vote in the General Assembly about the issue.[14] Following the vote, the Portuguese delegate stated his vote was a matter of principle, claiming that 'the life and stability of international relations will be seriously jeopardized if discriminatory interests of a political character are allowed to disrupt activities of a purely technical nature and worldwide scope whose efficiency for the welfare and progress of humanity rest upon their universality and unrestricted cooperation between nations,'[15] once again advocating keeping politics away from ICAO. The Spanish delegate did not take the floor.

The expulsion of Spain did not last long. On November 4, 1950, the UN General Assembly revoked its recommendation from December 12, 1946, on debarring Spain from specialized agencies. The President of the ICAO Council immediately took steps to resume relations with Spain.[16] When the Spanish delegation was back at the 5th Assembly in 1951, its chief delegate addressed the Assembly, saying they had returned without any resentment. He thanked the organization and many countries for collaboration and support, thanks to which its isolation did not damage Spain's civil aviation policy.[17] During the same session, Spain filled the vacancy in the Council, being the only candidate.[18] It is important to note that even when Spain was beyond the organization, ICAO worked behind the scenes to maintain relations,[19] so it was not entirely isolated from the international aviation system.

The developments surrounding the expulsion of Spain were a harbinger of the future use of depoliticization rhetoric on ICAO's forum. Debates were not particularly fierce and confrontational, probably because they did not result directly from an international estrangement, with Spain not being actively engaged in the war. As a result, Spain was not subject to direct verbal attacks and even those in favor of its expulsion justified it by the need to enter into relationship with the UN. Some delegations simply argued that technical ICAO should not be subject to political decisions. Such statements bear the hallmarks of preference-shaping depoliticization, with a prevailing argument that the works of technical ICAO should not be disrupted by political matters that lie beyond its scope. Naturally, defensive depoliticization was also present, with delegates from Spain and several other countries arguing that it was more important to keep Spain in ICAO than to follow the UN's political expectations.

Chinese membership in ICAO

A prolonged membership controversy concerned the Republic of China (Taiwan). The debate surrounding the so-called Chinese question occurred in numerous IOs, both intergovernmental and non-governmental. The controversy originated from the civil war in China, which led to the establishment of two Chinese governments, with the former Kuomintang government fleeing to Taiwan and the new Communist government of the People's Republic of China residing in Beijing. The developments resonated with the Cold War tensions, with Communist countries supporting the PRC while the majority of capitalist countries favoring Taiwan. This situation was also reflected in IOs. In the UN, it was Taiwan that enjoyed the membership, including the permanent seat on the Security Council. Mainland China, in turn, was excluded from mainstream international politics.[20] After the Communist revolution, the PRC's leaders anticipated that the United Nations and its specialized agencies would support its claim for Taiwan's replacement. They even demanded in September 1949 that the UN expelled the nationalist delegation. However, the UN Charter did not provide guidelines for the situation of a change of political regime, whereas the Western bloc did not recognize the PRC, leading the Security Council to defeat the Soviet proposal to admit the PRC in 1950.[21] The Soviet Union even boycotted the UN SC in protest against the refusal to seat the UN ambassador from the PRC.[22] A similar situation occurred in other UN agencies and even in international sports organizations such as the International Olympic Committee (IOC), which was open to accepting two Chinese National Olympic Committees, but until the late 1970s, the PRC did not agree to a joint membership.[23] ICAO was not different, and similarly to other IOs, it became a forum for numerous controversies and heated debates regarding the status of China.

China was a founding member of ICAO, signed the original version of the Chicago Convention, and participated in its meetings from the beginning.[24] The Chinese Revolution did not change this situation, but soon, controversies began to arise. On May 28, 1950, ICAO received a telegram from Beijing, informing that Kuomintang's government should be barred from organs and meetings of the organization. Three days later, the government in Taiwan gave notice of denunciation of the Chicago Convention taking effect one year from that date[25] because of difficulties with paying contributions.[26] Already then, Taiwan was facing some difficulties in ICAO. For example, during a meeting of the Executive Committee of the 4th Assembly in 1950, the delegates from the United Kingdom and India claimed the denunciation was not valid since their governments no longer regarded the Chinese Nationalist Government 'as responsible government of China.'[27] Either way, the Taiwanese withdrawal from ICAO temporarily allowed further controversy to be avoided, with no Chinese presence in the organization at the time as the PRC was still absent from the UN system.

The stable situation in the ICAO was disrupted in 1953 when Taiwan announced its intention to rejoin the organization. The Taiwanese observer, in an address to the 7th Assembly, spoke about financial reasons for temporal withdrawal from ICAO and willingness to re-enter,[28] which took effect on January 1, 1954.[29] Taiwanese return to ICAO soon led to voices about the absence of Communist China and the politicization of its deliberations. During the 10th Assembly in 1956, the India's delegate said that he regretted that China's seat was not occupied by the PRC, arguing there was 'no reasonable ground for ignoring the basic facts of the situation in regard to China,' a view backed by the delegates of Egypt and Indonesia and opposed by the American delegate.[30] During the 11th Assembly in 1958, the India's delegate requested to be recorded as abstaining on the report of the Credentials Committee because of his inability to accept the report concerning the credentials of the Chinese delegation. The delegates of the United Arab Emirates, Czechoslovakia, and Poland also raised similar requests. In response, the Taiwanese delegate said the mission of the Credentials Committee was to examine the credentials rather than go into political questions and that he represented a government that was a member of ICAO, UN, and other specialized agencies. The delegate added, referring to the statement by the India's delegate from the previous 10th Assembly, that 'the Government in Peking was the only Government entitled to represent China,' asked whether any of the delegations 'consider worthy of membership in ICAO a Government that less than four years ago had deliberately authorized the shooting down of a civil aircraft (…) and the strafing of rescue operations at the scene of the crash?' He added that he represented the only government of China elected under the constitution, that it maintained diplomatic relations with 45 countries and was represented in all major IOs, concluding that 'as long as it spoke for China in the councils of nations, international Communism would never be able to complete the political conquest of the Chinese people in spite of military domination over the mainland.'[31] The India's delegate responded that he did not want to introduce political considerations beyond the scope of ICAO as the Chinese delegate did, while the reason for bringing the matter to the Assembly, which he knew had political overtones, was to explain the reasons for his abstention at the second meeting on the interim report of the Credentials Committee.[32] The discussion from the 11th Assembly thus constitutes a clear example of depoliticization rhetoric employed in defense. Following criticism over RoC's membership, its delegate employed a depoliticizing move, arguing that political matters should not be raised in ICAO. Interestingly, in his intervention, the Taiwanese delegate also used political arguments, attacking the government in Beijing and Communism. At the same time, in the words of the delegate of India, we can observe elements characteristic for discursive depoliticization. After raising an issue that the delegate acknowledged to have political overtones and could be interpreted as politicizing the deliberations, he claimed it was not for political purposes but only to explain his abstention.

Similar developments took place during the 12th Assembly in 1959, with the delegate of India wishing to dissociate himself from the report of the Credentials Committee, saying that his government 'recognized the Government of the People's Republic of China as the only legitimate Government of China.'[33] A similar request was expressed by the delegates from Indonesia, Poland, the United Arab Republic, Czechoslovakia, and Afghanistan, whereas the British delegate said he would approve the report, but it should not imply recognition of authorities issuing the credentials. The Chinese delegate then responded that questions of a political nature were outside the province of the Credentials Committee and that 'the Government of the Republic of China was the only legal and constitutional government of China.' Delegations from Korea and the United States supported this view.[34] The discussion thus mirrored the deliberations from the previous Assembly.

The situation kept repeating itself during subsequent Assemblies, with delegations usually from the same countries expressing reservations regarding the interim or final reports of the Credentials Committee because of RoC's presence,[35] although there were also occasions when RoC's presence was criticized already during the opening statements of delegations.[36] Every time, RoC's delegates were employing, among other things, depoliticization rhetoric to defend their presence. During the extraordinary 13th Assembly in 1961, the RoC's delegate said he did not want to raise political or juridical issues, but his government represented a UN member state despite the repeated attempts by the Soviet bloc to undermine its position, adding that RoC's government was represented in other IOs, maintained diplomatic relations with most of the free nations, and that because of the Cold War context, some states raised the issue of Chinese representation in a political conference for the sake of propaganda or its political purposes.[37] During the 14th Assembly in 1962, the RoC's delegate once again referred to its status in the UN, criticized the PRC's regime as 'representing nothing but (…) enslavement, misery and starvation,' and concluded that the question of representation of the Republic of China should not arise in any IO, and particularly not in ICAO.[38] During the discussion, the Korean delegate also said he was surprised by some countries raising political questions.[39] The discussion reemerged after the final report was presented. The delegate of RoC responded to India's position by recalling a message from several years before from India's Prime Minister Jawaharlal Nehru to Chiang Kai-shek about the friendship between India and China, commenting that China that Nehru spoke about was 'not the puppet regime that the Delegate of India had referred to.'[40] As we can see, just as the criticism against Taiwanese presence was similar during subsequent sessions of the Assembly, the line of defense was also repeated, with arguments about the Taiwanese right to participate in the Assembly, remarks about the political character of the accusations that made them unfit for ICAO, and with critical remarks about the PRC and Communism.

Subsequent Assemblies were no different when it came to questioning RoC's presence and the attempts by its delegations to defend it. During the 15th Assembly in 1965, the RoC's delegate assured that the credentials of the Chinese delegation were in perfect order, while the government of the Republic of China 'was the only legitimate government of China,' the founding member of the UN, party to the Convention having every right to be represented at the Assembly.[41] Further debate developed, with subsequent delegations either supporting or opposing RoC's presence. An important point from the perspective of this study was made by the delegate of Vietnam, who claimed the discussion should not take place in the ICAO Assembly, adding that ICAO as a specialized agency should not undertake political questions such as the representation of China, which should be discussed in the UN, and that Communist China had never sought ICAO membership so only the RoC could represent the people of China.[42] It was, therefore, another delegation that used depoliticization rhetoric to defend RoC, which, from the perspective of Cold War geopolitical divisions, should presumably be considered an attempt to support an ally. At the 16th Assembly in 1968, the RoC's delegate argued that discussing such political questions was beyond the competence of the Assembly, that the RoC was the founding member of the UN, and its government was the only legitimate and constitutional government of China represented in all the UN organs, practically repeating the arguments from the previous Assembly. He added that the Chinese Communist regime 'was an oppressor and enemy of the Chinese people' and was not entitled to represent them. He also mentioned that the question raised had been decided many times in the UN what should be considered by its agencies.[43] Also, the Japanese delegate said it was a political question that should not be discussed in the Assembly.[44] Defensive depoliticization was thus employed by the delegations that wished to support Taiwanese presence. It is worth mentioning that these delegations represented pro-Western governments.

Even though extraordinary Assemblies normally were convened to discuss important and urgent civil aviation issues exclusively, with little reference to side topics, they were occasionally used to wage political conflicts. This was the case of the 13th Assembly mentioned earlier, as well as the extraordinary 17th Assembly in 1970 and 17th-A Assembly in 1971, both used by some delegations as a forum to question RoC's right to be represented in ICAO and subsequent defensive moves in response. During the 17th Assembly, the delegate of RoC said he found it strange that such a question was raised during the extraordinary session and argued that the RoC delegation had no less right than any other to be represented at the Assembly and that it was the only legal government to represent China. He mentioned RoC's UN membership, its friendly relations with the majority of states, and that Mao Tse Tung's regime was imposed by force.[45] During the subsequent 17th-A Extraordinary Assembly, following reservations by a number of delegations regarding the interim report of the Credentials Committee, the RoC's delegate responded that the report of the Credentials Committee had nothing to do with the question of representation of contracting states and that the Assembly was not a political place to discuss such things. He also noted how enthusiastic some speakers were in looking for every opportunity 'of pleasing the enemy of Chinese people and championing its cause' and added that the government of the Republic of China was the only legitimate government of China,[46] again repeating the same arguments in response to similar statements against Taiwanese presence.

The 17th-A session of the Assembly in 1971 was the last one to feature discussions over the status of China in the ICAO, with voices against RoC's presence expressed after the presentation of the interim and final reports of the Credentials Committee,[47] as well as during the address of the Romanian delegation to the Assembly.[48] The year 1971 marked the end of this lasting saga of debates in ICAO regarding RoC's membership, reflecting the developments in the UN where, following the US–Chinese rapprochement initiated by the famous Ping-Pong diplomacy, the PRC took the seat formerly occupied by RoC. Accordingly, in 1971, the ICAO Council decided to recognize the representatives of the PRC's government as the only legitimate representatives of China to the ICAO.[49] From that point, RoC was no longer an ICAO member, but for practical reasons concerning provisions of aviation services and facilities, the ICAO regional office in Bangkok entered an unofficial agreement with Taiwan through third parties.[50]

The developments concerning the Chinese question in ICAO between 1950 and the early 1970s were similar to what was happening in other IOs at the time, as well as in certain non-governmental organizations. Though Taiwan for a long time managed to secure its position within such organizations, mainly owing to the American support, there were many countries that consequently argued in favor of the membership of Communist China, which, as a result of the character of mutual relations between the PRC and RoC, would mean the expulsion of the latter. The controversy had a clearly Cold War character, although not only Communist countries argued that the PRC should be represented in ICAO rather than RoC. Such an argument was also raised by several delegations from the developing world and from Western countries, such as the United Kingdom and France. Taiwanese delegations and occasionally others attempted to defend Taiwanese presence, often referring to the political character of arguments against it. Besides the issue of political alliances visible on the ICAO forum, the Chinese issue also reveals political matters being injected into the organization, which offered a forum for political declarations of particular states. Despite the technical character of the organization, delegations against Taiwanese membership were employing such trivial issues as the reports of the Credentials Committee as a rationale for engaging in political debates, even though they sometimes argued they were not politicizing the deliberations, which corresponds with the concept of discursive depoliticization. The delegates of RoC, in an attempt to defend their ICAO presence, employed various techniques. They argued about their government's legal standing, the UN membership, and diplomatic relations with many countries worldwide. Among these defensive techniques, they also used depoliticization rhetoric, within which they argued that ICAO was not a proper place for political debates and declarations. Like in many other cases analyzed in this book, the RoC delegates, on many occasions, also attacked and criticized the government in Beijing, referring to its illegitimate character or various misconducts, thus arguing against referring to politics and doing this at the same time. This observation corresponds with the argument about depoliticization as a governing strategy, thus something highly political.[51] Such depoliticization rhetoric was not about withdrawing from politics but an argument used predominantly for defense.

South Africa's ICAO membership

The conflict between South Africa and African states over the apartheid policy pursued by the former constitutes another of the international controversies that was turning ICAO into a forum for hitting political opponents by questioning their right to ICAO membership. The problem emerged when many African countries, following decolonization, became independent and started joining the organization. Similarly as in the cases analyzed earlier in this chapter, ICAO was just one of the many multilateral forums where such tensions occurred. The country was isolated in sports, visas were refused to South Africans, South African products were boycotted, etc.[52] South Africa was also facing problems in multiple IOs. In the UN, the first resolutions against racial policy in South Africa, then the Union of South Africa, were adopted already in the late 1940s, whereas since the 1960s, growing membership of the African states led to pressure within the UN to impose economic sanctions against Pretoria for failing to heed with earlier UN General Assembly (GA) resolutions on apartheid. Internal debates in the UN led to the establishment of the Commission on the Racial Situation in the Union of South Africa in 1952, the Security Council's resolution on South Africa from 1960, which called for the personal intervention of the Secretary-General, or the establishment of the unit on apartheid (later renamed Centre Against Apartheid) within the UN Secretariat in 1967[53] if the early activities against apartheid in South Africa are considered. Some NGOs went even further, for example, between the 1950s and 1970s, many international sports governing bodies expelled South African national sports organizations.[54] Despite its vastly technical character, ICAO was also not immune from becoming a forum for attacking the South African regime.

Controversies surrounding South Africa within the ICAO spanned multiple issues, primarily concerning membership rights. Over time, these controversies focused on isolation and condemnation due to the argument that South Africa's racist regime deserved international censure. This effort aligned with a broader campaign where, beginning in 1960, African states sought to exclude South Africa from IOs, especially those operating by majority vote[55] where it was easier for them to outvote the states that were more tolerant toward South Africa. In ICAO, during the 15th Assembly in 1965, 31 African states' delegations submitted a paper proposing the addition of an item to the agenda concerning the question of South African continued membership in the organization.[56] According to their draft resolution, Article 93 ter of the Convention should be amended so that any contracting state violating the Preamble of the Convention, which practices apartheid and racial discrimination, shall be suspended or excluded from ICAO membership and only reinstated after renouncing its policy of apartheid and racial discrimination.[57]

In the Executive Committee, many delegates argued that ICAO could not ignore feelings of a third of its members, that continued South African membership would make it difficult to hold meetings in Africa, that South African policy was a threat to general security and therefore to safe and orderly development of international civil transport, and that South Africa violated article 44 (g) of the Convention through denying certain aircraft the right to land on its territory because it carried persons that the South African regime did not accept. The delegates from Argentina, Australia, Brazil, Canada, Colombia, Denmark, France, Israel, New Zealand, the Philippines, Sweden, the United Kingdom, the United States, and Spain opposed the proposal. They argued that the ICAO, as a technical organization, was an inappropriate forum for discussing political issues, and that such matters should be addressed within the UN. Additionally, without opposing the proposal, the delegates of Malawi and Mexico also stated that political questions should be considered by political bodies of the UN. The South African delegate focused on the procedural defect of the proposal but also argued that declaring South Africa a threat to the general peace and security would mean arrogating to itself the responsibilities of the UN Security Council. Despite such arguments, the Executive Committee voted in favor of the draft resolution and recommended adopting it.[58] As demonstrated, depoliticization rhetoric emerged as the primary tactic for those opposing South Africa's expulsion. Both the South African delegation and delegations lending their support employed defensive depoliticization arguments. In turn, discursive depoliticization was used by delegations in favor of South African expulsion, who, despite bringing the issue with clear political overtones, made arguments about a link between South African policy and aviation. More neutral statements were also employed by the two delegations not opposing the draft resolution but cautioning against the politicization of ICAO, with a prevailing argument that such issues should be dealt with in the UN, which should be interpreted as neutral depoliticization rhetoric employed to defend ICAO from politicization rather than South Africa from expulsion.

Deliberations about the draft resolution on South African membership resumed during the plenary sessions, with similar arguments being used. For example, the delegate of Cameroon argued that it was clear that the policy of apartheid and racial discrimination was universally condemned and that it should be an objective of ICAO to ensure the rights of all people are respected, despite its technical character. He then added that 'the South African policy of apartheid and racial discrimination, this dangerous threat to the peace, progress and security of the world, must be fought and defeated on all fronts.' The Cameroonian recognized that the resolution addressed more than technical issues but maintained that the severity of the violations warranted it.[59] The statement was then seconded by the delegates from Guinea and several other African countries.[60]

Some delegations spoke against the draft resolution. The Israeli delegate said the main reason why he opposed it was not the technical character of ICAO, but the fact that the question was an important political one and the United Nations should first take the decision. The British delegate stated that his government strongly condemned apartheid, but this was a political question and ICAO was not a proper forum for discussion of such issues, and that the decisions of the UN should guide specialized agencies. The delegate of Ecuador stated that ICAO was not competent to take the position for or against the policy of apartheid and that even though the UN General Assembly has often supported the African countries on the issue, ICAO was not in the position to expel any of its members.[61] The South African delegate did not take the floor this time, but those against the expulsion were basically unanimous in the sense that they all used the argument about the political character of the draft resolution, unfit for technical ICAO that was not a proper forum for such issues, which should be discussed elsewhere. Those against South African membership acknowledged the political context of the draft resolution, which was extraordinary compared to other cases analyzed in this book, although it made the defensive depoliticization arguments presumably more persuasive.

The discussion was followed by a vote requiring a two-thirds majority to pass. With 42 votes in favor of the draft resolution, 30 against, 15 abstentions, and 13 states absent, the resolution failed. After the vote, the delegate of Guinea announced that 31 African states were submitting another resolution that would reaffirm the condemnation of the apartheid policy, requesting all nations and people to exert pressure on South Africa to abandon its apartheid policy and to urge South Africa to comply with the aims and objectives of the Chicago Convention.[62] Apparently, after failing to expel South Africa, African delegations sought to achieve at least a symbolic rebuke against the country.

During the discussion on the new draft resolution, the South African delegate said that his delegation had consistently maintained that there was no place for political issues in the ICAO Assembly while the discussed resolution was such an issue. The delegate argued that the Assembly had already indicated its position on political issues and raised reservations about procedural and substantive aspects of the motion. The South African concluded that South Africa complied with the aims and objectives of the Convention and that it was not South Africa that had banned the aircraft of other contracting states from using its airports and airspace. Several other delegates also took the floor to explain why they would abstain from voting. The delegate of Belgium said his government had condemned the apartheid policy of South Africa, but specialized agencies of the UN were not a proper forum for such discussion. A similar view was raised by the delegates from Denmark, Norway, Sweden, Australia, the United Kingdom, the Netherlands, West Germany, the United States, France, the Philippines, and Peru. The resolution was ultimately adopted with 39 votes in favor, 1 vote against, 40 abstentions, and 20 members absent from the vote,[63] thus predominantly because most of those that considered ICAO as not a proper place for such issues abstained instead of voting against it, apparently since it would be difficult to justify a vote against condemning racial discrimination. Regardless of the outcome, depoliticization rhetoric played a key role in the discussion. Many delegations which opposed the draft resolutions, including South Africa, used it to attempt to dismiss the resolution critical of South Africa. Besides the latter, which used it for direct defense, in many other cases, it can be interpreted as an attempt to justify lack of support for the draft resolutions concerning an objective difficulty in challenging the argument about racial discrimination in South Africa and the roll call votes on both resolutions. Open opposition to condemning apartheid could consequently face a negative reception from parts of the international community.

The problem of minority-ruled South Africa's ICAO membership emerged again during the 18th session of the Assembly in 1971. In his address to the Assembly, the Tanzanian delegation chief said that it had been argued that ICAO was not the proper forum to discuss the question of apartheid and racial discrimination, but it should be noted that despite the UN General Assembly's Resolution 2704 asking specialized agencies to discontinue collaboration with South Africa, nations which did not sponsor the resolution were employing various interpretations of the issue. He argued that South Africa should be excluded from all ICAO activities, meetings, conferences, and seminars, which cannot be achieved without expelling South Africa from ICAO.[64] The strategy of the African countries changed compared to the 15th Assembly. Instead of just seeking to expel South Africa based on the apartheid policy, the expulsion was to be a way to realize the UN GA resolution, potentially dismissing the argument that such issues should be dealt within the UN.

During various meetings of the 18th Assembly, the problem of South African ICAO membership was discussed together with the problem of Portuguese membership – in reference to the UN GA resolutions 2555 and 2704 asking specialized agencies to take measures to discontinue any collaboration with the governments of both countries.[65] In the Executive Committee, the delegate of Guinea proposed recommending the adoption of resolutions calling to withhold invitations to ICAO meetings from both countries, as well as communication and documentation, except when the Convention required their provision. The proposal was supported by many delegations, particularly from Africa and the socialist block. The main argument of those opposing, including such countries as Canada, France, New Zealand, Portugal, South Africa, Spain, Sweden, the United States, and the United Kingdom, was that it was a political question that should be left to the UN. In contrast, supporters of the resolutions claimed the political decisions have already been taken in the UN. Despite differences in views by different delegations, the Executive Committee eventually recommended the adoption of the resolutions.[66]

Deliberations on the issue were further proceeded at the plenary session. Delegations opposing the resolutions, such as the United States or Sweden, claimed it would pose a serious threat to civil aviation safety.[67] Eventually, in the secret ballot, the Assembly only adopted the resolution concerning South Africa,[68] a decision that the South African delegate commented as unconstitutional and one that the Assembly had no right to vote.[69] The resolution did not explicitly mean striping it from the ICAO membership, but that the country would be barred from attending ICAO meetings apart from the Assembly and receiving official documents,[70] so its ICAO involvement became very limited despite formal membership. Similarly as during the earlier debates on South African ICAO membership, the delegations that did not wish to expel South Africa from ICAO or otherwise isolate it in the organization, including the South African delegation, argued that such political questions should not be dealt in ICAO. The domestic political system admittedly has a political character, but this time the proposal was based on UN GA resolutions and did not assume formal expulsion from ICAO, thus was more difficult to oppose and easier to defend, paving the way for African states to deepen South Africa's international isolation despite defensive depoliticization employed by several delegations.

Despite the limitation of South Africa's involvement in the ICAO's work, the 1971 decision did not mean the end of the controversy. African countries unsuccessfully kept pressing to expel South Africa from the UN and the specialized agencies.[71] On the forum of ICAO, delegations from several African countries once again attempted to hit South Africa (and Rhodesia, another African state ruled by a white minority) in 1977 during the 22nd Assembly. The chief delegate of Nigeria addressed the Assembly, saying that 'political stability was one of the essential ingredients of a steady growth of air transportation' and that it could not develop if people were oppressed, adding that Nigeria and other countries of the Organization of African Unity banned South African aircraft, and aircraft operating to South Africa and Rhodesia from traversing their airspace. He then expressed his hope that other contracting states could do the same.[72] The problem of the regimes in South Africa and Rhodesia was also raised by the chief delegate of Tanzania, who said that his delegation was saddened that the people of Azania (South Africa), Namibia, and Zimbabwe were still denied ICAO membership.[73] During the same meeting, the chief delegate of Upper Volta said it was difficult to speak of friendship and understanding among nations and peoples as put in the preamble of the Chicago Convention without condemning the apartheid policy and referred to the recent death in jail of the founder of South African Students Organization Steve Biko.[74] These were mere statements without further political or diplomatic implications, but the representatives of the African countries apparently tried to keep the problem of apartheid in South Africa on the agenda in the ICAO, similarly as it has been on the forum of the UN General Assembly and other IOs. On the one hand, these statements politicized ICAO by bringing political conflicts on its forum, but at the same time, featured discursive depoliticization when speakers drew a link between the political situation in minority-ruled countries and the objectives of the Chicago Convention. Such statements, however, did not lead to the employment of defensive depoliticization.

The problem of South Africa reemerged again in ICAO during the 26th Assembly in 1986. The delegate of Congo, on behalf of several African states, presented a draft resolution reiterating the UN call to all nations to exert pressure on South Africa to abandon apartheid policy and urging ICAO member states to ban air links and suspend or terminate bilateral air transport agreements with South Africa, as well as instructing the Council to review the developments on the matter. During the discussion in the Executive Committee, many speakers expressed their support, but some, while stressing their governments' condemnation of apartheid, claimed the ICAO Assembly was not appropriate for a question of political nature. Ultimately, the Executive Committee approved recommending the draft resolution to the Assembly.[75] At the plenary sessions, the issue was first raised by the delegate of Tanzania, who called for comprehensive mandatory sanctions, including severing all air links and shipping links.[76] The British delegate claimed it was an inappropriate subject for the discussion in the Assembly, but despite this and several other voices against the draft resolution, it was eventually adopted.[77] This marked the further sharpening of the pressure on South Africa in the area of aviation, after limiting its ICAO presence. African states, supported by many others, including the Communist bloc, used their majority in ICAO to articulate expectations from other states to join the boycott. Some delegations used depoliticization rhetoric, though not the South African delegation, in a rather neutral attempt to defend ICAO from politicization, but such voices were less common than before, reflecting a progressive change in the global approach to apartheid, but also the quantitative level of support for the call in the Assembly.

Adopting the resolution mentioned above did not remove the South African question from ICAO's agenda for long. During the subsequent 27th Assembly in 1989, the implementation of the resolution was reviewed. According to the information presented, a large number of states indicated having no air links with South Africa. However, several delegations claimed such an issue should not be discussed in ICAO. The Executive Committee recommended amending the earlier resolution according to the proposal from Tanzania to keep the issue 'in constant review.'[78] During the plenary session, the delegate of France, speaking on behalf of the European Community, said it never ceased condemning the regime of apartheid, but this was a political question that did not fall within the competence of ICAO, and as a result they would not support the draft resolution. The delegate of Switzerland also said that his government strongly condemned apartheid but considered ICAO not to be an appropriate forum to discuss such issues, a statement supported by the delegate of Austria. Despite such voices, the Assembly adopted the resolution[79]. The voices that apartheid in South Africa was a political question unfit for ICAO were raised by delegates of several Western countries, who also claimed that their position did not mean their approval of such a policy. It is not clear, though, whether expressing condemnation of apartheid was meant to conceal defensive depoliticization or was simply an expression of attempting to move political issues away from ICAO in a more neutral manner and, at the same time, an attempt to avoid being accused of supporting apartheid.

The debates concerning how to deal with the situation in South Africa in ICAO ceased once the country underwent the democratic transition in the early 1990s.[80] In 1993, the Council suspended the implementation of resolution A27-5 adopted during the 27th Assembly as a response to the UN GA decision to end all restrictions on economic relations with South Africa,[81] whereas in 1994, the Council suspended with immediate effect further implementation of resolution A18-4 which limited SA's participation in ICAO meetings and its receipt of ICAO documentation. South Africa thus resumed full membership rights.[82] All the developments, as mentioned earlier, reflected similar processes occurring in other IOs, and generally in international relations, that led to the international isolation of South Africa. In the field of civil aviation, like in others, its government managed to bypass some of the restrictions caused by the international boycott. For example, when African states closed their airspace to South African airlines in 1962s, the country built and equipped Cape Verde airport in exchange for landing rights and acquired long-haul Boeing 747s, while later it provided assistance to Equatorial Guinea in exchange for the possibility to use its international airport.[83] As to the ICAO membership, South Africa remained a formal member state with severe restrictions. However, as the delegate of South Africa said in an address to the 31st Assembly in 1995, owing to diplomatic efforts by President of the Council Assad Kotaite, 'South Africa was able to continue as a State Party of the Convention while being censored for its political policies.'[84]

The history of controversy regarding South Africa's participation in ICAO's work reveals many similarities to situations in other international forums. African states were taking every opportunity to exert pressure on South Africa, increasing the country's functioning costs and eventually contributing to the peaceful transition. Despite the technical and declaratively apolitical character of ICAO, the conflict between African countries and the minority-ruled regime in South Africa was more effectively played on its forum by the former. The South African delegates, particularly in the early years when their presence in ICAO was not limited, and delegations of some other countries, predominantly Western, very often used typical depoliticization rhetoric, referring both to the political character of the issues under discussion and the technical character of the ICAO, as an argument against debating or supporting the condemnation, expulsion, or other forms of limitation of South African presence in ICAO. It appeared to be one of few arguments available since it was difficult to defend apartheid policy on a multilateral forum. As we could read in many of the statements, even the delegates attacking South Africa sometimes acknowledged that the motions were going beyond mere technical issues, but at the same time, they attempted to link them with aviation-related problems, for example, by referring to the preamble of the Chicago Convention. However, in most cases, the defensive depoliticization was not successful. Delegations from the African countries took advantage, besides objective argument of racial discrimination, of their number, particularly since they were receiving support from the Communist bloc, and in most cases were able to secure the desired result of Assembly votes.

The conflict between Cyprus and Turkey

The last membership controversy discussed in this chapter concerns the conflict between Turkey and Cyprus. This case is somewhat similar to the one regarding China, as one of the main arguments used against the Republic of Cyprus was its legitimacy. As in the Chinese case, controversies featured reservations about the credentials of its delegations, although not exclusively. The problem was connected with the existence of two ethnic communities in Cyprus, subsequently two centers of power, and the Turkish invasion of the island. The developments regarding the Cypriot–Turkish conflict in ICAO are thus complex and could be studied in different parts of this book as well – in particular in reference to international conflicts discussed at the forum of ICAO. Still, because of the very clear link to the questioning of the statehood of Cyprus, we have decided to include it into the chapter on membership controversies.

The Cypriot problem in ICAO resulted from the political tensions on the island. A former British colony, Cyprus, was granted limited independence according to the Zurich Agreement of 1959 between the United Kingdom, Turkey, and Greece. However, the ethnic differences between Greek and Turkish–Cypriot communities exacerbated the internal situation, leading to clashes. All this led to the 1974 coup against President Makarios, the subsequent invasion by Turkey to 'restore constitutional order,'[85] and the declaration of independence by the Turkish Republic of Northern Cyprus in 1983.[86] These developments created a conflicting situation, unsettled until today, with the UN still guarding the demarcation line.

The situation in Cyprus led to several controversies within ICAO, for example, an attempt to assert control over the airspace by Turkey after the establishment of the Turkish–Cypriot government in 1974, which led to complaints to ICAO by Greece, Cyprus, pilots' associations, and airlines.[87] There were also multiple situations when the ICAO Assembly was becoming a forum for mutual political accusations between Turkey and Cyprus, including debates regarding the statehood of Cyprus. For the first time, such a controversy took place during the 21st Assembly in 1974, held shortly after the Turkish intervention in Cyprus. In a similar manner as earlier in the case of China, after the presentation of the interim report of the Credentials Committee, the delegate of Turkey entered a reservation about the representation of the government of Cyprus in the Assembly, whereas the delegate of Cyprus, with the support from the Greek delegation, thanked the Credentials Committee for accepting the credentials of his delegation, adding that they could not be legitimately challenged.[88]

The debate resumed during the addresses by both delegations when the delegate of Cyprus referred to acts committed by Turkey against his country. As he stated, Turkey had used the air force to attack targets of civil aviation importance, damaging runways and communication installations, concluding that Turkey threatened to occupy the airport area, leading the UN peacekeeping force to place the airport under its protection.[89] The Turkish delegate responded in his address to the Assembly a day later. He rejected the claims of the delegate of Cyprus, reiterated the Turkish statement concerning the report of the Credentials Committee, and said the delegation of Cyprus represented the Greek Cypriot Administration, which had limited representative powers. The Turk continued that his delegation objected to the Cypriot delegation's presence, which contrary to international treaties was only representing the Greek Cypriot community. He said that as a country guaranteeing the independence of the Republic of Cyprus, Turkey had to intervene when another guarantor tried to annex Cyprus on July 15, 1974. The intervention, according to the Turk, was preceded by peaceful and diplomatic attempts and allowed to prevent genocide. He concluded that the intervention had implications for civil aviation, but immediate measures were taken for the safety of air traffic.[90] As we can see, attempts to question the right of the Cypriot delegation to represent the country were raised even in the general addresses, not only in reference to the reports of the Credentials Committees. The Turkish delegate made several points with clear political overtones, although the delegate of Cyprus mentioned the invasion in the first place.

The discussion reemerged after the final report of the Credentials Committee was presented. The delegate of Cyprus stated that Turkey had an accredited mission in Nicosia and received a Cypriot ambassador in Ankara and mentioned the UN General Assembly resolutions concerning Cyprus calling to respect the sovereignty, independence, and territorial integrity of the Republic of Cyprus.

He concluded that his delegation rejected the Turkish reservations concerning its statehood. The Turkish delegate responded that the Greek Cypriot administration posing as the government of the Republic of Cyprus had decided unilaterally to take part in the Assembly, which it had no right to according to the Turkish government. The delegate has also once again referred to the Turkish intervention in Cyprus, claiming it was a response to the coup d'état of July 15, 1974, carried out by the 'Greek Fascists.' Other delegates also joined the discussion. The delegate of Greece endorsed the Cypriot position and assured the Assembly that Greece had officially recognized Cyprus as an independent state and never sought to unite it with Greece. The Greek added that he was astonished by what the Turkish delegate had said, claiming he had never heard of a minority of 18 percent seeking representation at an international meeting and the majority of 82 percent being considered a particular administration. He also noted that the resolutions of the UN Security Council were, in principle, against the Turkish intervention and occupation.[91] The Turkish delegate responded that the Greek delegate should 'look at the international agreements his country had signed' and stated that what he had said proved in what spirit Greece has signed international agreements.[92] At this point, both parties and the Greek delegation focused on accusing each other. Neither of the parties used depoliticization rhetoric directly, while both sides referred to clearly political arguments in their discussion.

Similar verbal attacks were repeated numerous times in ICAO in the subsequent years. In his address to the 22nd Assembly in 1977, the delegate of Cyprus spoke about the Turkish invasion, continued occupation of almost 40 percent of Cyprus, restoring the aviation infrastructure that took three years, 'wasteful detours' that aircraft were forced to and further disruptions caused by Turkey by 'setting up a puppet Flight Information Region (FIR) within the Nicosia FIR.'[93] In his response, the delegate of Turkey spoke about his Cypriot counterpart as 'the Representative of the Greek Cypriots' and defended the establishment of air services, which were to fill the vacuum and provide air safety. He concluded that the issue was raised by the Cypriot delegation only for political purposes.[94] Despite admittedly strong mutual accusations and reference to political developments by both sides, it was the first time that a representative of one of the parties employed so directly depoliticization rhetoric by accusing the other of bringing political issues before the Assembly.

The Cypriot delegation also mentioned the situation in Cyprus during the 23rd Assembly in 1980, when its delegate, in the context of rebuilding the tourist and travel infrastructure and reaching the pre-invasion levels of air traffic, referred to the occupation of 40 percent of the island.[95] In turn, after the presentation of the report of the Credentials Committee, the Turkish delegate reserved his delegation's position concerning the delegation of 'Greek Cypriot Administration,' claiming it did not represent the whole of Cyprus. The Cypriot responded that the Turkish attitude was not surprising since Turkey, in violation of certain principles of international relations, invaded Cyprus in July 1974 to destroy the sovereignty and integrity of the country, adding that the Republic of Cyprus had been recognized internationally and member of IOs such as UN and others. This position was backed by the delegate of Greece. The Turkish delegate responded that Turkey, as a guarantor country safeguarding the independence and sovereignty of Cyprus, was forced to intervene after diplomatic and political means failed to stop deprivations, displacements, and loss of life of Turkish–Cypriots.[96] Again, both sides accused each other and did not attempt to defend themselves through arguments about the political character of the accusations.

The subsequent 24th Assembly in 1983 was also used by Turkish and Cypriot delegations to make mutual accusations in a similar manner as before. The Turkish occupation of Cyprus was brought up by the delegate of Cyprus in his address, in which, among other things, he mentioned that FIR services provided by Nicosia were being hampered by an illegal station 'ERCAN' operating in the occupied part of Cyprus. The Turkish delegate replied that the delegate of Cyprus mentioned the problem from the political point of view. He said he disagreed with the statement but wished not to politicize issues in ICAO since such problems should be solved at the negotiations table under the auspices of the UN Secretary-General.[97] Mutual attacks then returned in reference to the Credentials Committee's report. The Turkish delegate said that the delegation of the Greek Cypriot administration did not represent the whole of Cyprus. The delegate of Cyprus responded by speaking about the Turkish invasion and attempt to destroy Cypriot independence and concluded he did not represent any of the communities but the Republic of Cyprus. The Turkish delegate responded that he only wanted to make a reservation, but the Cypriot delegation used every opportunity to talk about the history of the Cyprus problem, adding that only after the Turkish intervention were the Turkish–Cypriots living in peace and without fear.[98] The 24th Assembly thus marked an increased employment of depoliticization rhetoric by the Turkish delegations, which used an argument about the political character of Cypriot statements to dismiss them, and at the same time claiming their interventions were not political, a denial typical for discursive depoliticization.

The 25th Assembly, probably due to its extraordinary character, did not become an arena for the Turkish–Cypriot political clash, which reemerged during the 26th Assembly, with a very similar course of events as during previous sessions. In the address to the Assembly, the Cypriot delegate spoke about the progress of aviation in his country being hampered by invasion by 'another Contracting State' and mentioned the recent establishment of a new illegal airport at Lefkoniko, appealing to all governments to ensure no flights be allowed to operate there.[99] The Turkish response came in reference to the initial report of the Credentials Committee, when after making reservations regarding the Cypriot delegation, the Turkish delegate said the Assembly was not the place to discuss the Cyprus problem and that the delegate of the Greek Cypriot Administration attempted to inject politics into a purely technical forum. The Turk also defended the new airport as being within the limits of the Turkish State of Northern Cyprus. The Cypriot responded that it was the Turkish delegate to have turned the technical forum into a political one and argued that the Turkish Republic of Northern Cyprus was an entity that did not exist.[100] The development during the session, besides mutual accusations, featured the use of depoliticization rhetoric, this time by both parties. Each side made some political statements – the Cypriot regarding invasion and occupation, the Turkish regarding limited legitimacy of the Cypriot delegations, and each accused the other of injecting politics into ICAO, a situation which demonstrated the pejorative connotations of politics and politicization.

The 26th session of the Assembly in 1986 was the last time when the Cypriot problem was discussed so intensively. It has been raised several times during future ICAO meetings[101] but did not lead to heated discussions. At the same time, Turkey stopped using the Credentials Committee's reports to attempt to question the legitimacy of the Cypriot delegation. The developments concerning the situation in Cyprus and the Cypriot–Turkish conflict within ICAO were pursued under a specific scheme, in which, on the one hand, the Cypriot delegations were attacking Turkey for its intervention and several unilateral decisions concerning aviation in the region, whereas Turkey, apart from justifying its intervention, kept questioning the right of the Cypriot delegation to represent Cyprus, usually by voicing its reservations concerning the Credentials Committee's reports and claiming the Cypriot delegation only represented the Greek Cypriot community of the island. Although not from the beginning, first Turkish and then both delegations gradually started employing depoliticization rhetoric to downgrade arguments used by the other side, which eventually developed into mutual accusations of politicizing ICAO during the 26th Assembly. That reveals an important quality of politics on the forum of IOs. Considered as something explicitly pejorative and unfit for a technical organization such as ICAO, accusing others of undertaking political issues appeared to be a convenient form of demeaning claims of counterparts, regardless of the gravity and context of the offenses, and thus defending oneself.

Conclusions

The controversies regarding ICAO membership of Spain, the Republic of China, South Africa, and, to a lesser extent, Cyprus, all grew from international conflicts: World War II, legitimacy rivalry between Beijing and Taipei, conflict between South Africa and most of the other African countries over the policy of apartheid pursued by the former, and conflict between Turkey and Cyprus. All these controversies in ICAO included attempts by one or more delegations to question the right of a particular delegation to participate in the ICAO works, connected with calls for expulsion and declarative questioning of the legitimacy or statehood of political adversaries. This was done in several ways. Delegates made accusations against other states during addresses to the Assembly, by presenting draft resolutions against them, and making reservations regarding the Credentials Committee's reports or suggesting that their acceptance did not mean recognition of contested states. Although with varying intensity, all these cases featured the employment of depoliticization rhetoric in usually ineffective attempts to defend the positions of those being attacked, to demean the credibility of the accusations, or to persuade other delegations that the issues or items should not be discussed. Politics was explicitly referred to as something negative and unfit for ICAO, so in some cases both parties accused each other of politicizing ICAO. Also, it was not unusual for a delegation to accuse others of politicizing the debate and, at the same time, using political arguments themselves. All this clearly indicates depoliticization rhetoric to be a technique, one of many used in ICAO, with the purpose of improving one's position, particularly if such state was in fact guilty of offenses, and undermining the position of adversaries as those who politicize ICAO.

Defensive depoliticization was not the only one to be observed in the controversies regarding ICAO statehood and membership. On several occasions, delegates who brought politically related issues to the forum of ICAO attempted to justify them by building links with aviation matters, like in the case of delegations of African countries arguing in the context of South Africa that lack of political stability hampered the growth of air transportation, or by denying the political character of their interventions, thus trying to discursively depoliticize the deliberations. There were also voices against politicizing ICAO not directly linked to the attempts to defend the countries under verbal attack. Depoliticization in its various forms was therefore frequently employed in the ICAO debates regarding membership in the organization, including the most crucial from the perspective of this study defensive depoliticization, considered a diplomatic technique.

Notes

1 Antonio Marquina, "The Spanish Neutrality during the Second World War," *American University International Law Review* 14, no. 1 (1998): 171.
2 Eugene Sochor, *The Politics of International Aviation* (Basingstoke: Macmillan, 1991), 42.
3 John A. Houston, "The United Nations and Spain," *The Journal of Politics* 14, no. 4 (1952): 683–684.
4 Minutes of the First Plenary Meeting, First Assembly, May 6, 1947, 8, A1-P/18 DOC 4102, ICAO Archival Documents.
5 Minutes of 1st Meeting held in Council Chamber on Thursday, First Assembly, Commission No. 1 – Constitutional and General Policy Questions, May 8, 1947, 5, A1-CP/32, DOC 4232, ICAO Archival Documents.
6 Ibid., 4–5.
7 Ibid., 7.
8 Ibid., 7–11.
9 Ibid., 9.
10 Ibid., 5–11, 15.
11 Minutes of the First Plenary Meeting, First Assembly, May 6, 1947, 11, A1-P/18, DOC 4102, ICAO Archival Documents.
12 Ibid., 29.
13 Minutes of the Second Plenary Meeting, First Assembly, May 7, 1947, 4, A1-P/21, DOC 4155, ICAO Archival Documents.
14 Minutes of the Third Plenary Meeting, First Assembly, May 13, 1947, 2–6, A1-P/24, DOC 4184, ICAO Archival Documents.
15 Ibid., 6.
16 Report of the Council to the Assembly of the Activities of the Organization in 1950. Supporting documentation for the 5th Session of the Assembly, June 1951, 72, A5-P/1, DOC 7148, ICAO Archival Documents.

17 Minutes of the First Plenary Meeting, Assembly – Fifth Session, June 5, 1951, 5–6, A5-P/2-1, DOC 7168-1, ICAO Archival Documents.
18 Minutes of the Fourth Plenary Meeting, Assembly – Fifth Session, June 18, 1951, 59, A5-P/2-4, DOC 7168-4, ICAO Archival Documents.
19 Sochor, *The Politics of International Aviation*, 43–44.
20 Ann Kent, "China's International Socialization: The Role of International Organizations," *Global Governance* 8, no. 3 (July–September 2002): 344.
21 Eadem, *Beyond Compliance: China, International Organizations, and Global Security* (Stanford: Stanford University Press, 2007): 36–37.
22 Edward Sharp, "Soviet Security Council Boycott," in *The Encyclopedia of the Korean War*, ed. Spencer C. Tucker and Paul G. Pierpaoli Jr. (Bloomsbury: New York, 2002), 797.
23 See: Michał Marcin Kobierecki, *Sports Diplomacy: Sports in the Diplomatic Activities of States and Non-State Actors* (Lanham: Lexington Books, 2020).
24 See: "Convention on International Civil Aviation." Signed at Chicago on 7 December 1944; Minutes of the First Plenary Meeting, First Assembly, May 6, 1947, 30, A1-P/18, DOC 4102, ICAO Archival Documents.
25 Sochor, *The Politics of International Aviation*, 49.
26 David MacKenzie, *ICAO: A History of the International Civil Aviation Organization* (Toronto: University of Toronto Press, 2010), 220–221.
27 Executive Committee Minutes of the Eighth Meeting, Assembly – Fourth Session, June 8, 1950, 51, A4-WP/213, EX-Approved Min. 8, ICAO Archival Documents.
28 Minutes of the Second Plenary Meeting, Assembly – Seventh Session, June 17, 1953, 34–35, A7-P/2, DOC 7409, ICAO Archival Documents.
29 Report of the Council to the Assembly on the Activities of the Organization in 1953, Supporting Documentation for the 8th Session of the Assembly, June 1954, 50, A8-P/2, DOC 7456, ICAO Archival Documents.
30 Minutes of the Second Plenary Meeting, Assembly – Tenth Session, June 20, 1956, 8, A10-P/17-2, DOC 7708-2, ICAO Archival Documents.
31 Minutes of the Fourth Plenary Meeting, Assembly – Eleventh Session, June 2, 1958, 44, A11-P/11, DOC 7886, ICAO Archival Documents.
32 Ibid.
33 Minutes of the Second Plenary Meeting, Assembly – Twelfth Session, June 17, 1959, 29–30, A12-P/2, DOC 7996, ICAO Archival Documents.
34 Ibid., 130.
35 Minutes of the Second Plenary Meeting (Draft), Assembly – Thirteenth Session (Extraordinary), June 19, 1961, 1–3, A13-Draft Min. P/2, ICAO Archival Documents; Minutes of the Second Plenary Meeting, Assembly – Fourteenth Session, August 22, 1962, 57, 97–99, A14-P/21, DOC 8269, ICAO Archival Documents; Minutes of the Third Plenary Meeting, Assembly – Fifteenth Session, June 23, 1965, 63–64, A15-P/5, DOC 8516, ICAO Archival Documents; Minutes of the Eleventh Plenary Meeting, Assembly – Fifteenth Session, July 16, 1965, 174–175, A15-P/5, DOC 8516, ICAO Archival Documents; Minutes of the Seventh Plenary Meeting, Assembly – Sixteenth Session, September 24, 1986, 85–87, A16-Min. P/7, DOC 8775, ICAO Archival Documents.
36 Minutes of the Second Plenary Meeting, Assembly – Sixteenth Session, September 3, 1968, 8–9, A16-Min. P/2, DOC 8775, ICAO Archival Documents.
37 Minutes of the Second Plenary Meeting (Draft), Assembly – Thirteenth Session (Extraordinary), June 19, 1961, 1–2, A13-Draft Min. P/2, ICAO Archival Documents.

38 Minutes of the Second Plenary Meeting, Assembly – Fourteenth Session, August 22, 1962, 57–58, A14-P/21, DOC 8269, ICAO Archival Documents.
39 Ibid., 58.
40 Minutes of the Seventh Plenary Meeting, Assembly – Fourteenth Session, September 14, 1962, 97–99, A14-P/21, DOC 8269, ICAO Archival Documents.
41 Minutes of the Third Plenary Meeting, Assembly – Fifteenth Session, June 23, 1965, 64, A15-P/5, DOC 8516, ICAO Archival Documents.
42 Ibid., 54–65.
43 Minutes of the Seventh Plenary Meeting, Assembly – Sixteenth Session, September 24, 1986, 86–88, A16-Min. P/7, DOC 8775, ICAO Archival Documents.
44 Ibid., 87–88.
45 Minutes of the Third Plenary Meeting, Assembly – Seventeenth Session, June 18, 1970, 14, A17-Min. P/3, DOC 8893, ICAO Archival Documents.
46 Minutes of the Second Plenary Meeting, Assembly – Seventeenth Session (A), March 11, 1971, 23–25, A17 A-P/7, DOC 8931, ICAO Archival Documents.
47 Minutes of the Second Plenary Meeting, Assembly – Eighteenth Session, June 15, 1971, 5, 6–7, 11, A18 Min. P/2, DOC 8963, ICAO Archival Documents; Minutes of the Fourteenth Plenary Meeting, Assembly – Eighteenth Session, July 6, 1971, 167–168, A18 Min. P/14, DOC 8963, ICAO Archival Documents.
48 Minutes of the Third Plenary Meeting, Assembly – Eighteenth Session, June 16, 1971, 36, A18 Min. P/3, DOC 8963, ICAO Archival Documents.
49 Annual Report of the Council – 1970, Documentation for the session of the Assembly in 1974, 83, A19-P/1, DOC 8982, ICAO Archival Documents.
50 Sochor, *The Politics of International Aviation*, 50–51.
51 See: Peter Burnham, "Globalization, Depoliticization and 'Modern' Economic Management," in *The Politics of Change*, ed. Werner Bonefeld and Kosmas Psychopedis (London: Palgrave Macmillan, 2002), 22, https://doi.org/10.1057/9780333993798_2
52 Douglas Booth, "Hitting Apartheid for Six?: The Politics of the South African Sports Boycott," *Journal of Contemporary History* 38, no. 3 (2003): 477–493.
53 Newell M. Stultz, "Evolution of the United Nations Anti-Apartheid Regime," *Human Rights Quarterly* 13, no. 1 (1991): 2–10.
54 Bruce Kidd, "The Campaign against Sport in South Africa," *International Journal: Canada's Journal of Global Policy Analysis* 43, no. 4 (1988): 644, https://doi.org/10.1177/002070208804300406
55 Audie Klotz, *Norms in International Relations: The Struggle against Apartheid* (Ithaca: Cornell University Press, 1995), 48.
56 Report of the Executive Committee on Agenda Item 41, Assembly – Fifteenth Session, July 12, 1965, 1, A15-WP/212, P/43 – Item 41, ICAO Archival Documents.
57 Draft resolution, Agenda Item 41: The question of South Africa's continued membership in ICAO, Executive Committee, Assembly – Fifteenth Session, July 8, 1965, A15-WP/183, ICAO Archival Documents.
58 Report of the Executive Committee on Agenda Item 41, Assembly – Fifteenth Session, July 12, 1965, 2–4, A15-WP/212, P/43 – Item 41, ICAO Archival Documents.
59 Minutes of the Tenth Plenary Meeting, Assembly – Fifteenth Session, July 14, 1965, 140, A15-P/5, DOC 8516, ICAO Archival Documents.
60 Ibid., 141.
61 Minutes of the Tenth Plenary Meeting, Assembly – Fifteenth Session, July 14, 1965, 137–141, A15-P/5, DOC 8516, ICAO Archival Documents.
62 Ibid., 141–143.

63 Minutes of the Twelfth Plenary Meeting, Assembly – Fifteenth Session, July 16, 1965, 185–191, A15-P/5, DOC 8516, ICAO Archival Documents.

64 Minutes of the Third Plenary Meeting, Assembly – Eighteenth Session, June 16, 1971, 42, A18 Min. P/3, DOC 8963, ICAO Archival Documents.

65 In the case of Portugal, the African attempts to isolate it were resulting from the colonial wars it was engaged in.

66 Report of the Executive Committee on Agenda Item 39, Assembly – Eighteenth Session, July 5, 1971, 39-1-39-5, A18-WP/177, P/55, ICAO Archival Documents.

67 Minutes of the Thirteenth Plenary Meeting, Assembly – Eighteenth Session, July 6, 1971, 138–140, A18 Min. P/13, DOC 8963, ICAO Archival Documents.

68 The problem of Portuguese membership reemerged during the extraordinary 19th Assembly in 1974, with a similar resolution being adopted as regarding South Africa during the 18th Assembly. However, by 1974 Portugal underwent democratic transition and resigned from its African colonies, with the pressure to expel it from ICAO gradually fading. See: Working Paper, Agenda Item 4: Completion of the consideration of the United Nations General Assembly Resolutions 2555 and 2704, Assembly – Nineteenth Session (Extraordinary), February 28, 1973, A19-WP/7, ICAO Archival Documents; Decisions Taken by the Assembly at Its Fifth and Sixth Meetings, Assembly – Nineteenth Session (Extraordinary), March 1, 1973, 1, A19-Decisions 5&6, ICAO Archival Documents; MacKenzie, *ICAO,* 236–237.

69 Minutes of the Fourteenth Plenary Meeting, Assembly – Eighteenth Session, July 6, 1971, 143, 148, A18 Min. P/14, DOC 8963, ICAO Archival Documents.

70 Sochor, *The Politics of International Aviation*, 46–47.

71 Ibid., 46.

72 Minutes of the Fourth Plenary Meeting, Assembly – 22nd Session, September 14, 1977, 58, A22 Min. P/4, DOC 9216, ICAO Archival Documents.

73 Minutes of the Sixth Plenary Meeting, Assembly – 22nd Session, September 15, 1977, 89–90, A22 Min. P/6, DOC 9216, ICAO Archival Documents.

74 Ibid., 92.

75 Report of the Executive Committee, Assembly 26th Session, 21–22, A26-EX, DOC 9489, ICAO Archival Documents.

76 Minutes of the Sixth Plenary Meeting, Assembly 26th Session, September 25, 1986, 106, A26-Min. P/6 DOC 9494, ICAO Archival Documents.

77 Minutes of the Thirteenth Plenary Meeting, Assembly 26th Session, October 10, 1986, 203–204, A26-Min. P/13 DOC 9494, ICAO Archival Documents.

78 Report of the Executive Committee, Assembly 27th Session, 21, A27-EX, DOC 9545, ICAO Archival Documents.

79 Minutes of the Fourteenth Plenary Meeting, Assembly 27th Session, October 6, 1989, 199–200, A27-Min. P/14 DOC 9550, ICAO Archival Documents.

80 Minutes of the Ninth Plenary Meeting, Assembly 29th Session, September 26, 1992, 127, A29-Min. P/9 DOC 9601, ICAO Archival Documents.

81 Annual Report of the Council – 1993, Documentation for the Session of the Assembly in 1995, 91, DOC 9622, ICAO Archival Documents.

82 Annual Report of the Council – 1994, Documentation for the session of the Assembly in 1995, 87, DOC 9637, ICAO Archival Documents.

83 Sochor, *The Politics of International Aviation*, 47.

84 Minutes of the Third Plenary Meeting, Assembly – 31st Session, September 20, 1995, 3–4, DRAFT A31-Min. P/3, ICAO Archival Documents.

85 Maria Hadjipavlou-Trigeorgis, and Lenos Trigeorgis, "Cyprus: An Evolutionary Approach to Conflict Resolution," *Journal of Conflict Resolution* 37, no. 2 (1993): 343–344.

86 James Ker-Lindsay, "Great Powers, Counter Secession, and Non-Recognition: Britain and the 1983 Unilateral Declaration of Independence of the 'Turkish Republic of Northern Cyprus'," *Diplomacy & Statecraft* 28, no. 3 (2017): 432, https://doi.org/10.1080/09592296.2017.1347445

87 Sochor, *The Politics of International Aviation*, 116–117.

88 Minutes of the Second Plenary Meeting, Assembly – 21st Session, September 24, 1974, 9, 11, A21 Min. P/2, DOC 9119, ICAO Archival Documents.

89 Ibid., 19.

90 Minutes of the Third Plenary Meeting, Assembly – 21st Session, September 25, 1974, 47–48, A21 Min. P/3, DOC 9119, ICAO Archival Documents.

91 Minutes of the Eleventh Plenary Meeting, Assembly – 21st Session, October 15, 1974, 137–140, A21 Min. P/11, DOC 9119, ICAO Archival Documents.

92 Ibid. 141.

93 Minutes of the Second Plenary Meeting, Assembly – 22nd Session, September 13, 1977, 20–22, A22 Min. P/2, DOC 9216, ICAO Archival Documents.

94 Minutes of the Sixth Plenary Meeting, Assembly – 22nd Session, September 15, 1977, 85, A22 Min. P/6, DOC 9216, ICAO Archival Documents.

95 Minutes of the Fourth Plenary Meeting, Assembly 23rd Session, September 17, 1980, 49, A23 Min. P/4, DOC 9317, ICAO Archival Documents.

96 Minutes of the Thirteenth Plenary Meeting, Assembly 23rd Session, October 6, 1980, 153–154, A23 Min. P/13, DOC 9317, ICAO Archival Documents.

97 Minutes of the Sixth Plenary Meeting, Assembly 24th Session, September 22, 1983, 100, 105, A24-Min. P/6, DOC 9415, ICAO Archival Documents.

98 Minutes of the Fourteenth Plenary Meeting, Assembly 24th Session, October 7, 1983, 178–180, A24-Min. P/14 DOC 9415, ICAO Archival Documents.

99 Minutes of the Seventh Plenary Meeting, Assembly 26th Session, September 26, 1986, 144, A26-Min. P/7 DOC 9494, ICAO Archival Documents.

100 Minutes of the Eighth Plenary Meeting, Assembly 26th Session, September 26, 1986, 156–158, A26-Min. P/8 DOC 9494, ICAO Archival Documents.

101 See: Minutes of the Eighth Plenary Meeting, Assembly 29th Session, September 25, 1992, 121, A29-Min. P/8 DOC 9601, ICAO Archival Documents; Minutes of the Fifth Plenary Meeting, Assembly – 31st Session, September 21, 1995, 25–26, DRAFT A31-Min., ICAO Archival Documents.

4 The Arab–Israeli conflict in the ICAO

The conflict between Israel and Arab states for years has been one of the most crucial preoccupations regarding international security and is considered one of the most intractable and tragic in contemporary history.[1] The origins and history of this conflict have been the subject of extensive scientific publications, making a detailed introduction in this volume unnecessary and impractical. In short, it is a conflict over land between Jewish and Arab peoples. Following the proclamation of Israel in 1948, the conflict covered not only violence between Israelis and Palestinians but also five wars between Israel and its Arab neighbors. The conflict is still far from being solved. At the time of writing (April 2024), a full-scale military operation is taking place in the Gaza Strip following the attack by the Palestinian organization Hamas on Israel. However, on a state-to-state level, the conflict has been mitigated since the late 1970s. Key milestones include the bilateral peace treaty between Israel and Egypt (March 1979), which followed the Camp David Accords, and the Madrid/Oslo peace process (September 1991), which led to the creation of the Palestinian National Authority.[2] This contributed to the gradual decrease of the intensity of the conflict being waged in International Civil Aviation Organization (ICAO), with the last of the controversies under analysis having occurred in 1986.

The Arab–Israeli conflict frequently led to intense clashes on the forum of international organizations. According to David Forsythe, the UN dedicated more attention to the Arab–Israeli conflict than any other matter in history.[3] The character of the conflict thus led to the politicization of multiple international forums. As Di Mauro argued in a book dedicated to the conflict in the UN, its events were politicized, becoming issues for which the member states aggregate their solutions in opposing groups.[4] Even though the UN was a natural multilateral forum for waging the Arab–Israeli conflict, by no means was it the only one. On the contrary, most international organizations, to some extent, were becoming arenas for tensions between Arab states and Israel, featuring also strong engagement of other states. As Abba Eban put it, 'No other theme has come before so wide a range of tribunals, forums, and institutions.'[5] ICAO was not an exception. Like other UN agencies such as United Nations Educational, Scientific and Cultural Organization (UNESCO) or World Health Organization (WHO),[6] it was

DOI: 10.4324/9781032695402-5

a frequent arena for tensions surrounding the conflict. Various controversies with the political background were brought before the organization by both Israel and the Arab states. On numerous occasions, both sides engaged in attempts to strike at each other within ICAO, although many of the controversies were tangentially related to aviation matters, with clear culpability often attributable to one side. At the same time, both sides (and sometimes other states) typically employed defensive depoliticization.

Political controversies stemming from the Arab–Israeli conflict in ICAO started emerging almost immediately after Israel joined ICAO in April 1949. Since then, Arab states attempted to boycott Israel in the field of aviation. For example, when Israeli delegates were present at regional meetings, the Arab states refused to accept reports and recommendations to which Israel was a party. Israel was also complaining that Arab states were withholding flight information, jamming air communications, and denying Israeli aircraft permission to overfly their territories.[7] Animosity toward Israel by Arab states was evident within ICAO even before Israel officially joined the organization. At the beginning of the 3rd Assembly in June 1949, during the plenary session, it was discussed whether Cuba and Israel, two non-contracting states, could attend the session as observers since they were invited by the Council and their governments deposited instruments of ratification of the Chicago Convention, but it happened less than the required 30 days before the opening of the Assembly. The proposition was opposed by the delegate from Egypt. Eventually, the Assembly voted to accept observers from both states, with Egypt and Iraq being against.[8] These events foreshadowed the political tensions that were soon to intensify.

The cases analyzed in this chapter do not cover all political controversies in ICAO connected to the Arab–Israeli conflict. Like in other empirical chapters, we decided to focus on the instances that featured a direct use of depoliticization. That means that several highly politicized deliberations were not considered, such as regarding the shootdown of the Libyan Boeing 727 over Sinai occupied by Israel on February 26, 1973. The Israeli air defense assumed it was on a hostile mission as a sandstorm grounded commercial flights in the area, while at the time, terrorists threatened to use commercial flights to attack Israeli cities. Israel expressed regret and offered compensation, but Libya, Egypt, Lebanon, and Saudi Arabia requested the Council's immediate action. The Council called an extraordinary Assembly, which condemned Israel and instigated an investigation.[9] The situation led to emotional disputes in the ICAO Council and during the 19th extraordinary session of the Assembly in 1973, with Israel being almost unanimously condemned.[10] The discussion in the ICAO Assembly included some claims about the political circumstances of the discussed issues,[11] but attempts to use it to defend the Israeli action were not very direct. The cases selected for analysis in this chapter include Israeli complaints about difficulties created by the Arab states, the Israeli attack on Beirut airport in 1968, the interception of the Lebanese civil aircraft by the Israeli Air Force in 1973, the Jerusalem airport controversy, Palestine's ICAO observer status, and the interception of Libyan Arab Airlines flight by Israel 1986.

Israeli complaints about civil aviation difficulties created by the Arab states

One of the first situations when the Arab–Israeli conflict was waged on the forum of ICAO and featured the use of depoliticization took place in 1955 during the 9th Assembly. The Israeli delegate spoke about the difficulties Israel was encountering in the field of aviation in the ICAO Middle Eastern Region. In particular, he complained about disturbing radio waves, pooling weather information, problems with coordinating rescue situations, and reported that the ICAO regional office for Israel was located in a country denying Israel any access or communication. In response, the delegate from Egypt protested 'against the improper reference to certain political matters in the Middle East Area,' naming it propaganda aimed 'to satisfy a political aim' and injecting irrelevant political issues into the atmosphere of friendly cooperation.[12] The exchange occurred only at the stage of statements by delegations and was not discussed further. However, already this early example of the Arab–Israeli conflict on the forum of ICAO showed a pattern that was frequently repeated in the future. One side, Israel in this case, complained about the behavior of the other. The complaint was not separated from the aviation matters, and despite the political context of the entire controversy, it was not particularly politicized. Still, instead of responding substantively, the accused party attempted to depreciate the accusation by pointing out its political character, unfit for the organization, which is a characteristic example of depoliticization rhetoric used for defense. Like in other cases, politics was pictured as something highly pejorative.

A similar situation occurred during the subsequent 10th Assembly in 1956. The Israeli delegate spoke about 'serious infringements of the Convention' and 'practices applied by certain States (…) as part of their economic warfare against Israel.'[13] Specific examples mentioned by the Israeli included the refusal to allow any aircraft bound for or coming from Israel to fly over their territories, with one state even announcing publicly that it would shoot down such aircraft regardless of its nationality. He also referred to a situation when three Israeli passengers were arrested and held in prison for four months after a British aircraft en route to Tehran made an emergency landing in Baghdad.[14] The Israeli also spoke about flight information being withheld from planes flying to or from Israel, radio messages between such aircraft and Israeli airports being frequently jammed, and the refusal to cooperate in establishing a single Flight Information Centre for the Eastern Mediterranean region. In response, the Lebanese delegate said that 'problems of this nature can only do harm to the cordial atmosphere for which so many speakers have expressed their desire,' which referred to the opening addresses of various delegations, that the accusations were of political nature and 'should never have been raised in this Assembly.'[15] Also, the Egyptian delegate, in his statement, referred to the Israeli intervention, saying that he could also mention several facts in support of an opposite view, but unlike the Israeli delegate, he 'would rather refrain from introducing irrelevant elements into our discussion.'[16]

Unlike the 9th Assembly, the 10th session, besides plenary statements, also featured actual discussion in the Executive Committee (EC). The issue was earlier dealt with by the Council, which, in its report on the situation, concluded that 'although the situation had technical aspects, it was part of a larger political problem outside the purview of ICAO.'[17] The Israeli delegation argued in the EC that since the Council's report failed to note the situation in the Middle East, he felt obliged to bring it to the attention of the Assembly. He also referred to the comments by the Lebanese and Egyptian delegates during the plenary session that the problems were either irrelevant to civil aviation or political in nature, while according to him, it was obviously the opposite. The Egyptian delegate responded that his delegation refrained from undertaking the issue throughout the Assembly since it was a political matter and should be brought before a political organization so that it could receive appropriate political treatment. However, as the Israeli delegate continued to undertake the issue, he had no alternative but to take the floor. He then described a situation of a Sudanese aircraft flying over Israel in April 1956 that was approached by Israeli Spitfires, concluding that two months after

> committing the crime of attacking a civilian aircraft at the high seas, the Government of Israel had sent a delegation to the ICAO Assembly to accuse them (Arab states) of serious infringements of the Convention and to pretend that Israel was not in a state of war with them.[18]

The Egyptian delegate then mentioned three similar incidents and argued that jamming radio messages from Israeli airports was not true that the regional office in Cairo was not depriving Israel of its services since it has been granted immunities similar to diplomatic missions. The Egyptian admitted that withholding flight information from aircraft flying to and from Israel was partly true, but only in normal conditions and not in reference to planes in distress. Finally, the delegate added that the refusal to allow aircraft en route to or from Israel to fly over their territories was entirely true and was part of the Arab states' boycott against Israel, though not a blockade. He concluded that all these issues were political and should not be dealt with by the Assembly. The discussion was dismissed by a vote following a suggestion by the Peruvian delegate, who claimed it had a political nature.[19] Besides a more intensive discussion instead of pure statements and engagement of a third-party delegate, the arguments were similar. Israeli delegation was complaining about the behavior of Arab states in the field of aviation, whereas the Arab states' delegations, despite admitting some of the accusations, employed defensive depoliticization to successfully adjourn the discussion. Contrary to some of the cases discussed in Chapter 3, the Israeli delegation did not argue that the issues discussed were not political, although it has to be admitted that their link with aviation was clear from the beginning. Ironically, the Arab delegations undertook the political dimension of the conflict and, at the same time, argued against discussing such an issue. In turn, the Peruvian delegate's statement and the result of the vote reveal qualities of neutral depoliticization and apparently a genuine attempt to protect ICAO from political controversies.

Similar issues were raised during the 12th Assembly in 1959. In his address at the first plenary meeting, the Israeli delegate said that he had hoped the situation of political interference with aviation in the Middle East would improve after the promise of one of Israel's neighboring states during the 10th Assembly to cooperate in matters of search and rescue, but this hope had not been realized. He referred to the problem of access to the Regional Office of the ICAO in the Middle East and the lack of cooperation, which may lead to danger to the lives of crews and passengers.[20] This time, it did not spark wider discussions. It was also the end of this kind of debates in the ICAO. In all these instances, Israeli delegations raised aviation-related problems stemming from the Arab–Israeli conflict, whereas the Arab states defended themselves by claiming that such political issues should not be discussed in ICAO. During one of the Assemblies, the Egyptian delegate also mentioned several events related to politics, apparently provoked by the Israelis. Generally, the argumentation by the Arab states proved successful and the discussions did not lead to any decisions in favor of Israel, although at the same time Israeli delegations did not always expected a formal action. The defensive depoliticization by Arab states featured arguments that the issues raised by the Israeli delegation lied beyond ICAO's scope, the latter also voiced by the delegate from Peru, a country not engaged in the conflict, whose interventions have been interpreted as neutral.

Israeli attack on Beirut airport in 1968

Subsequent cases of politicization of ICAO as a result of the Arab–Israeli conflict more often were initiated by the Arab states, though usually in reference to actual misconduct by Israel. However, the situations were usually far from being absolutely clear in terms of ICAO jurisdiction. This was the case of the extraordinary session of the Council convened in 1969 to consider Lebanese complaint against Israel. On December 28, 1968, Israeli helicopters flew into Lebanese territory, destroyed 13 civil aircraft at the Beirut airport, and set on fire airport facilities. The Israeli action was a response to the December 1968 attack when terrorists threw bombs on an El Al airliner at Athens airport, killing one passenger, with no action by the Council.[21] Importantly, before the ICAO Council considered the issue, it was dealt with by the UN Security Council (SC). Already on December 29, Lebanon requested its emergency session to consider its charge that Israel had committed an attack upon Beirut airport. In turn, Israel requested an urgent SC meeting to consider its countercharge that Lebanon was assisting warfare, violence, and terror against Israel. The UN SC acted only in reference to the Lebanese charge.[22] In the unanimously adopted resolution 252 from December 31, 1968, the SC, among other things, 'condemned Israel for its premeditated military action' and 'issued a solemn warning to Israel that if such acts were to be repeated, the Council would have to consider further steps to give effect to its decisions.'[23] Though the decision has been made by the SC, according to Falk, both Israel and Lebanon were displeased with the outcome, with Lebanon having sought more definite action such as sanctions, whereas Israel having claimed the condemnation was without significance because of the one-sided composition of the SC. Israel was also dissatisfied that the resolution did not refer to the Athens raid and the Lebanese role in tolerating the use of its territory to mount terrorist activities against Israel.[24] However, it was the Lebanese dissatisfaction that paved the ground for bringing the issue before ICAO.

Before the beginning of deliberations of the ICAO Council, the Israeli representative made the first attempt to defend his country, requesting to include in the order of business its complaint against Lebanon for violation of its obligations. However, without the necessary majority, the issue was not included.[25] The Israeli representative tried to include a motion against the adversary in the deliberations despite Israel being the main object of scrutiny during the Council's meeting. Apparently, 'the best defense is a good offense' approach has been adopted here rather than depoliticization, but it has to be admitted that defensive depoliticization sometimes also featured offensive argumentation, accusing the adversary of politicizing the debate.

When the actual deliberation on the Lebanese complaint to the Council began, its representative and future President of the ICAO Council Assad Kotaite strongly criticized Israel. He spoke about the Council facing 'a case of total destruction of the Chicago Convention, without precedent in the entire history of the Organization.'[26] The Lebanese referred to the condemnation of Israel by the UN Security Council and called for the condemnation and sanctions by ICAO. In his speech, the Lebanese representative also said that a state 'that does not behave in accordance with the principles and objectives of this Organization should not be a member of ICAO.' He concluded calling the Israeli action 'the most perfidious aggression' which was 'premediated, carefully planned, coldly calculated.'[27]

The representative of Israel responded in a long and equally strong statement. Besides complaining about the Council's lack of objectivity in regard to not including the Israeli complaint in the agenda, the Israeli accused the Lebanese representative of describing the developments without the background and of reading the parts of the UN SC resolutions that suited him and put aside others.[28] He argued that the Lebanese government was 'asking the Council to deal with a political matter'[29] and that since the UN did not impose sanctions on Israel or called its action an act of aggression as expected by Lebanon, it now tried to 'embroil ICAO "into political and military matters of grave moment"' despite the fact that it is a technical UN specialized agency. The Israeli continued that ICAO's constitution did not permit it to deal with political and military matters and recalled the already mentioned decision from the 10th Assembly when the Executive Committee refused to consider the problem because 'it was part of a larger political problem – the problem of the Middle East – which did not fall within the competence of this Organization.'[30] Other points mentioned by the Israeli included the fact that Lebanon defined itself as being in a state of war with Israel, and in such a situation, provisions of the Chicago Convention do not affect the freedom of action of the belligerent states and spoke about the interconnection between the Israeli action and the attack on Israeli civil aircraft by organizations operating from Lebanon recognized by the UN SC. He said that Israeli position on the event was already explained in the UN SC but wanted to add that Beirut International Airport was also used by military aircraft and that the action was performed with great care to avoid loss of life.[31]

As to the Lebanese call for sanctions, the Israeli called them 'redolent with political overtones' and having 'transparent political character.'[32] The representative concluded by accusing the Lebanese government of passivity and tolerance toward terrorists.[33] The statement featured accusations against Lebanon, but most of all, numerous arguments about the political character of the accusations against Israel and claims that the issue was beyond ICAO's jurisdiction because of its political character, providing a clear example of defensive depoliticization, regardless of the ICAO legal jurisdiction over the incident.

The statements described above were followed by a discussion in which similar arguments were used. The Lebanese representative said the representative of Israel was bringing into discussion 'purely political elements that were outside the competence of ICAO Council and had already been considered in the Security Council' and that he had not referred to the Lebanese complaint, which had no references to political considerations. He then added that they were ready to discuss the question of Palestine, but the discussion should remain within the limits of the Chicago Convention and should concern only the Lebanese complaint.[34] The Israeli representative responded by saying that his goal, like that of the representative of Lebanon, was to improve the safety of civil aviation. He spoke about the danger posed by terrorists, particularly the Palestine Liberation Front, and that it was not his delegation to introduce political matters to the discussion and not the Israeli government to start interference with civil aviation in the region. The Israeli then accused Lebanon of supporting terrorist organizations and said that if the Council was to consider the Lebanese request, it should impose pressure on Arab and other states so that civil aviation was not 'allowed to become target of political dissenters.'[35] Both statements represent a common example of defensive depoliticization, with the two sides accusing each other of trying to politicize the deliberations but at the same time making arguments with more or less direct political overtones, demonstrating an explicitly pejorative connotation of the word 'politics' in the 'technical' ICAO, which connects with the so-called ideology of depoliticization discussed in Chapter 2. In principle, the Israeli argument was that it was a belligerent situation beyond the scope of the organization and a response to the Lebanese misdoings, whereas the Lebanese standpoint was that an attack on a civil airport was making the matter aviation-related and that it should not be held responsible for the actions of non-state actors. Israel was also trying to justify its action with the circumstances in the region. Depoliticizing moves were used on an operational level to undermine the arguments of the adversary.

During the subsequent discussion, the alternate representative of Lebanon made several points on the deliberations of the UN SC on the issue, claiming the Israeli representative only said half-truth. The Lebanese called Israeli claims about Lebanese engagement in the Athens incident as 'unfounded allegations' and an attempt to project Israel as 'the gendarme of international aviation.' The Lebanese added that he did not want to inject political issues, underlined that the Lebanese government did not permit training or establishment of fedayeen units in its territory, and concluded that, unlike Israel, Lebanon accepted and obeyed the Armistice Agreement.[36] In response, the representative of Israeli, among other things, confirmed Israeli reservations concerning the SC Resolution but said he would not talk about it because 'what goes on in the Security Council does not come within the competence of this Organization' but repeated that Lebanese delegation was not satisfied with the UN SC decisions.[37] Both sides thus employed similar tactics, intertwining substantive arguments with more political ones, and in the case of Israel, referring to the incident being outside ICAO's jurisdiction, which also constitutes a characteristic move of defensive depoliticization.

At this stage, representatives from other member states joined the discussion. Statements by some of them featured strong accusations against Israel. The representative of Tunisia expressed support for the Lebanese complaint against 'premeditated and inglorious aggression,' spoke about state terrorism practiced by Israel, called for condemnation and sanctions, and accused the Israeli representative of bringing 'political digressions and old partisan cliches' to the ICAO.[38] The representatives of Tanzania and the United Arab Emirates called for condemnation of Israel. The representative of Czechoslovakia condemned the Israeli act as in a complete conflict with the fundamental principles of the Chicago Convention and stated that interventions by the Israeli representative suggest Israel believes ICAO members can order aggressive acts that violate the Convention, an attitude that should be rejected.[39] On the other hand, there were also statements underlining the need to separate politics from technical matters in a more impartial and neutral manner. The representative of Spain said the Council was dealing with 'both a political and a technical problem' but should only deal with the technical one of ensuring the safety of civil aviation but also spoke about the need to eliminate the danger posed by terrorists and condemn states' acquiescence for their acts.[40] In a similar tone, the representative of Italy said the Council should confine itself to technical aspects, meaning 'everything that falls within the Chicago Convention' as the political aspects had already been discussed in the UN SC, and that everything possible should be done to avoid acts of violence against civil aviation.[41] The representatives of Australia, the Netherlands, Colombia, Denmark, France, Nigeria, and Guatemala advocated that the Council should focus on aviation aspects and not refer to the political ones. The representative of the United Kingdom said the Council should express general concern, but any sanctions would be outside the constitutional powers of ICAO and the UN SC was the proper forum for such issues with political implications. The representative of India, although called for condemning the act, claimed it was looked at from a political perspective in the UN SC, so the ICAO should do it from the perspective of ensuring the safety of civil aviation.[42] Such depoliticization arguments were, in principle, used in two contexts: as a genuine attempt to limit the Council's activity to aviation matters and combined with revealing some form of defense of Israel, although virtually every speaker criticized its attack on the Beirut airport. Still, the statements by the representatives of the countries not criticizing Israel bear the hallmarks of depoliticization aimed to remove the political problems from consideration, among other things through calls to focus on the technical aspects of the incident.

After all the major positions were revealed, the representatives of Lebanon and Israel engaged in the discussion again. The representative of Lebanon responded to those against discussing political issues, saying that his delegation did not come to discuss the political questions, which have their own forums, that an attack of one state against the other cannot be compared to the acts of individuals, and that the request was only concerned with technical, economic, and legal considerations relating to the Convention.[43] In turn, the Israeli representative argued that the Convention was not violated and spoke about innumerable violations of Israeli airspace by its neighbors, including Lebanon, which Israel did not bring before the Council because of their political and military implications. He then argued that, unlike the terrorists who committed the recent attack, Israeli soldiers had the strictest order not to hurt any person and repeated that ICAO was not empowered to consider the event. The Israeli concluded that it was not Israel to introduce violence into civil aviation in the region and appealed to the Council members 'not to let political or other secondary considerations obscure the main tasks before us – the promotion of the safety of civil aviation.'[44] Both statements demonstrate clearly the negative connotation of 'politics.' The attacking side argued that an issue was not political and should be dealt with, which bears the hallmarks of discursive depoliticization, whereas the defending side claimed it was political and should be discussed elsewhere. Additionally, both sides accused each other of politicizing the deliberations, while at the same time, both used arguments that can be interpreted as more or less directly political.

As a response to the last intervention from the representative of Israel, the representative of Tunisia asked for specification of the violations of Israeli airspace by Arab countries and wondered why Israel did not lodge a complaint about them, and that if Israel was able to implicate Lebanon in the Athens affair, it could have brought it before the Council. After that, the representative of Lebanon repeated that his delegation was not speaking of politics and only wanted to consider Israel's violation of the fundamental principles of the Convention. He then said Israel sought ICAO protection in some cases, reminding the case of El Al aircraft diverted to Algiers on July 23, 1968, but spoke about the state of war when it violated the Convention. The representative concluded that Israel accused Lebanon of actions of individuals, while during the Eichmann affair,[45] Israel denied state responsibility for acts of individual citizens outside Israel.[46]

Eventually, after three meetings of the Council, it decided not to take action.[47] Like in the case of the Israeli complaints against Arab states, depoliticization argumentation proved effective in preventing ICAO from taking a more severe stance. Naturally, such an outcome can also be interpreted from the legal point of view, with an argument about the state of war being an objective premise for the situation lying beyond the provisions of the Chicago Convention. However, as argued particularly by the representative of Lebanon, Israel itself did not follow such an interpretation consequently. From the perspective of this study, it is crucial that the argument about the political character of the discussed issue that made it unfit for ICAO was used to defend from international condemnation. Politics was consequently interpreted as not proper for ICAO, with each side claiming they were not injecting it into the deliberations and accusing the other of doing so. Thus, depoliticization was employed on several levels, most directly as a defensive diplomatic tool, but also to imply the validity of discussing the issue which was to be not political, and more neutrally calling for limiting the discussion to technical and economic matters.

Interception of the Lebanese civil aircraft by the Israeli Air Force in 1973

The year 1973 was very tense regarding the Arab–Israeli conflict on the forum of ICAO. First, on February 21, 1973, Israeli fighters shot down Libyan civil aircraft over Sinai. Israeli action was condemned by the ICAO Assembly on February 28, 1973, at its extraordinary session, whereas later, when the Council considered the report of the investigation team, it found no justification for the Israeli action and strongly condemned it.[48] The incident, although highly controversial, did not result in an extensive effort to depoliticize the deliberations. During the debates in the Assembly, the Israeli delegate only called for not making political capital out of the tragic occurrence, which should be an occasion for searching for ways to prevent such tragedies in the future, although he also called for waiting with the condemnation until the investigation is completed.[49] The reason for not employing defensive depoliticization by Israel was probably its unequivocal fault combined with the incident's clear link to civil aviation. Either way, soon another controversy occurred, this time leading to the explicit use of defensive depoliticization.

The 20th extraordinary session of the Assembly was convened on August 10, 1973, to consider proposals for the amendment of the Chicago Convention. However, shortly before its opening, the Israeli Air Force forcibly diverted Lebanese Middle East Airlines aircraft chartered by Iraqi Airways, leading to international reactions. According to the Lebanese side, after the aircraft took off from Beirut, two Israeli Mirage fighters intercepted it and forced it to land in Israel. Passengers were inspected and interrogated, and after 1.5 hours, the pilot was instructed to fly back to Beirut with the passengers.[50]

Before ICAO undertook the issue, it was first considered by the UN SC, which on August 15, 1973, unanimously condemned the government of Israel for violating Lebanon's sovereignty and territorial integrity, considered the action as a violation of the Lebanese–Israeli Armistice Agreement and other international documents, called ICAO to 'take due account of this resolution when considering adequate measures to safeguard international civil aviation,' and called Israel to desist from such actions.[51] ICAO Council considered the issue a few days later and, on August 20, 1973, also condemned Israel for its action, considering that it had violated the Chicago Convention. The Council had also recommended to the Assembly to include considerations of these actions in its agenda.[52] Dealing with the issue by the Assembly was thus not an initiative of Lebanon or any other state seeking to attack Israel but a consequence of deliberations on other forums – the UN SC and ICAO Council.

In the Assembly, the first discussion referred to whether the item should be added to the agenda. The Libyan delegate described the event as 'an act of air piracy,' arguing that the aircraft had been hijacked by the military authorities, undoubtedly on order by the Israeli government. The delegate of Israel responded that lengthy debates held in the UN Security Council and ICAO Council were to be repeated and that if the item was added to the agenda, he would explain in detail the real circumstances and which states were the guilty ones.[53] At this stage, Israel did not employ depoliticization, confining itself to questioning the need to discuss the action once again in multilateral forums. Still, the Assembly decided to consider the item.

During the actual discussion in the Assembly, 31 states, predominantly from Africa and the Middle East, proposed a draft resolution strongly condemning Israel, urgently calling it to stop committing such acts and warning that further measures might be taken if Israel continues committing such acts.[54] Israeli action was criticized by the delegate of Lebanon and by the delegate of Egypt, who, among other things, talked about the threat posed by the Israeli action, claiming that 'Israel now had a government-organized terrorist system called "God's Wrath" (…) supervised personally by the Premier, Mrs. Golda Meir.' He said that the declared Israeli motive was to apprehend some Palestinian leaders expected to be onboard, commenting that if such practice is accepted, 'nobody would be safe from the agents of some ruthless foreign power.'[55] The tone of some statements against Israel was very strong, but at the same time, considering earlier international reactions, the international community was rather unanimous in criticism of the Israeli act.

The delegate of Israel responded in a long statement, several times interrupted by the delegates of Lebanon, Qatar, Tunisia, and the United Arab Emirates. At the beginning, he said that such a debate should not be held in ICAO because of its political nature, but his delegation was compelled to engage in it. He then said that the issue was dealt with by the UN Security Council and the ICAO Council, and then the Assembly was asked to take up the same discussion in order to condemn Israel for the third time. In contrast, other states or political organizations guilty of attacks on the security of civil aviation have not been condemned. According to the Israeli, the interception was to be conducted because George Habash of the Popular Front for the Liberation of Palestine, responsible for hijacking and murder of passengers flying on international routes, alongside other terrorists, was supposed to have been on board. The delegate then gave a few examples of interceptions of civil aircraft to capture particular individuals, to which neither the Security Council nor ICAO reacted. The Israeli delegate then accused governments of Algeria, Syria, Egypt, Lebanon, Yemen, Iraq, and Libya of cooperating with terrorists or not putting charges against them and said that the UN Security Council and ICAO remained inactive and silent regarding the violations of the conventions by the Arab states. He concluded that the Israeli government's objective in its action was to protect international aviation from terrorists and that the draft resolution presented by Lebanon 'was a grotesque distortion of the real situation.'[56] This was one of the strongest and most accusatory statements on the forum of ICAO of all analyzed within this research. The Israeli employed depoliticization rhetoric to support the argument that the issue should not be discussed but, at the same time, strongly attacked Arab states, directly referring to political arguments. Before doing this, the Israeli used an oft-repeated statement that he/she did not want to engage in the political debates but was forced to by the other side. It should also be underlined that contrary to many deliberations analyzed in this volume, discussing the issue in the Assembly was assumed already by the Council, whereas the UN SC resolution assumed ICAO engagement. Therefore, the Israeli argument about no need to deliberate on the issue has little merit. Under such circumstances, there was less space for defensive depoliticization, but the Israeli delegate still employed it.

During the subsequent discussion, several delegates spoke about the need to make the resolution more general instead of being focused on the Israeli act, but eventually, the resolution was adopted, with only Israel being against it and just a few delegations abstaining but arguing they were against the interception.[57] In this sense, we can say that the condemnation of Israel for its actions was almost universal. Moreover, the resolution of the Assembly 'strongly condemned' the Israeli act, which was an even stronger phrasing than used in previous resolutions of the UN SC and ICAO Council. Unlike some previous cases, depoliticization rhetoric proved ineffective, although taking into consideration the circumstances, with the action being condemned both in the UN SC and the ICAO Council, such outcomes could have been anticipated. The intervention of the Israeli delegate provided a good example of using political arguments and arguing that politics had no place in the technical organization, which proved to be a common tactic by those engaged in conflictual discussions in ICAO.

Jerusalem airport controversy

The following year marked the beginning of a new controversy arising from the Arab–Israeli conflict within the framework of ICAO. This time, it concerned the use of Jerusalem airport by Israel, which, according to Arab states, was illegal. The issue was first brought up during the 21st Assembly in 1974 by delegations from Iraq and Jordan. According to the draft resolution presented by them, since the airport lied in the occupied Arab territories under the jurisdiction of Jordan in the ICAO Middle East Air Navigation Plan, all contracting states should take all measures to refrain from operating or giving permissions to airlines to operate to and from it unless prior permission is granted.[58] The delegate of Israel opposed adding the item to the agenda, claiming it raised the issue of ICAO competence and gave rise to conflicting interpretations of the Chicago Convention, and that if the issue was to be dealt with by ICAO, it should be the Council to have the exclusive competence. The Israeli then argued that Transjordan occupied part of Jerusalem in 1948 but lost these territories in 1967, so the proposal was an attempt to indirectly obtain pseudo-recognition of theoretical Jordanian sovereignty over Jerusalem, which was then Israeli territory. The Israeli summarized that ICAO had not been created to paralyze airports in the name of politics, that it was not qualified to pronounce on territorial disputes, and even if it assumed such competence, it would be the Council to address such issues.[59] Although the subject matter of this dispute was entirely different from those discussed above, the argumentation used by Israel did not change much and was built around defensive depoliticization. The Israeli position assumed that political issues should have no place in ICAO, whereas the issue of the Jerusalem airport was strictly political. The situation is slightly different from the previous instances of the Arab accusations against Israel. There was a clear link to civil aviation, but this time, the situation was more complex, and we cannot speak unequivocally of Israeli aviation-related misconduct. Regardless of the merit of the claims by Arab states, they used the forum of ICAO to hit its political adversary. Israeli argument was that the issue of the Jerusalem airport was an issue of territorial sovereignty, thus political and unfit for ICAO, and especially unfit for the Assembly. Still, the Israeli delegate did not avoid political statements to support his argument either.

During the subsequent discussion on the addition of the item to the agenda, the delegate from Nicaragua shared the argument about limited ICAO powers. Delegates of Egypt and Tunisia claimed the question was not of territorial rights and within ICAO competence, whereas the US delegate argued that such debate should not be held in a technical organization and that it could be harmful to the negotiations being held at the time. Eventually, the item was included in the agenda.[60] The statements of the delegates from Egypt and Tunisia have the qualities of discursive depoliticization, typically based on denial, arguing that the question was not political and thus fit for ICAO. Moreover, their statements reveal the close link between discursive and preference-shaping depoliticization, in line with the theoretical considerations on the issue. The American argumentation that such a debate should not be held in the technical organization has been interpreted as neutral since it did not feature direct statements about Israel's innocence, although it also bears some hallmarks of defending Israel. Also the general circumstances might suggest Americans were seeking to lend support to Israel. For example, in 1974 the United States was a country which voted most similarly to Israel in the UN GA, with the voting coincidence at the level of 85.3 percent,[61] which suggest that also on other forums the Americans might have been supportive of Israel, while depoliticization argument was to conceal this support.

The actual discussion featured many voices on the technical matters relating to the draft resolution, but also such that referred to more political arguments or used depoliticization rhetoric. The Israeli delegate said the statements of those being against the use of Jerusalem airport were of a political nature, spoke about the good management of the airport, and that ICAO should deal with real life rather than with 'dreams, hopes, or past memories, or with the political mood of any of the great powers.'[62] Among those supporting the resolution, the delegate of Syria said it was a matter of preventing infractions of the Chicago Convention, that each state should freely exercise its right to grant permission to operate on its own territory, and that a state occupying territory should be prevented from making use of it for the civil aviation purposes. The Tunisian delegate said the objective of the resolution was to protect passengers, while the Egyptian delegate stressed that the Jerusalem airport was located in the occupied Arab territories and that operating from it implied aggression against Arab sovereignty and violated the ICAO Convention and UN resolutions. After the discussion, the resolution which among other things called all contracting states to refrain from operating to and from Jerusalem airport was adopted with 52 votes in favor, 3 against, 38 abstentions, and 26 delegations absent.[63] The discussion once again demonstrated how Israel attempted to prevent the adoption of an unfavorable resolution by one of ICAO bodies using arguments that the issue under discussion was political. Though effective at the beginning if the Arab–Israeli conflict on the forum of ICAO is considered, at some point, critical decisions were made regardless of these arguments. Even when making points about the political character of the accusations, Israeli delegates also made political arguments against their adversaries themselves, demonstrating that defensive depoliticization as a diplomatic strategy was more about defense than about sparing ICAO from politicization.

The issue of the Jerusalem airport kept returning to the forum of ICAO. The Council dealt with it during its 86th session on December 17, 1975, deciding to deeply deplore Israel's disregard of the Assembly resolution discussed above.[64] In the Assembly, the problem was discussed again during the 23rd session in 1980 after the delegate of Jordan, on behalf of 20 states, introduced a proposal to add an item that referred to the Israeli continued use of the airport.[65] According to the draft resolution, the Assembly reaffirmed ICAO's earlier decisions, considered the alteration of character and status of Jerusalem as null and void,[66] deeply deplored Israel's formal annexation of Jerusalem, urged Israel to abide ICAO decisions, and directed the Council to take necessary measures to implement them.[67] As previously, the delegate from Israel opposed considering the issue, claiming the item was of political nature, that the proposal attempted to politicize ICAO, that an attempt to involve ICAO in the determination of sovereignty constituted a dangerous precedent, and that the proposal went beyond the UN SC resolution 478 of August 20, 1980.[68] Still, the majority of states supported adopting the item. The discussion was also joined by the observer from the Palestine Liberation Organization (PLO),[69] who said the proposal dealt with the technical and humanitarian aspects resulting from the annexation of Jerusalem.[70] Israeli argumentation did not change and was still centered around claims that the issue was political and unfit for the ICAO.

During the actual discussion in the Assembly, the Israeli delegate accused the Libyan of forcing others to support the inclusion of the item and claimed that his delegations tried to prevent ICAO from involving in purely political issues. Responding to the text of the draft resolution, he said that the historical character and status of Jerusalem had never changed and would never change, that the Jewish community had always composed the largest community of Jerusalem, and that the Jerusalem airport was an integral part of the city, but it did not mean ICAO could concern issues of territorial rights. The Israeli delegate concluded that the Assembly was being used in an attempt to delegitimize the State of Israel. Regardless of such argumentation, which again focused on using defensive depoliticization combined with political arguments, the Assembly adopted the resolution.[71]

The events surrounding ICAO deliberations on the Jerusalem airport did not differ much from other instances of the Arab–Israeli conflict in the organization. Arab states were accusing Israel of acting contrary to international aviation norms, whereas Israel attempted to avoid unfavorable decisions of the organization through arguments about the political character of the issues discussed and ICAO having no competence to consider them. Heated discussions surrounded both the issue of adding the items to the agenda and the actual deliberations. While accusing Arab states of politicizing ICAO, delegates of Israel also referred to political arguments, although in some cases, this might have been understandable concerning the content of the resolutions being discussed. At that time, the distribution of votes in the Assembly became favorable to the Arab states, making it more difficult for Israel to avoid the adoption of such documents and depoliticization tactics less effective.

Observer status of the Palestine Liberation Organization

The 21st session of the Assembly in 1974, besides the issue of the Jerusalem airport discussed above, was also an arena for the beginning of another controversy connected to the Arab–Israeli conflict, this time regarding the observer status of the PLO. The controversy was connected to the UN General Assembly resolutions inviting liberation movements to attend the meetings of specialized agencies.[72] In the ICAO Assembly, the issue was first discussed in the Executive Committee. According to the proposal presented by the delegate of Tunisia, liberation movements recognized by the Organization of African Unity and the Arab League could be invited to ICAO meetings dealing with matters pertaining to their respective territories. The proposal was seconded by a number of delegations, mostly from Africa, Asia, and the Communist bloc. The delegate of Israel responded that the Tunisian delegate opened a political debate inappropriate to ICAO. He claimed Israel was against inviting the PLO, the only liberation movement recognized by the Arab League, to any ICAO meeting. As the delegate said, it would be 'a grotesque and an aberration to invite representatives of the PLO, whose name was identified with terrorism.'[73] The Tunisian responded by recalling acts committed by Israel against civil aviation and said that PLO had officially disavowed all acts of air piracy and that the proposal was not motivated by hostility but 'by a concern to prepare a better future based on understanding and justice.'[74] The Israeli delegate replied that ICAO had no competence concerning acts by states and that Israel and its people had aspired to peace. Israel proposed amending the proposal by removing the reference to the Arab League, but the amendment failed in a vote, garnering support only from Israel, Ecuador, Nicaragua, and the United States. Eventually, the Executive Committee recommended that the Assembly adopt the Tunisian proposal.[75] This initial discussion already featured a typical scenario for the Arab–Israeli conflict in the ICAO, although in this case, it did not refer to any particular activity by Israel. Rather, it can be interpreted as another attempt by the Arab states to hit Israel in the multilateral forum. As to the Israeli argumentation, like before, it included claims that the issue was political and should not be discussed, or at least to exclude the liberation movements recognized by the Arab League so that PLO could not be invited. The Tunisian delegate, in turn, employed discursive depoliticization by describing the proposal as not connected to the Arab–Israeli conflict.

The discussion resumed during the plenary meetings. The Israeli delegate made a statement against authorizing the Council to invite representatives of PLO to the ICAO meetings. The Israeli stated that ICAO was not competent to take any decision in favor of PLO and repeated his arguments from the Executive Committee meetings. In response, the Lebanese delegate deplored the Israeli argument that the PLO controlled fractions of Lebanese territory. The delegate from Syria refuted the claims that PLO was responsible for acts of brutality and crimes, whereas the Tunisian delegate said he did not wish to engage in the political debates and that the proposed resolution was to underline peace.[76] Neither minutes of the plenary session nor the list of resolutions reveal the result of the vote, but from the context and according to other sources, we can assume the vote was in favor of granting the observer status to liberation movements as parts of delegations from the Organization of African Unity or the Arab League. PLO never used that right[77] but soon received individual rights to participate in ICAO meetings.

The discussions regarding the PLO's participation in ICAO meetings as an observer resurfaced during the 22nd Assembly in 1977. This time, the discussion concerned the PLO directly. As could have been expected, the proposal to include the issue in the agenda was objected to by the delegate of Israel who, in principle, repeated Israeli arguments from the 21st Assembly, including that inviting the PLO to act as an observer would be a purely political act, and that since ICAO was not a political forum, it should not 'allow itself to be transferred into an instrument of policy of certain states.' The Israeli continued that the acts and aims of PLO were contradictory to those of ICAO and that PLO was neither a state nor an international organization, so inviting it would be against the Standing Rules and Procedure of the Assembly. Regardless of these arguments, the item was included in the agenda.[78] During the actual deliberation, the delegate of Saudi Arabia, on behalf of Arab states, requested the Assembly to agree for PLO's participation as an observer in ICAO meetings. In turn, the delegate of Israel repeated that representatives of the PLO should not be allowed to enter the ICAO deliberations since its aims and history were opposite to the ICAO goals of promoting the safety of aviation. He spoke about security costs for aviation caused by the threats and acts of the PLO, about the territories being the domain of the PLO, enumerated the terrorist incidents committed by the PLO, and concluded that such terrorist organizations should not receive the observer status in ICAO. The arguments did not find support, and the Assembly voted in favor of the proposal. In a roll-call vote, the resolution was supported by 70 states, with 33 abstentions and 20 delegations absent. Only South Africa, the US, and Israel voted against.[79] The resolutions were supported specifically by Arab, African, and Communist countries, which apparently were able to outvote Israel and its allies. Arab states thus succeeded in getting PLO to be invited to ICAO meetings despite Israeli arguments about the political character of the decision and about the terrorist past of the organization. As in several previous cases, depoliticization rhetoric was used to defend from unfavorable decisions, although it was presumably the vote majoritythat played an overriding role.

As a result of these decisions, PLO could send an observer to ICAO meetings. Unsurprisingly, already during the subsequent 23rd Assembly in 1980, the observer from PLO made a statement with apparent political overtones. He spoke, among other things, about Palestinian land being 'usurped by the racist Israeli Zionist entity, that seizes the land and loots the heritage and civilization,' about Israel legalizing terror and occupation, and acting against the ICAO resolution of 1974 by using the Jerusalem airport for international aviation. Finally, the observer requested an urgent resolution to suspend the Israeli membership in ICAO. The Israeli delegate responded that the statement bore no relevance to the agenda items, regretted that the Assembly was made into a political forum, and requested that the PLO statement be considered out of order. Later, the Israeli delegate also added that his government considered the attendance of the PLO as illegal and contrary to the ICAO foundations.[80] In a similar manner, at the 26th Assembly in 1986, the PLO observer talked about state terrorism against civil aircraft, giving several examples of Israeli actions,[81] while at the 27th Assembly in 1989, the PLO observer spoke about the birth of the State of Palestine 10 months earlier, with Jerusalem as its capital, whose legitimacy had been recognized by 107 states, concluding that 'stone-throwing children must one day lead a happy life.'[82] Regardless of their reason, statements like these can undoubtedly be assessed as having political overtones. Israeli delegates did not always respond, but when they did, their central argument was that the PLO's observer was turning the Assembly into a political forum, thus employing defensive depoliticization.

Israel manifested its opposition against the presence of the PLO also through the path used by various states questioning the statehood or legitimacy of member states (see Chapter 3) – by making reservations to the reports of the Credentials Committee. After its presentation during the 23rd Assembly in 1980, the Israeli delegate said that the PLO 'was an illegal body unfit and unqualified to participate in the Assembly.'[83] A similar statement was made by the Israeli delegate after the presentation of the Credentials Committee's report at the Extraordinary 25th Assembly in 1984. At the time, the observer from the PLO responded by expressing regret that his first intervention was to 'reply to the accusations of the delegation of an enemy which has usurped the land of his country.'[84] The same happened during the 27th Assembly in 1989 when, after the presentation of the Credentials Committee's report, the delegate of Israel reiterated his delegation's reservation concerning the invitation issued to the observer delegation from Palestine to attend the Assembly for the reasons expressed already at the 22nd Assembly.[85] Israeli diplomatic tactics regarding PLO thus combined defensive depoliticization with questioning PLO's observer status.

According to Sochor, there was no justification for PLO to become an observer in the ICAO Assembly, contrary to the UN General Assembly, a political body. It controlled no territory and operated no aviation facilities, while its presence reflected the political climate of the time.[86] The global character of ICAO and the democratic character of the Assembly provided a convenient, cheap, and visible ground for waging the conflict and for the Arab states another opportunity to hit Israel. At the same time, the vote distribution at the time, which in the ICAO Assembly was not connected to the power of respective countries, with each state having one vote, allowed Arab states to outvote Israel and its allies. Throughout the controversy Israel attempted to prevent granting PLO an observer status, arguing about its terrorist past and claiming the discussions and eventual decision were bringing politics into the ICAO. These deliberations sometimes also featured using political arguments, but depoliticization proved to be the most crucial defensive tool. Once PLO began to send its observers to the Assembly, on several occasions they attacked Israel, not necessarily in reference to aviation matters. In turn, Israel started voicing reservations about Credentials Committee reports, which can also be considered a form of politicizing the deliberations. The entire controversy not only provides more evidence for treating depoliticization rhetoric as a defensive diplomatic tactic in multilateral organizations but also further reveals a close link between politicization and depoliticization.

Interception of Libyan Arab Airlines flight by Israel 1986

The last controversy regarding the Arab–Israeli conflict held in the ICAO analyzed in this book occurred in February 1986 and is connected with the interception of Libyan Arab Airlines aircraft en route from Tripoli to Damascus with Syrian diplomatic personnel by the Israeli Air Force over international waters. The aircraft was forced to land in an Israeli military base after Israel had mistakenly suspected that terrorists were on board. After it was revealed that there were no terrorists, the plane was allowed to continue its journey.[87] The occurrence was thus similar to the one from 1973 when Lebanese aircraft was intercepted, after which Israeli was condemned by both the Council and the Assembly. However, this time, the UN Security Council did not adopt the resolution condemning Israel due to the American veto.[88] The issue then moved to ICAO.

In ICAO, the issue was discussed in the Council after Libya lodged a formal complaint, featuring discussions on the political character of the matter and the ICAO's jurisdiction. In particular, it was discussed whether it was a civil or a state aircraft – in the latter case, the issue would be beyond the Council's scope. Such a doubt was first raised by the representative of the United States, whereas the British representative spoke about the need not to go beyond Council's mandate. Apart from that, there were also statements about the political character of the matter. The Canadian representative said the issue undoubtedly had political implications and should be dealt with in political forums such as the UN Security Council or General Assembly and that the Council should not be asked to look at political considerations. The Norwegian representative warned about undermining the Council's credibility if it allowed itself to become a political forum, although for safety reasons, he deplored the interception. The Italian representative said the situation was serious, but the Council should not act if it was beyond its scope and should avoid political considerations. The Spanish representative called to avoid political considerations and the need to look for the compromise solution.[89] Many of these statements do not seem to have aimed to defend the Israeli action. Rather, they implied that the issue should first be determined if it felt within ICAO's competence. If it did, then it should have been addressed. Therefore, the discussion was principally legal, but some statements referred to the possible political character of the matter, making it unfit for ICAO. Some of the statements revealed qualities of neutral depoliticization, with calls to focus on issues within ICAO's jurisdiction.

Some speakers seemed genuinely interested in safeguarding ICAO from politicization or defending Israel by citing ICAO's limited jurisdiction. Others argued that since the aircraft was civilian, the Council had jurisdiction over the issue. Additionally, there were arguments reflecting broader international tensions. For example, the representative from Madagascar compared the act to terrorism, whereas the Libyan observer said that raising a question of whether the incident was within the scope of the Chicago Convention was an attempt of the US representative to divert the Council's attention from the main issue of state air piracy and state terrorism against international civil aviation.[90] Statements like this can be considered a backlash to defensive depoliticization and examples of discursive depoliticization, describing the occurrence as aviation-related and thus fit for consideration in ICAO.

The Israeli observer undertook the defensive strategy based on the legal argument that it was a state aircraft that was intercepted. According to that standpoint, the Convention did not carry an exclusive list of state aircraft, so its use should be the criterion, while the said aircraft was used exclusively by the Libyan government to ferry its guests. Moreover, the call sign LN777 was to be used exclusively by the Libyan government. At that stage, the Israeli did not speak about the political character of the accusation, focusing on legal arguments. In response, the Libyan observer drew attention to Article 35 of the Convention, which states that civil aircraft 'might be used for the carriage of military effects' and still remain civil aircraft governed by the provisions of the Chicago Convention.[91]

Further discussion sparked after the Lebanese representative presented a draft resolution calling the Council to take action to protect civil aviation from acts of unlawful interference. The Israeli observer addressed the Libyan threat to civil aviation, citing an announcement made by the Libyan leader Muammar Khadaffi in the media on February 7, 1986. According to the Israeli, Khadaffi had ordered Libyan air forces to intercept all Israeli civilian aircraft over the Mediterranean in search of Israeli terrorists. The Israeli argued that such threats should receive equal consideration by the Council and asked the President to use his influence with the Libyan government.[92] Israel thus attempted to draw attention to the Libyan behavior, which, on the one hand, referred to the reasons for its action according to the Israeli standpoint, while on the other hand, can be interpreted as an attempt to divert the Council's attention elsewhere.

A number of speakers responded to the Israeli request. The British delegate said that, according to his opinion, press reports and interviews were not sufficient for the Council to deal with the issue, whereas the Libyan observer called the Israeli request 'an attempt to confuse and divert attention from the legitimate Libyan complaint' and said that his government had always supported security of civil aviation and peace and had never threatened or endangered civil aviation. The Libyan concluded that if the international community failed to prevent Israeli aggressive behavior, his government reserved the right to self-defense and spoke about the disappointment after the UN Security Council failed to act because of the American veto.[93] The Soviet representative categorically objected to examining the Israeli request by the Council, associated himself with the British position, and added that the issue was beyond the Council's scope and its purpose was to divert attention from the interception, a view shared by several other representatives. In turn, in defense of the Israeli position, the US delegate claimed it was wholly inappropriate for ICAO to consider the interception by Israel, which harmed no one, while ignoring disregard for human life by terrorists and states supporting them, such as Libya.[94] The discussion demonstrated several characteristic features typical for politicized discussions in the ICAO. Regardless of the actual fault of either of the sides, both attacked each other, also resorting to political arguments. At the same time, both claimed the motions against them should not be considered because of their political character or, in this case, because the subject lied beyond the scope of the Chicago Convention.

The discussion resumed at the next meeting of the Council. The British representative reminded that many representatives shared the desire to reach a consensus on the matter and the importance of maintaining the integrity of the Council by avoiding politically oriented action. He also argued that the Council should only deal with technical issues and mentioned that he had circulated an alternative draft resolution informally.[95] Such argumentation can be interpreted as reflecting a genuine objective to distance ICAO from politics. Further deliberations, among other things, were about the phrasing of the resolution and the level of condemnation since, in this case, no one died, and the aircraft was not in danger.[96] In turn, the Israeli observer said that the draft resolution was 'clearly and blatantly politically inspired,' did not reflect the discussion about the character of the aircraft, and did not refer to the background of the Israeli action, which, according to him, was 'part of a legitimate act in the struggle against air piracy.'[97] Still, the Council adopted the resolution condemning the Israeli act, but several representatives stated they voted against or abstained because of the problem of politics in the technical ICAO.[98]

The issue was also mentioned by the Libyan delegate during the subsequent 26th Assembly in 1986, together with other accusations against Israel and the United States.[99] However, they did not initiate any heated discussion. In the analyzed case, the Israeli argumentation received some support in the Council from other member states. As in many previous instances, Israel and the United States employed depoliticization rhetoric as a defensive tactic, but there were also several delegations that spoke about the need to separate politics from the deliberations or focus on the provisions of the Convention, though without attempts to defend Israel, which can be interpreted as manifestations of more general depoliticization. The final arrangement was unfavorable to Israel, though, with one of the strongest phrasings being used in the resolution.

Conclusions

As in other international organizations, for many years, the Arab–Israeli conflict was one of the prime reasons for the politicization of ICAO deliberations. Both the Council and the Assembly were becoming frequent arenas for expressing Arab–Israeli hostility. However, it was not only the conflictual character of the Arab–Israeli relations that was raised in ICAO. For example, during the 14th

Assembly in 1962, the delegate of Israel spoke of the role of aviation in the evolution toward peaceful cooperation worldwide and in the Middle East.[100] During the 25th Extraordinary Assembly in 1984, the delegate of Israel declared Israeli civil air corridors 'open to all civil aircraft of all countries – including our neighbouring States' – and expressed 'hope that mutual recognition among States concerning the importance of civil aviation will bring a break-through toward peace in the world, and especially here in this region, which has seen enough war.'[101] During the 31st Assembly in 1995, the delegate of Israel said that after signing a Peace Treaty in 1994 with Jordan, both countries had been implementing an overflying agreement and soon would sign a bilateral air transport agreement and spoke about the development of aviation relations between Israel and other countries of the region over the past three years.[102] Such a change definitely can be attributed to the general improvement of Arab–Israeli relations at the time. Still, it cannot be denied that for many years, it was the conflict that dominated the Arab–Israeli relations on the forum of ICAO, multiple times turning it into a place of politicized, confrontational debates.

The general pattern of the Arab–Israeli conflict waged on the forum of ICAO was that one of the sides, Israel or the Arab states, complained about the actions perpetrated by the other side, hoping that ICAO would take action against their adversary, but there were also instances of bringing the issue to ICAO which should rather be interpreted as attempts to hit the political opponent on another of the multilateral forums, like in the case of granting PLO observer status. Such attempts were initiating highly politicized debates, often already at the point of adding an item to the agenda. Although in most cases, the accusations had at least some reference to aviation, which justified raising them, speakers often also mentioned political circumstances surrounding the events, sometimes in an emotional way.

The parties subject to criticism have employed various defensive tactics, whether or not they were actually guilty of offenses. Representatives of such states spoke about the political character of the accusations which were unfit for the technical ICAO or referred to legal constraints regarding ICAO's jurisdiction, which was limited by the provisions of the Chicago Convention. Alternatively, representatives stroke back through making accusations against those attacking them or submitting motions against the adversary despite being subject to scrutiny. Usually, such tactics were employed by the side being criticized, but on some occasions, similar arguments were used by states supporting them. Apart from that, in several cases, representatives of states that were not aligned in the conflict also spoke about the need to separate politics from ICAO, focus on the technical dimensions of the discussed issues, or not to go beyond the provisions of the Convention, which can be interpreted as the genuine desire to sustain the technical and unbiased character of the organization, although potentially they also could have been aimed to defend, though in a more concealed way. Such unclear character of depoliticization arguments can be considered their potential merit, although probably only effective if there are no close political links between such states.

The Arab–Israeli conflict on the forum of ICAO demonstrated in a glaring way the link between politicization and depoliticization. Depoliticization used as a

Table 4.1 Instances of Arab–Israeli conflict in ICAO

Subject	*Forum*	*Year*	*Attacking side*	*Defending side*	*Result*	*Did defensive depoliticization succeed?*
Creating difficulties in aviation	Assembly	1955	Israel	Egypt/Arab states	N/A	N/A
Creating difficulties in aviation	Assembly	1956	Israel	Lebanon / Arab states	No action	Yes
Israeli attack on Beirut airport	Council	1969	Lebanon	Israel	No action	Yes
Interception of the Lebanese civil aircraft by Israeli Air Force	Assembly	1973	Lebanon	Israel	Resolution against Israel	No
Jerusalem airport	Assembly	1973	Iraq and Jordan	Israel	Resolution against Israel	No
Jerusalem airport	Assembly	1980	Jordan	Israel	Resolution against Israel	No
PLO's observer status	Assembly	1974	Tunisia	Israel	Vote in favor of observer status for liberation movements	No
PLO's observer status	Assembly	1977	19 Islamic states	Israel	Vote in favor of granting PLO observer status	No
Interception of Libyan Arab Airlines flight by Israel 1986	Council	1986	Libya/Syria	Israel	Resolution against Israel	No

Source: Own study.

defensive tactic was not meant to remove politics but for self-defense. In multiple instances, state representatives claimed they did not wish to engage in political discussions but were compelled to do so. They argued that certain issues were political and should be disregarded, yet subsequently made arguments with political overtones, thus supporting this claim. It should be noted that in some cases, making political statements was provoked by the other party. Instances of the Arab–Israeli conflict in ICAO also reveal examples of discursive depoliticization when speakers argued that the issues under discussion were about civil aviation and not about politics and thus adequate for consideration in ICAO, even though it was factually leading to the politicization of deliberations. Additionally, references to neutral depoliticization could be observed when delegations of states not engaged in the conflict called for considering only the technical and economic aspects of the events.

One of the observations derived from the analysis in this chapter was that the Arab states more often brought political issues into the ICAO and were more successful in making their ideas and claims realized through the Council's or Assembly's resolutions (see: Table 4.1). This dependence was growing over time, reflecting a more favorable distribution of votes in ICAO following the decolonization and entering into the organization by the Communist countries, although it should also be noted that in many cases, the Israeli offenses were so evident that it was difficult for any state to defend them. Either way, a review of the depoliticization used as a defensive tactic in the context of the Arab–Israeli conflict in ICAO suggests its relative ineffectiveness. The higher success rate of the Arab states should probably be linked with ICAO's more democratic character compared to some other international organizations. It should be noted that the cases analyzed here do not cover all instances of the Arab–Israeli conflict, only those where depoliticization was identified according to the accessible documents, which in reference to Council minutes were limited.

Notes

1 T. G. Fraser, *The Arab-Israeli Conflict* (Basingstoke: Palgrave Macmillan, 2004), 2.
2 Charles Smith, "The Arab-Israeli Conflict," in *International Relations of the Middle East*, ed. Louise Fawcett (Oxford: Oxford University Press, 2005), 230; Michael C. Hudson, "The United States and the Middle East," in *International relations of the Middle East*, ed. Louise Fawcett (Oxford: Oxford University Press, 2005), 290.
3 David P. Forsythe, "The UN and the Arab-Israeli Conflict: What Has Been Learned in 25 Years," *International Organization* 26, no. 4 (1972): 705.
4 Danilo Di Mauro, *The UN and the Arab-Israeli Conflict: American Hegemony and the UN Intervention since 1947* (London: Routledge, 2012), 4.
5 Abba Eban, "Multilateral Diplomacy in the Arab-Israeli Conflict," in *Multilateral Negotiation and Mediation: Instruments and Methods*, ed. Arthur S. Lall (New York: Pergamon Press, 1985), 40–41.
6 Gene M. Lyons, David A. Baldwin, and Donald W. McNemar, "The "Politicization" Issue in the UN Specialized Agencies," *Proceedings of the Academy of Political Science* 32, no. 4 (1977): 82, 89.

7 Eugene Sochor, *The Politics of International Aviation* (Basingstoke: Macmillan, 1991), 125–126.
8 Minutes of the First Plenary Meeting, Third Assembly, June 7, 1949, 5–6, A3-P/25, DOC 6456, ICAO Archival Documents.
9 Sochor, *The Politics of International Aviation*, 134.
10 David MacKenzie, *ICAO: A History of the International Civil Aviation Organization* (Toronto: University of Toronto Press, 2010), 280–281.
11 See: Resolutions and Minutes, Assembly – Nineteenth Session (Extraordinary), February 27–March 2, 1973, A19-Res., Min., DOC 9061, ICAO Archival Documents.
12 Minutes of the Second Plenary Meeting, Assembly – Ninth Session, June 1, 1955, 24-25, 36, A9-P/13-2, DOC 7596-2, ICAO Archival Documents.
13 Minutes of the Second Plenary Meeting, Assembly – Tenth Session, June 20, 1956, 14, A10-P/17-2, DOC 7708-2, ICAO Archival Documents.
14 In 1954, three Israeli passengers travelling on British aircraft from Nicosia to Tehran were detained in Baghdad. The Council President Warner transmitted Israeli protest to Iraq requesting 'any observation on this matter.' Release of the passengers in exchange for seven Iraqi soldiers was arranged by UN Secretary General Dag Hammerskjöld. Sochor, *The Politics of International Aviation*, 126.
15 Minutes of the Second Plenary Meeting, Assembly – Tenth Session, June 20, 1956, 14–15, 17–18, A10-P/17-2, DOC 7708-2, ICAO Archival Documents.
16 Ibid., 33.
17 Annual Report of the Council to the Assembly for 1956, Supporting Documentation for the Eleventh Session of the Assembly, 1958, 49, A11-P/1, DOC 7788, ICAO Archival Documents.
18 Executive Committee Minutes of the Sixteenth Meeting, 10th Session of the Assembly, July 11, 1956, 142–145, A10-WP/150, Min. Ex-16, ICAO Archival Documents.
19 Ibid., 145–147.
20 Minutes of the First Plenary Meeting, Assembly – Twelfth Session, June 16, 1959, 7, A12-P/2, DOC 7996, ICAO Archival Documents.
21 Sochor, *The Politics of International Aviation*, 127–129.
22 Richard A. Falk, "The Beirut Raid and the International Law of Retaliation," *The American Journal of International Law* 63, no. 3 (July, 1969): 416–417, https://doi.org/10.2307/2198865
23 UN Security Council Resolution 262 (1968) of December 31, 1968, available from https://digitallibrary.un.org/record/90758, accessed February 7, 2024.
24 Falk, "The Beirut Raid," 421.
25 Minutes of the First Meeting, Council – Extraordinary Session, January 20, 1969, 2–7, C/982-1 C-Min. EXTRAORDINARY/1, DOC 8793-1, ICAO Archival Documents.
26 Ibid., 8.
27 Ibid., 9–10.
28 Ibid., 13.
29 Ibid., 14.
30 Ibid., 15.
31 Ibid., 15–17.
32 Ibid., 19.
33 Ibid., 19–20.
34 Ibid., 20–21.
35 Ibid., 21–23.
36 Ibid., 25–30.

37 Ibid., 30–31.
38 Ibid., 32–33.
39 Minutes of the Second Meeting, Council – Extraordinary Session, January 21, 1969, C/982-2 C-Min. EXTRAORDINARY/2, DOC 8793-2, 43–44, 46, 48–49, ICAO Archival Documents.
40 Minutes of the First Meeting, Council – Extraordinary Session, January 20, 1969, 35, C/982-1 C-Min. EXTRAORDINARY/1, DOC 8793-1, ICAO Archival Documents.
41 Minutes of the Second Meeting, Council – Extraordinary Session, January 21, 1969, C/982-2 C-Min. EXTRAORDINARY/2, DOC 8793-2, 39, ICAO Archival Documents.
42 Ibid., 39, 40–42, 45–47, 49–50.
43 Ibid., 51–52.
44 Minutes of the Third Meeting, Council – Extraordinary Session, January 23, 1969, 58–60, C/982-3 C-Min. EXTRAORDINARY/3, DOC 8793-3, ICAO Archival Documents.
45 Reference to the capture of Nazi war criminal Adolf Eichmann by Israeli secret service. See: Isser Harel, *The House on Garibaldi Street* (New York: Routledge, 2013).
46 Minutes of the Third Meeting, Council – Extraordinary Session, January 23, 1969, 61, 63–64, C/982-3 C-Min. EXTRAORDINARY/3, DOC 8793-3, ICAO Archival Documents.
47 Sochor, *The Politics of International Aviation*, 129.
48 Annual Report of the Council – 1973, Documentation for the session of the Assembly in 1974, 97, DOC 9085, ICAO Archival Documents.
49 Minutes of the Fourth Plenary Meeting, Assembly – Nineteenth Session (Extraordinary), February 28, 1973, 53–54, A19-Res., Min., DOC 9061, ICAO Archival Documents.
50 Minutes of the Fifth Plenary Meeting, Assembly – Twentieth Session (Extraordinary), August 30, 1973, 91–92, A20-Min. P/5, DOC 9087, ICAO Archival Documents.
51 UN SC Resolution 337 (1973) of August 15, 1973, available from https://digitallibrary.un.org/record/93465?v=pdf, accessed April 17, 2024.
52 Annual Report of the Council – 1973, Documentation for the session of the Assembly in 1974, 97, DOC 9085, ICAO Archival Documents.
53 Minutes of the First Plenary Meeting, Assembly – Twentieth Session (Extraordinary), August 28, 1973, 21–22, A20-Min. P/1, DOC 9087, ICAO Archival Documents.
54 Working Paper, Agenda Item 2: Diversion and seizure by Israeli military aircraft of a civil aircraft, Assembly – 20th Session (Extraordinary), August 29, 1973, A20-WP/12, 1–2, ICAO Archival Documents.
55 Minutes of the Fifth Plenary Meeting, Assembly – Twentieth Session (Extraordinary), August 30, 1973, 91–93, A20-Min. P/5, DOC 9087, ICAO Archival Documents.
56 Ibid., 94–101.
57 Minutes of the Sixth Plenary Meeting, Assembly – Twentieth Session (Extraordinary), August 30, 1973, 103–115, A20-Min. P/6, DOC 9087, ICAO Archival Documents.
58 Working Paper, Agenda Item 5: Adoption of the Agenda (Presented by Iraq and Jordan), Assembly – 21st Session, October 14, 1974, A21-WP/191, P/63, ICAO Archival Documents.
59 Minutes of the Twelfth Plenary Meeting, Assembly – 21st Session, October 15, 1974, 155–157, A21 Min. P/12, DOC 9119, ICAO Archival Documents.
60 Ibid., 157–159.
61 Pardee Centre for International Futures, UNGA Coincidence Score, February 20, 2024, available from https://public.tableau.com/app/profile/pardeecenterifs/viz/VotesterTableauDashboard_16529835337750/UNGACoincidenceScores?publish=yes, accessed April 17, 2024.

62 Minutes of the Twelfth Plenary Meeting, Assembly – 21st Session, October 15, 1974, 160–163, A21 Min. P/12, DOC 9119, ICAO Archival Documents.
63 Ibid., 163–165.
64 Resolutions of the Assembly, A23-5: The airport of Jerusalem, Assembly Resolutions in Force (as of October 8, 1992), 1–28, ICAO Archival Documents.
65 Minutes of the Tenth Plenary Meeting, Assembly 23rd Session, October 3, 1980, 129, A23 Min. P/10, DOC 9317, ICAO Archival Documents.
66 The statement refers to the decision by Israeli Knesset to change the character and status of Jerusalem. UN Security Council did not recognize these actions by Israel. See: UN Security Council Resolution 478 (1980) of August 20, 1980, available from https://digitallibrary.un.org/record/25618, accessed February 7, 2024
67 Working Paper, Agenda Item 5: Adoption of the Agenda, September 26, 1980, A23-WP/97, P/42, ICAO Archival Documents.
68 Minutes of the Tenth Plenary Meeting, Assembly 23rd Session, October 3, 1980, 130, A23 Min. P/10, DOC 9317, ICAO Archival Documents.
69 The controversy surrounding participation of an observer from PLO will be discussed later.
70 Ibid., 130–132.
71 Minutes of the Eleventh Plenary Meeting, Assembly 23rd Session, October 3, 1980, 133–136, 137–138, A23 Min. P/11, DOC 9317, ICAO Archival Documents.
72 UN General Assembly resolutions regarding the observer status of liberation movements were being adopted since 1972. Working Paper, Agenda Item 17: Resolutions of the United Nations concerning invitations to liberation movements to attend meetings of the Specialized Agencies, Appendix A, Assembly – 21st Session, May 23, 1974, A21-WP/36 EX/9, ICAO Archival Documents; UN General Assembly Resolution 45/37 of 28 November 1990: Observer status of national liberation movements recognized by the Organization of African Unity and/or by the League of Arab States, accessed June 5, 2023, www.un.org/unispal/document/auto-insert-186275/.
73 Report of the Executive Committee, Assembly – 21st Session, 31–32, A21-EX, DOC 9113, ICAO Archival Documents.
74 Ibid., 32.
75 Ibid., 32–33.
76 Minutes of the Ninth Plenary Meeting, Assembly – 21st Session, October 11, 1974, 110–112, A21 Min. P/9, DOC 9119, ICAO Archival Documents.
77 Jewish Telegraphic Agency, "PLO Gets Observer Status in the Icao," accessed October 30, 2023, www.jta.org/archive/plo-gets-observer-status-in-the-icao
78 Minutes of the Twelfth Plenary Meeting, Assembly – 22nd Session, October 3, 1977, 145–147, A22 Min. P/12, DOC 9216, ICAO Archival Documents.
79 Ibid., 147–151.
80 Minutes of the Seventh Plenary Meeting, Assembly 23rd Session, September 19, 1980, 98, 101, A23 Min. P/7, DOC 9317, ICAO Archival Documents.
81 Minutes of the Eighth Plenary Meeting, Assembly 26th Session, September 26, 1986, 162, A26-Min. P/8 DOC 9494, ICAO Archival Documents.
82 Minutes of the Tenth Plenary Meeting, Assembly 27th Session, September 23, 1989, 167–168, A27-Min. P/10 DOC 9550, ICAO Archival Documents.
83 Minutes of the Thirteenth Plenary Meeting, Assembly 23rd Session, October 6, 1980, 154, A23 Min. P/13, DOC 9317, ICAO Archival Documents.
84 Minutes of the Seventh Plenary Meeting, Assembly 25th Session (Extraordinary), May 10, 1984, 94, A25-Min. P/7 DOC 9437, ICAO Archival Documents.

85 Minutes of the Fourteenth Plenary Meeting, Assembly 27th Session, October 6, 1989, 196, A27-Min. P/14 DOC 9550, ICAO Archival Documents.

86 Sochor, *The Politics of International Aviation*, 129.

87 Ibid., 95.

88 Provisional Verbatim Record of the 2655 Meeting, UN Security Council, February 6, 1986, 114–115, S/PV.2655, accessed February 2, 2024, https://digitallibrary.un.org/record/112779.

89 Minutes of the Sixth Meeting, Council – 117th Session, February 26, 1986, 58–61, 64, C-Min. 117/6, ICAO Archival Documents.

90 Ibid., 57–61.

91 Ibid., 63.

92 Ibid., 64–65.

93 Ibid., 65–66.

94 Ibid., 66.

95 Minutes of the Seventh Meeting, Council – 117th Session, February 27, 1986, 72, C-Min. 117/7, ICAO Archival Documents.

96 Minutes of the Eighth Meeting, Council – 117th Session, February 28, 1986, 75–76, C-Min. 117/8, ICAO Archival Documents.

97 Ibid., 77.

98 Ibid., 79–80, 83.

99 Minutes of the Third Plenary Meeting, Assembly 26th Session, September 24, 1986, 45–46, A26-Min. P/3 DOC 9494, ICAO Archival Documents.

100 Minutes of the Second Plenary Meeting, Assembly – Fourteenth Session. August 22, 1962. A14-P/21, DOC 8269. ICAO Archival Documents.

101 Minutes of the Third Plenary Meeting, Assembly 25th Session (Extraordinary), April 25, 1984, 54, A25-Min. P/3, DOC 9437, ICAO Archival Documents.

102 Minutes of the Fifth Plenary Meeting, Assembly – 31st Session, September 21, 1995, 22, DRAFT A31-Min. P/5, ICAO Archival Documents.

5 The political context of shootdowns of civil aircraft

One of the most controversial situations with political overtones that can occur in international civil aviation is associated with the shootdown of civil aircraft in connection to international conflicts and estrangements. In history, there were multiple situations when, for various reasons, civil aircraft were shot down. The post-World War II period witnessed numerous tragedies of this nature. Brian E. Foont enumerated 11 such occurrences from between 1952 and 2001.[1] More recent civil aircraft shootdowns include Malaysia Airlines Flight 17, shot down over Eastern Ukraine by pro-Russian separatists in 2014,[2] and Ukraine International Airlines Flight 752, shot down by Iran in 2020. Such situations were usually dealt with not only by International Civil Aviation Organization (ICAO), but also by the UN Security Council, which, in many cases, was the first to react. As to the ICAO's reactions and activities, they differed in reference to a particular situation and the violator.[3]

Many of the shootdowns of civil aircraft were the result of a mistake and, though tragic, carried less political controversy. However, some of them occurred in the circumstances of international tensions or conflicts, sometimes in connection to the problem of state sovereignty over airspace, the protection of which caused hazards to civil aircraft.[4] In virtually any of the occurrences of the shootdown of civil aircraft, ICAO became interested and engaged, but when they were surrounded by wider political tension, deliberations regarding them were also subject to politicization. This chapter is dedicated to the issue of shootdowns of civil aircraft by the military using the examples of the Korean Air Lines Flight 007, shot down by the Soviet Union in 1983, and Iran Air Flight 655, shot down by the United States in 1988, two occurrences that as a result of interstate tensions and hostilities initiated intensive politicization of ICAO and attempts to use depoliticizing moves in defense.

Shootdown of the Korean Air Lines Flight 007 by the USSR in 1983

A significant portion of the period analyzed in this book focuses on the Cold War era, characterized by tensions between two superpowers, the United States and the Soviet Union, along with their respective allies. The Cold War rivalry manifested

DOI: 10.4324/9781032695402-6

in various arenas, including the arms race, sports, and competition for spheres of influence. Naturally, ICAO was not immune to Cold War tensions, but for several reasons, they appeared there somehow later than in other multilateral bodies. For some time, the Soviet Union was not interested in the ICAO membership. At the same time, in the early years of ICAO's existence, two of its satellite states, Czechoslovakia and Poland, strongly limited their presence and resumed it only in the second half of the 1950s,[5] providing Communist countries representation in ICAO. Soon, other Communist states followed, with Romania joining in 1965 and Hungary in 1969.[6] As to the Soviet Union, it had been rejecting the ICAO membership for many years even though the United States wanted them in. Such an attitude began to change in the late 1960s when the USSR began sending observers to ICAO meetings. Eventually, it became an ICAO member state in 1970.[7] This marked a new situation in ICAO, with the two major superpowers being present, leading to the initiation of the Cold War alliance-based diplomacy within ICAO, particularly in the Assembly.

ICAO deliberations with Cold War overtones, though not very common, began with the resumption of the membership of Czechoslovakia and Poland. In January 1956, Czechoslovakia complained about the release of balloons carrying leaflets into its airspace.[8] When international sanctions were imposed on Poland after its government declared martial law in 1981, during the 24th Assembly in 1983, the Polish delegate brought the case, claiming that one of the ICAO member states unilaterally broke off air transport agreement with Poland, motivated solely by political reasons and intending to exert political pressure.[9] Communist states also became frequent seconders of the Third World countries, as shown in Chapters 3 and 4. Tensions with a direct Cold War background were happening from time to time, but none of them can be compared to the level of politicization associated with the Soviet shootdown of Korean Air Lines aircraft in 1983.

The tragedy that paved the way for one of the most politicized deliberations to be held in the ICAO occurred on September 1, 1983. Korean Air Lines Flight 007, traveling from New York to Seoul with a refueling stop in Anchorage and carrying 269 people, including an American congressman, deviated from its planned route and entered Soviet airspace.[10] The aircraft flew over a restricted military area in Sakhalin after it entered Soviet airspace over Kamchatka, left it, and re-entered while approaching Sakhalin Island. Several miles before leaving the Soviet airspace again, it was shot down[11] after it was mistaken with the US Air Force RC-135 reconnaissance aircraft on a surveillance mission. Two missiles were fired at the airliner by Soviet fighters. At least one struck the aircraft, which eventually crashed.[12] The occurrence caused emotional reactions worldwide, particularly in Western countries. Among other things, it led to the imposition of sanctions against the USSR by such countries as the United States, Canada, or Japan, including boycotts, refusing landing rights to Aeroflot flights for a couple of weeks, restrictions on flights to the Soviet Union.[13]

The incident had multidimensional significance from the perspective of the US–Soviet relations. In the field of aviation, the tragedy occurred after the period of improved relations, marked by the signing of the protocol in 1973, which amended the original air transport agreement from 1966 and expanded air links between both countries. However, the improved aviation relations soon got worse because of the reported unfair practices by the Soviet side, leading to estrangements.[14] In international political relations, the incident occurred when tensions increased following the Soviet invasion of Afghanistan after the détente of the 1970s, marked by the processes surrounding the Conference on Security and Cooperation in Europe. The increased tensions had many manifestations, with the boycott of the Los Angeles Olympic Games in 1984 by the Soviet Union and other Communist countries being one of the prime examples.

Alongside the general increase of East–West tensions in the early 1980s, the incident is believed to have led to the fight between the United States and the USSR for world public opinion,[15] 'one of the strangest and least expected confrontations between the superpowers in the annals of U.S. postwar diplomacy' according to *Time*. Within the clash, both sides were accusing each other of propaganda and news manipulation.[16] Rhetorically, the United States sought to use the incident to win a moral victory over the USSR, whereas the Soviet Union defended itself by employing a rhetoric based on its ideology.[17] The struggle for hearts and minds primarily took place in the media but also within multilateral organizations, particularly the UN and ICAO. Deliberations in ICAO, besides mutual accusations featuring confrontational and emotional tones, featured the employment of depoliticization rhetoric as a defensive diplomatic tool.

On a multilateral level, the incident was first dealt with by the UN Security Council, but the Soviet Union vetoed a resolution on that matter.[18] International attention then turned to ICAO. For the United States, it was a unique opportunity to condemn the USSR internationally, while the Soviet Union did not have the right to veto in the ICAO Council. At the same time, ICAO had no power to impose sanctions, so turning to ICAO was a way to avoid additional sanctions and provide an opportunity for both sides to cool down.[19] Still, the confrontational tones appeared to have been dominating, particularly in the first years after the shootdown.

Extraordinary Session of the Council, 1983

ICAO Council was the first to deal with the issue. It held an extraordinary meeting shortly after the incident, in mid-September 1983, at the request of South Korea and Canada. The Soviet act was strongly criticized by many delegations, particularly by the South Korean, whose observer called the incident 'an act of the most unprecedented outrage in the history of civil aviation,' and spoke about the evolution of the Soviet position from not knowing anything to admitting the facts that were already known. The observer accused the Soviet Union of shooting down a civil plane, rejected Soviet claims that the plane was on an espionage mission, and demanded an apology, compensation, punishing those responsible and guaranteeing the prevention of such incidents, concluding that it was 'high time for the world to learn the true nature of the Soviet regime' in which 'amorality borders beastliness.'[20] The Japanese alternate representative said the shooting down of an unarmed aircraft was a violation of humanitarian principles and rules of international law, that the Soviet action should be strongly condemned, and that 'the USSR stubbornly refused to admit the fact of the shooting down of the aircraft,' which it did only after hard evidence was provided by Japan, but it had never admitted 'responsibility of its unlawful and barbarous action,' attempting to divert 'its own responsibility to third countries through various false allegations.'[21] The West German alternate representative said the event represented 'an inhuman act and a clear violation of international law and the principles of international civil aviation community,'[22] whereas the Italian representative called the incident an 'act of frightening brutality' and expressed astonishment that the perpetrators did not at least assure they understood the gravity of the problem.[23]

A very strong statement against the Soviet Union was also made by the US alternate representative, who spoke about the outrage expressed at the highest level of the US government. According to the alternate representative, the 'Soviet action constitutes a grave threat to the safety of the international civil aviation system requesting urgent measures.'[24] Later, the American also said that in contrast to the Soviet Union, the United States and other ICAO members 'do not use deadly force against off-course civilian airliners of other countries' and mentioned situations when Soviet planes strayed off-course over the American territory and were assisted back to their original path.[25] The British representative was also very critical, calling the incident a serious challenge to the ideal of peace and safety travelers have been enjoying thanks to the efforts of ICAO, and that the Soviet response to the plane off-course has ignored the moral dimensions of the incident. The representative criticized the Soviet Union for invoking its internal legislation despite its responsibilities stemming from international law and for its veto in the UN Security Council, which blocked the investigation.[26] These statements echoed accusations leveled against Israel by Arab states, combining logical arguments with emotional weight. The Soviet Union was portrayed as a ruthless force, disregarding human lives, a rhetoric aligned with US objectives regarding the crises.

Besides statements and debates typical for this kind of situation, with respective representatives speaking in favor of one side or another or adopting a more balanced position, some representatives, both critical of the act and more sympathetic toward the USSR, called for keeping politics away. The Canadian alternate representative called for the investigation to be 'divorced, to the extent possible, from political considerations.'[27] The Algerian representative spoke about the need to avoid partisan emotions. The Colombian representative, besides condemning the act, called for an impartial investigation. The representative of Indonesia said the Soviet Union should bear full responsibility for the incident, adding that this tragic incident should not further exacerbate East–West tensions. The Egyptian representative said the Council's approach and treatment of the accident should disregard all the political considerations, adding that the success of ICAO within the UN family stemmed from succeeding in isolating its mainly technical activities from political aspects. The representatives of France and Mexico also mentioned the need for an impartial investigation.[28] Many of these statements, especially when made by diplomats not representing either of the geopolitical blocs, reveal an apparently genuine will to keep politics away from ICAO, focus on the incident, and seek a solution that would increase the safety of civil aviation, thus exemplifying rather neutral depoliticization, although as mentioned earlier, we cannot be certain of the true motivation. Interestingly, some of the representatives presenting such a position were coming from Western countries and could have been expected to present a more critical approach toward the Soviet Union.

Depoliticization as a defensive tactic, as could have been expected, was employed by the Soviet side. Its representatives took the floor for the first time after most other speakers made their statements. The Soviet representative spoke about regret over the deaths of innocent people expressed by the Soviet government, the Soviet investigation of the circumstances surrounding the violation of Soviet airspace, and the intrusion into the prohibited area over the Soviet territory. The representative mentioned five US intelligence aircraft in the area and said that the Soviet Air Defence concluded that the plane on the radars was an intelligence aircraft approaching Soviet airspace. The representative spoke about interception procedures that had failed, leading to the decision to terminate the flight, and said that the US and Japanese air traffic control must have known about the deviation of the flight but did not take any steps. The Soviet representative concluded that the Council should not examine the issue until the Soviet inquiry was completed. Additionally, he criticized the observer from Korea and the representatives of the United States and Japan for neglecting to mention their countries' responsibility regarding the safety of the flight. He also condemned the countries that organized and sanctioned the use of passenger airplanes for intelligence purposes. Then the floor was taken by the Soviet alternate representative, who, among other things, argued that the Council should refrain from making any decisions on the incident, raising attention to the problem of violation of the Soviet airspace and repeated claims about the responsibility of the crew and the providers of air traffic control, and that the plane was used for intelligence purposes. Then he spoke about discrimination against Aeroflot stemming from anti-Soviet hysteria.[29] These statements did not include depoliticization yet besides references to anti-Soviet hysteria, which could also be interpreted this way. Instead, it was more about promoting the Soviet standpoint on the event. The Soviet representatives have also used the defense through offense tactics, accusing other states of certain misconduct. Techniques used by the USSR in the early days of the KAL007 controversy in ICAO also correspond with the diplomatic techniques of the Soviet Union proposed by Kulski,[30] in particular adopting the role of an injured party.

The Soviet standpoint was criticized by the observer from South Korea, who claimed it had no credibility and that the reasons for straying off-course could only be known from the crew, and such knowledge would have been available if the Soviet Union had made the effort to make it land. The observer added that the Soviets were trying to make others responsible and that shooting the plane after hours of tracking was indefensible. The US alternate representative spoke about previous Soviet statements that were untrue and highlighted inconsistencies in the Soviet version, while the Japanese disagreed with the Soviet accusations that its traffic controllers knew about the deviation, concluding that the Soviet charges were completely groundless. In defense of the USSR, the representative of Czechoslovakia spoke, stating that many aspects remained unclear following previous statements, and emphasized the necessity for a thorough investigation into the incident that should focus on the reasons for the plane's deviation,[31] thus trying to direct the deliberations in accordance with the Soviet line of defense.

During subsequent meetings, the Council considered two draft resolutions. The first one was submitted by Canada and co-sponsored by delegations from Western countries and several others like Nigeria, Jamaica, Argentina, Senegal, El Salvador, which was critical of the Soviet Union. The USSR, supported by Czechoslovakia, submitted the second one which reflected the Soviet standpoint mentioned earlier.[32] The representative of Czechoslovakia, due to a lack of time to study the texts or obtain instructions from the government, requested suspension of the debate indefinitely according to the Council's Rules and Procedures, which the Soviet representative supported. The US representative responded that the situation was not a normal one and the world was awaiting Council's action, while after a break the Czechoslovak motion was defeated. By the decision of the President of the Council, both proposals were to be considered as alternatives. The Soviet representative then criticized the Western draft resolution for not reflecting the violation of Soviet sovereignty, while the Algerian representative claimed the Western proposal had emotional, political, and technical aspects, with the second one going beyond the Council debate. Eventually, the Council voted in favor of the Western draft resolution,[33] which, among other things, recognized the destruction of the Korean Air Lines civil aircraft by Soviet military aircraft as 'incompatible with the norms governing international behavior and elementary considerations of humanity.'[34] It is worth mentioning that postponing decisions on sensitive issues belongs to typical practices of depoliticization in IOs, although in this case it was rather used in defense of an ally than in an attempt to defend the organization from politicization.

The first stage of the KAL007 controversy in ICAO was subject to politicization and strong, emotional statements. Western countries were attacking the USSR for the shootdown, the USSR and Czechoslovakia hit back, trying to direct deliberations toward the issue of violation of airspace. Depoliticization as a defensive tool was used modestly, in particular through an attempt to postpone the decisions without arguments about the political character of accusations. References to depoliticization were more visible in the neutral statements of the representatives from states not directly engaged in the incident nor in the Cold War. Either way, the Council's decision did not reflect Soviet expectations.

24th Session of the Assembly, 1983

The Council's deliberations and decisions were merely the beginning of the politicized debates within ICAO on the issue. The 24th Assembly was scheduled to be held in September 1983, the very month of the tragedy. Although the original plans did not feature dealing with the incident, the issue had been raised. In the Executive Committee, a number of delegations supported the actions taken by the Council and made propositions on how to prevent such occurrences in the future. The Soviet delegation, on the other hand, opposed the endorsement of the Council's resolution because its provisions did not stress the violation of the Soviet airspace, and that the incident was being investigated by the Soviet government and the results would be transmitted to ICAO in accordance with the international law. This view was supported by delegates from other Communist states, namely Poland, Czechoslovakia, and Vietnam, but the Executive Committee voted in favor of the draft resolution, which endorsed the resolution of the Council from September 1983 and recommended its adoption by the plenary session.[35] Soviet line of defense did not change from the one used inthe Council and focused on sovereignty over the airspace, its violation by the aircraft, and the Soviet responsibility for the investigation.

The deliberations on the KAL007 incident in the Assembly then moved to the plenary sessions, where delegations presented several different attitudes, mostly during the opening addresses. The first group included the most fierce detractors of the Soviet Union, who often spoke about the shootdown in an emotional way. For example, the Japanese delegate spoke about a violation of humanitarian principles and international law and criticized the USSR for refusing to admit and accept responsibility. The delegate of Malaysia called the act 'highly irresponsible,' the delegate of Nepal spoke about the clock of international civil aviation having turned decades back, the delegate of New Zealand called the Soviet attack 'barbaric' and said it should call into question the re-election of the Soviet Union to the ICAO Council.[36] The South Korean delegate called the act 'despicable' and 'act of barbarism.'[37] These were just a few of the many highly critical statements against the USSR. As to the delegates from the key Cold War adversaries of the Soviet Union, the British delegate said his delegation shared grief and anger of those touched by the disaster 'at the shameless and callous nature of the statements made by the responsible Soviet authorities who have tried to excuse themselves by seeking to pin the blame on others.' He said that ICAO's joint responsibility was to demand that planes flying off-course are not shot down but provided assistance to get back safely to their route.[38] The American delegate added that the Assembly had seen the world civil aviation community united 'in deploring the senseless murder of 269 innocent travelers' and called upon the Soviet Union to 'forego its position of intransigence and challenge' and to declare the military attack against civil aircraft as unlawful.[39]

Although the tragedy was mentioned by most delegations, not all of them were as critical of the Soviet Union. Like during the extraordinary Council, there were also those advocating separation from politics. The Nigerian delegate, among other things, said that political capital should not be made out of the incident.[40] The delegate of Bangladesh said that politicization of the issue with charges and countercharges was wrong and that the main objective before the Assembly was to find means to prevent such occurrences in the future,[41] whereas the Algerian delegate argued that political confrontation should be rejected to reach the aim of safe aviation.[42] These statements were rather neutral in their tone, which means they at least appeared not to have aimed to defend the Soviet Union but to attempt to make the deliberations constructive and focused on technical matters. Naturally, defensive intentions might have been concealed, but there is no evidence for that.

The third of the main positions in reference to the incident was presented by the Communist states. In principle, it contradicted the views shared by most of the delegations that had been taking the floor during the discussion. The Polish delegate spoke about the incident as 'being a result of an evident violation of sovereignty of one state.'[43] The Soviet delegate said the incident was being 'exploited to aggravate the international situation and provoke anti-Soviet hysteria.' He then spoke of the 'criminal violation of the sovereignty of the USSR' by the spy aircraft and explained the Soviet version of the course of events, concluding that clearly the intrusion was organized by the US and that civil aircraft was employed 'regardless the possibility – and perhaps even in the calculated expectation – that human lives would be lost.' He then said the full responsibility fell upon those who organized the operation and spoke about the anti-Soviet campaign launched by the US and a number of other countries, discriminatory measures, and inimical acts against Aeroflot, including prohibition of flights, suspension of flights, restrictions on commercial flights, and other provocations.[44] Soviet arguments were, in principle, similar to those used in the Council. Depoliticization at the time was very subtle. The USSR did not seek to avoid deliberations but to set them in a more favorable direction, underlining the fault of others rather than the Soviet fault. Depoliticization at this stage could only be seen in the context of the reported anti-Soviet hysteria, accusations of aggravation of the international situation, and complaints about sanctions against Soviet aviation, in which we can see indirect accusations against others for politicizing the issue.

A number of delegations from Communist countries endorsed the Soviet standpoint. The delegate from Hungary said the Assembly session was held in a difficult international atmosphere, with attempts to aggravate the complex situation by threatening contacts between countries. He expressed hope that ICAO would resist pressure from some countries and focus the work on fostering better understanding among member states.[45] The delegate from Bulgaria underlined that the aircraft 'intruded deeply into USSR territory' and spoke against the restrictions imposed on Aeroflot.[46] The Czechoslovakian delegate condemned 'negative occurrences and restrictive measures in international civil aviation.'[47] The delegate from the Lao People's Democratic Republic spoke about 'lawbreaking' South Korean aircraft, the desire to know what was behind the tragic incident, and the hope that the conciliary attitude instead of attacking the Soviet Union would dominate the debate.[48] The observer from East Germany referred to the infraction of ICAO rules by pilots and incidents of unlawful interference with civil aviation, arguing that the analysis showed it was an action in which a civil plane was used for intelligence purposes.[49] As we can see, the prevailing argument presented by the Communist bloc was that it was the aircraft that was guilty of the incident, with accusations that it was on a spy mission. Like in the case of the Western states, the statements of different delegations were not similar in the level of criticism, but they were definitely more alike than those of the Western delegations and, in principle, reflected the Soviet arguments. Several speakers referred to the attacks against the Soviet Union in the Assembly, implying their political character.

Besides addresses of the delegations, the discussion on the issue occurred during the approval of the Executive Committee report on the Council's Extraordinary Sessions at the end of the 24th Assembly, when the Soviet delegate opposed the adoption of the resolution before the investigation was completed. He said the resolution was 'incriminating and politically tendentious,' ignoring the violation of Soviet sovereignty and failing to encompass all the aspects. He also called for objectivity and declared the USSR's desire to cooperate in measures enhancing civil aviation safety.[50] This was the first time defensive depoliticization was used in such a straightforward way, although, in fact, it was a development of the earlier arguments about the anti-Soviet attacks and hysteria.

As before, the Soviet argumentation was supported by delegations from Communist states. The Polish delegate, with the support of the Cuban delegation, formally proposed softening the phrasing of the resolution so that instead of 'endorsing' the resolutions and decisions of the Council, it would 'note' them. The Czechoslovak delegate supported the Polish proposition and opposed the original resolution as it failed to respect the sovereignty of states and because the investigation was not completed. Polish proposal was also supported by the delegates from Hungary and Nicaragua. In turn, a number of delegates spoke against the Polish proposition. As earlier, the Algerian delegate spoke about the confrontational spirit with political overtones and appealed for reconciliation and dialogue. Eventually, the Assembly voted in favor of the original text of the resolution.[51] The Assembly thus endorsed the Council's decision, which reflected a rather critical judgment of the Soviet act. Key observations from the review of the deliberations are that other Communist delegations strongly supported the USSR. The Soviet argumentation, as earlier, focused on the principle of sovereignty over airspace, the fault of the plane intruding on its territory, and unconcluded investigation. Communist states also referred to the political attack on the Soviet Union and the use of the incident to criticize it. Depoliticization as a defensive tool was increasingly being employed, with the intention to postpone the deliberations and to soften the anti-Soviet phrasing of the decisions.

111th Session of the Council, 1984

The next episode of the KAL007 ICAO controversy took place in the Council. During its 111th session in March 1984, the Council was to investigate the final report on the incident. The entire discussion revolved around two draft resolutions, one introduced by the United States and the other by the USSR. However, it was only the American proposal that received serious consideration. According to the US proposal, the Council condemned the use of armed force resulting in the destruction of the Korean airliner and loss of 269 lives, deeply deplored the Soviet failure to cooperate in the investigation and in the search and rescue efforts, and urged states to cooperate in adopting an amendment to the Chicago Convention to improve the measures for preventing such tragedies.[52] The proposal thus assumed a rather severe phrasing of such resolutions.

The discussion in the Council was very confrontational, with both sides accusing each other. The Soviet and the Czechoslovakian representatives argued that the conclusions of the available report by the Secretary General were tendentious and missing crucial evidence. As the representative of Czechoslovakia said, the report 'deliberately overlooked the pre-planned nature of the flight and tried to explain its deviation by some unspecified navigational error.' He also claimed the report did not properly account for the responsibility of US and Japanese Air Traffic Service (ATS) units.[53] Representatives of the Communist countries thus maintained the previous Soviet line of defense, this time in reference to the investigation report, which was not final. The statements critical of the Soviet Union also built on the earlier arguments, but their main theme was now the Soviet lack of cooperation. For example, the alternate representative of the United States reminded that the Soviet Union had six months to respond to the Secretary General's request for relevant information, and for six months it had refused to comply with the two Council's resolutions, concluding that he did not believe in the Soviet submission of the required evidence. The Italian representative said that the Soviet refusal to cooperate showed its lack of interest in helping international civil aviation use this case to avoid such incidents and criticized the Soviet representative for questioning the investigation by ICAO experts. The British representative said that additional questions could have been answered if the Soviet authorities had provided the information they claimed to have possessed but refused to make available and that full responsibility for the tragedy rested with the authorities of the Soviet Union. The French representative added that the use of force against civil aircraft was incompatible with the norms governing international conduct and inhumane. The Australian representative accused the USSR of not cooperating over the incident, contravening international law and humanitarian principles. The Korean observer also referred to the Soviet refusal to cooperate, referring to its inability to provide evidence that the aircraft was on a spy mission, that Korean pilots knew about the brutality of Soviet airmen so they would not have sent the plane on a suicide mission, referring to the Soviet shootdown of Korean civil aircraft in 1978. The Korean added that early Soviet claims about the incident disqualified them as impartial investigators.[54] A recurring theme in the Western argumentation was the lack of cooperation by the Soviet Union.

The Soviet alternate representative answered to the Western accusations, saying that the reason for the deviation of the Korean airliner, which had been the main issue, was not resolved in the report, so it could not serve as the basis for the Council's decision. He said that the US delegate made a biased interpretation of the incident and made attacks and insinuations against the Soviet Union. The alternate representative spoke about the Soviet right to conduct the investigation, accused the United States of not cooperating, and argued that the draft resolution presented by the United States was 'an impermissible attempt to use ICAO for political purposes and grossly distort the real state of affairs.' He said the proposal aimed to distract attention from the fact that those who premeditated and carried out the intelligence-gathering operation bore the entire responsibility and concluded that the Soviet response was in full accord with international law and that the draft resolution proposed by the United States only aimed 'to impose on the Council a political decision so as to use it in the future for further aggravating international tensions and pursuing the dangerous course of confrontation in international relations.'[55] This speech reveals certain evolution of Soviet argumentation. At first, it was oriented at underlining the guilt of the Western countries rather than its own. With the growing accusations, depoliticization as a defensive tool was increasingly being employed. This leads to a potential conclusion about the last resort character of such depoliticization for defense – with the lack or ineffectiveness of other arguments, diplomats may refer to defensive depoliticization.

As in the previous proceedings, there were also voices about the need to drop confrontational tones and focus on the ICAO's mission. The representative of India reiterated that ICAO was a technical forum and the resolution behind the Council 'did not make constructive contributions to dispassionate and result-oriented study of the question' and that the Council's task was to avoid confrontation and to cooperate in consideration of the issue.[56] Also, the representative of Indonesia said that cooperation was needed to avoid the repetition of the tragedy, whereas the Argentinian representative said it was necessary to develop a spirit of international peace and security.[57] These were other examples of an apparently neutral approach that seemed to have desired the ICAO to stay focused on its technical mission and not become subject to politicization.

Following the discussion, the Council adopted the resolution proposed by the United States, with 20 votes in favor, 2 against, and 9 abstentions. The Soviet alternate representative commented on the decision, saying that the vote was completely unjustified and incompatible with the facts, that it referred to the report by the Secretary General, which failed to establish the reasons for intrusion into the Soviet airspace, and repeated that the entry into the Soviet airspace was premeditated and organized by the US special services.[58] It can be observed that the deliberations in the Council resembled the previous ones in the Council and in the Assembly. Similar arguments were made, and three similar main themes of statements could be observed – accusatory of the Soviet Union by most Western countries, defensive and accusatory of the West by the Soviet Union and Czechoslovakia, and other Communist countries if the deliberations in the Assembly are considered, and several more neutral ones reflecting a presumed desire to keep politics away from ICAO. Depoliticization was visible in the second and third approach, with the apparently neutral motivation expressed in the third approach, while the Communist countries among other arguments have been employing defensive depoliticization. It was employed in a more glaring way during the latter instances of deliberations on the issue, which could have been the response to the ineffectiveness of previously used arguments. Apart from underlining the aspects of the incident that were more favorable for the Soviet Union, representatives of the Communist states argued that both the current version of the report and the decisions by the Council were politically motivated. References to politics were thus aimed at depreciating the gravity of the decisions and, on an operational level, to make the phrasing of the resolutions softer.

25th Session (Extraordinary) of the Assembly, 1984

Unlike similar cases of ICAO dealing with offenses in international aviation, the KAL007 controversy did not end with an investigation or simply with a condemnation. The problem returned during the subsequent 25th extraordinary Assembly in 1984, although this time, the deliberations focused not on responsibility for the tragedy but on the amendment of the Chicago Convention concerning the refraining from the use of force against civil aviation.[59] The deliberations centered around three amendment proposals: the Franco-Austrian, American, and Soviet. The deliberations were much more substantive compared to the more emotional previous ones, but two main standpoints stemming from the argumentation of various delegations could still be distinguished.

The first standpoint was presented by the Soviet delegation, which was much less confrontational than previously. The Soviet delegate spoke about no need to amend the Convention, arguing that the main problem concerned intrusions by foreign aircraft and the need to protect airspace by countries, with violations of sovereignty creating an atmosphere of mistrust and tension in international relations and posing a danger to flight safety and human rights. The delegate claimed the Assembly should find new means to increase international flight safety and prevent violations of state sovereignty or the illegal use of civil aircraft. The delegate said that other proposals only focused on the consequences of the violations committed and that the will of some states to amend the Convention was driven by political considerations. The Soviet proposal recognized the close link between ensuring the sovereign rights of states and improving the safety of international flights, which was to be driven by the desire to actively participate in the works of the Assembly.[60] Thus, the Soviet standpoint still focused on airspace sovereignty as the most crucial point. Defensive depoliticization was subtly visible in the claim that the desire of other states to amend the Convention was politically motivated, but unlike in earlier deliberations, the Soviet statement was not confrontational.

Delegations from other Communist states supported the Soviet standpoint. The Hungarian delegate argued the need to reduce tensions and enhance cooperation in ICAO, claiming there was no need to amend the Chicago Convention, which together with international law already provided adequate safeguards for the sovereignty of states and the safety of international aviation.[61] The Bulgarian delegate said there were two options on the table: to amend the Convention and seek a solution through administrative action, and to enhance the procedures to eliminate unintentional deviations and violations of sovereignty of states, claiming he was in favor of the second option. A comparable view was voiced by the Chinese delegate, who said the problem lied not in the lack of provisions but in the fact that they had not been strictly observed. Such a position was supported by delegations from Cuba and Czechoslovakia.[62] The Polish delegate added that the Assembly needed to ensure the maximum level of safety for civil aircraft and to prevent violations of the sovereignty of states in order to protect their security. The Vietnamese delegate argued that the Convention was a complete and perfect system.[63] Most radical was the statement of the East German observer, who claimed that anyone willfully crossing the border of another state, no matter whether on land or in the air, commits an illegal act, while sovereign states have the right to terminate an illegal intrusion into its airspace and take appropriate measures.[64] Communist states, like the Soviet Union, thus highlighted the importance of protecting the sovereignty of airspace. Their statements did not hold clear references to defensive depoliticization, although the East German position did carry some confrontational tone.

The second primary standpoint focused on the shootdown of civil aircraft as the main problem, assuming the need to amend the Convention, reflected in the American and Austrian–French proposals. As the British delegate said, the main concern was the safety of innocent men, women, and children, and therefore there was a need to codify international law to make it clear that no state is justified in using force against civil aircraft except in such circumstances of self-defense, while in such cases the degree of force must be appropriate to the danger.[65] Arguments about the need to strengthen states' obligation not to use force against civil aircraft were also raised by the delegates from Australia, Japan, the Netherlands, Austria, France, Israel, New Zealand, Canada, Italy, Belgium, the United States, Cyprus, and Switzerland.[66] Differences between delegations presenting such a standpoint generally centered around the details concerning the exceptions connected to permissible self-defense. Several delegations appreciated the principle of state sovereignty but still argued that it should not justify violence against civil aircraft.

A more radical position within the standpoint was presented by the Korean delegate, who spoke about the need to ban the use of force against civil aircraft, the need to reconcile the security interests of states and the interests of international civil aviation, and the settlement for the accident and incident in the air. The delegate also spoke about imposing sanctions on states violating the prohibition of the use of force against civil aircraft, which should be institutionalized rather than individual, as in the case of KAL007. The Korean proposed that such a state be suspended from its right to vote in ICAO Council and Assembly or expelled from ICAO.[67]

Despite considering several proposals and two major standpoints being present, in the end, the Assembly managed to reach a compromise worked out in the Executive Committee. The new article 3 bis of the Chicago Convention assumed, among other things, that every state must refrain from resorting to the use of force against civil aircraft. In case of interception, the lives of persons on board must not be endangered. States exercising their sovereignty can require the landing of an aircraft flying over its territory if relevant conditions are met, while the state in which the aircraft is registered shall take appropriate measures to prohibit its deliberate use for any purpose inconsistent with the aims of the Convention.[68] The resolution was then unanimously adopted.[69] The 25th Assembly has also adopted a resolution urging contracting states to ratify the protocol embodying the amendment and a resolution encouraging the taking of practical measures which would further enhance the safety of civil aviation.[70]

The extraordinary Assembly dealing with the issue of intercepting civil aircraft was far less focused on the Soviet shootdown of the KAL007. Unlike the 24th Assembly or the Council deliberations, there were no accusations directed at any specific party. This might be the reason why, despite two various standpoints being discussed, both the Communist and Western countries managed to reach a compromise, although we should also state the two standpoints were not entirely contradictory. The key objectives were similar, while the countries differed in how to reach them. There were no attempts to depoliticize the discussion besides the Soviet argument that the desire to amend the Convention was driven by political motivation, but it has to be admitted that the deliberations were not particularly politicized. The case of KAL007 thus suggests that it is the confrontational atmosphere that causes depoliticization attempts, an observation in line with the theoretical considerations on politicization.

The KAL007 incident revealed many gaps concerning international aviation system, with communication problems between civil and military flight control. It led to the adoption of several annexes to the Chicago Convention. Interestingly, when it came to the rules of intercepting aircraft, the United States and the Soviet Union joined forces, leading to the watering down of the initial project. As for the further developments, during the 26th Assembly, both the USSR and the United States spoke about their joint success together with Japan in establishing a voice communication link between the American, Soviet, and Japanese air traffic control centers over Northern Pacific – in Anchorage, Tokyo, and Khabarovsk, allowing them to exchange information on aircraft which might have in-flight emergencies or might have strayed from their routes.[71] The tragedy revealed the ICAO's role both as a diplomatic actor and a facilitator of diplomacy. Once the case was put before the Council at the request of contracting states, it took an active role, issuing an investigation and condemning the Soviet action. At the same time, despite tensions, the incident also led to direct contact between the countries concerned, leading to the increase of safety of civil aviation. In spite of these positive consequences, the KAL007 controversy was also a glaring example of the use of ICAO as a forum for confrontational diplomatic deliberations with political overtones. Cold War division was very clear, with delegations of Communist states actively defending the Soviet Union and repeating Soviet argumentation. In turn, the Western countries, often with the support from others, criticized the USSR for its action, often in a very emotional way. In an attempt to defend itself and to water down the phrasing of the ICAO resolutions or postpone the decisions, the USSR sometimes referred to depoliticization tactics, accusing Western countries of anti-Soviet hysteria and claiming Western draft proposals and reports from ICAO's investigation were biased and had political character. These attempts proved ineffective and the Soviet Union was condemned for the shootdown of the Korean Boeing 747. A review of the deliberations indicates that resorting to defensive depoliticization is often a final tool in the diplomatic playbook. The Soviet defense primarily relied on substantive arguments for a considerable period, turning to depoliticization only when other avenues were exhausted. Apart from this, as in many similar cases, depoliticization arguments were probably also used in attempts to genuinely keep politics away from ICAO – in this case, by several delegations from non-aligned countries.

Shootdown of the Iran Air Flight 655 by the United States in 1988

The second case analyzed in this chapter concerns another of the lasting rivalries in international relations – between the United States and Iran. Both countries were once close allies. The American involvement in Iran dates back to the 19th century, but it was only after the discovery of oil that Iran became important for American economic interests. The United States aided Mohammad Reza Pahlavi in replacing his father as the Shah of Iran and continued to escalate its involvement in Iran, a move that was viewed unfavorably by nationalist and Islamic forces. Americans backed the counter-coup after the Shah was removed by Mohammad Mosaddegh in 1953, while in the 1970s, Iran became the closest US ally in the Middle East. Even though the Shah stayed in power until 1979, the 1953 coup and counter-coup awakened the Islamic clergy in Iran,[72] a process that culminated in the Islamic revolution and the overthrowing of Pahlavi's regime by Ayatollah Khomeini in February 1979. The strained relations between the two states were epitomized by the hostage crisis, where American diplomatic personnel in Tehran were held captive from November 1979 to January 1981, resulting in a prolonged diplomatic standoff.

The Iranian Revolution changed the nature of Iran–US relations, with Iran rejecting the position of the regional gendarme.[73] From the US perspective, these changes had a deep Cold War context because of Iran's lasting importance to the American Cold War strategy and in the context of the decline in the US–Soviet relations.[74] Also, the outbreak of the Iraq–Iran war coincided with the end of the détente period in East–West relations. The United States saw it as a chance to limit Soviet growing engagement in the Third World, even though both the USSR and the United States found themselves in an odd situation of supporting the same side – Iraq.[75] For the United States, involvement in the war was difficult because it was held between two detestable regimes. According to Blight et al., it was the hostage crisis that drove the United States to support Iraq,[76] although Washington resigned from the initial non-involvement policy only in the second year of the war following Iran's military victories.[77] The context of the Iraq–Iran war, in which the United States supported Iraq, is believed to have given birth to mutual demonization between the United States and Iran. As Viola Vincze put it, when Iraq invaded Iran in 1980, US–Iranian relations were 'rocky and unpromising,' whereas after the war ended, 'self-righteous enmity' dominated in mutual relations.[78]

The shootdown of the IR655 flight is closely linked to the American presence in the area, which was not directly connected to its support to Iraq. During the conflict, both Iraqi and Iranian forces had been carrying out attacks against oil tankers in the Persian Gulf. This led the United States and some other countries to deploy warships in the Persian Gulf to ensure the flow of the oil.[79] The American–Iranian hostilities, the US support for Iraq in the war, the Cold War context, and the US military presence in the Persian Gulf all provide the background for the occurrence from 1988, revealing contextual similarities with the KAL007 incident, though different on the level of specific circumstances.

On July 3, 1988, Iran Air Flight 655 from Bandar Abbas to Dubai was shot down by American missile cruiser USS Vincennes while battling several Iranian speedboats. Two hundred ninety-eight people were killed.[80] Americans at the time allowed their ships to fire at aircraft after, in May 1987, the American frigate USS Stark was struck by a missile deployed from an Iraqi warplane. The Iranian Airbus was mistaken with an Iranian F-14 fighter, so the ship destroyed the plane. The Americans claimed it was an accident and the plane had violated several rules but offered compensation to the families of the victims.[81] As to the actual cause of the events, both flight IR655 and an Iranian F-14 departed from Bandar Abbas airport in close sequence. When the USS Vincennes noticed the plane on the radar, its crew made several attempts to identify it. Vincennes issued warnings on military channels not accessible to the pilot and eventually shot down the airliner.[82] The tragedy, despite being a result of a mistake and procedural problems, taking into consideration US–Iranian hostilities, led to highly politicized ICAO debates and attempts to employ defensive depoliticization.

Multilaterally, the tragedy was first dealt within the ICAO Council at an extraordinary meeting convened at the request of Iran in mid-July 1988 before the UN Security Council dealt with the matter. During the opening meeting, the Iranian observer called the event 'atrocious act of use of force against a civilian aircraft.' He said that contrary to previous cases, the US reaction was 'graduated and aimed at downplaying the gravity of its action and its consequences,' first denying the attack and claiming they had shot down an Iranian F-14 fighter. After the facts emerged, the United States initially revised its narrative without confirming the shootdown of the civilian airliner. When the facts became undeniable, the United States acknowledged that its forces had indeed shot down the airliner but persisted in claiming the presence of an F-14 in the vicinity, a claim that was later retracted. The Iranian observer also referred to American attempts to justify the act on the grounds of self-defense, with false claims that the plane was posing a threat to the ship, descending toward it and increasing speed, or that it was transmitting military signals. Apart from that, the Iranian referred to the question of what the aircraft was doing in the confrontation area, arguing that to him, the right question would be what the naval ship was doing near an international ATS route with regular scheduled flights. Concluding, the Iranian observer reminded that in the past, the ICAO Council and the United States rejected justifications that such incidents were caused either by mistake or in self-defense and requested explicit condemnation of the use of weapons against the Iranian aircraft by the United States and commissioning an investigation.[83] The statement was typical for this kind of situations. The Iranian observer was very critical of the United States but referred to political matters only subtly in reference to the US military presence in the area.

The US representative responded to the Iranian intervention, saying that immediately after the incident, the President of the United States expressed deep regret over the tragedy and announced that the United States was ready to provide compensation to the families of the victims. He added that the United States initiated a formal investigation immediately after the incident and described the events from the American perspective. He posited that the tragedy occurred within the context of the ongoing war between Iraq and Iran, despite the UN Security Council's mandatory call for an immediate ceasefire. The American claimed the US naval presence in the Persian Gulf was to preserve peace and contain the effects of the conflict. He called the incident an accident directly related to the unresolved Iraq–Iran conflict and referred to the general warning issued by the US government regarding flights in the region, emphasizing the importance of aircraft identification and the warnings to alter their courses issued to civil aircraft by the American naval vessels. The American then spoke about the developing threatening trend, referring to several recent Iranian attacks on the US military and other ships. In regard to the shootdown of the civilian airliner, the representative described the circumstances that led to the erroneous assumption by the captain of the Vincennes that an attack from the Iranian military was imminent. He also discussed the limitations of radars, concluding that the judgment of the situation should consider these circumstances. The American representatives also mentioned that Iranian civil aviation authorities must have known, or should have known, about the fighting and should have prevented an aircraft from flying into the area, so Iran should take some degree of responsibility. At the end of his intervention, the representative spoke about the need for a fact-finding investigation to identify measures for improvement, declaring cooperation from the US government and urging the Iranian government to cooperate. The American concluded that the risk of such tragedies would continue until the war between Iran and Iraq was in progress and that it was Iran that refused willingness to comply with the UN Security Council decisions.[84] The statement of the American representative leads to several observations. In the beginning, the representative focused on objective arguments concerning the incident and admitted US responsibility. Later, the American described political circumstances with the intention of shifting at least some of the responsibility to Iran and its engagement in the war with Iraq. What is interesting is that, being in a defensive position, rather than using depoliticization for defense, the representative took a reversed strategy and made political accusations against Iran.

As expected, subsequent discussions in the Council were tense, with most delegates deploring or condemning the act. Some of the interventions featured political argumentation. The representative of Czechoslovakia, after expressing condolences, said his government strongly condemned the 'tragic and unjustified act carried out by the United States military ship' and called the incident 'a gross violation of the fundamental principles of international civil aviation.' He also referred to the American active military presence in the Persian Gulf, which could have led to the escalation of the conflict and further danger to international civil aviation.[85] The Soviet representative was also very critical, calling the destruction of the aircraft 'barbaric' and 'inhuman.' According to his statement, the incident was not accidental but a consequence of the American intensification of its military presence in the Gulf region, confirming what 'a policy of power politics and of forcing tension can lead to.' He also called for the American navy to immediately withdraw from the Persian Gulf, while peace and security should be ensured by the

UN naval forces. Elimination of foreign military presence and bases, according to the Soviet representative, would allow such tragedies to be avoided in the future. He concluded by calling for the adoption of both political and technical measures. In a similar tone, the Cuban representative spoke about the conditions leading to the event that were still prevalent and that the primary cause of the tragedy was the growing US and NATO military presence in the region,[86] whereas the representative of China said the Chinese government opposed to big power involvement in the Gulf region as it did not foster peace and stability.[87] Interventions by representatives of the Communist states, though more critical than the majority, primarily revolved around a political argument attributing the shootdown to American military presence in the region, accompanied by calls for US withdrawal. Such politicization of the deliberations can be attributed to the particular goals and interests of the Soviet Union and its allies. As discussed in the introductory part of this section, US–Iranian relations in the 1980s and the American involvement in the region had a clear Cold War context, with the so-called Second Cold War increasing tensions and rivalry. Although neither the USSR nor other Communist countries were directly involved in the incident, they seemed to have attempted to achieve certain geopolitical gains with the use of the political context of the shootdown, an argumentation also embraced by the Iranian side.

Several delegations commented on the political context of the shootdown in a way that was less critical of the United States. The representative of Mexico, among other things, called states involved in the Gulf to reduce their military presence, and Iran and Iraq to cease hostilities immediately. The representative of Indonesia spoke about the need to end the Iran–Iraq war and argued that the presence of foreign forces in the Gulf increased the risk of widening the conflict, although this statement was not directly critical of American policy. The Nigerian representative presented an approach familiar from previously studied controversies, advocating for the Council's deliberations to focus solely on aeronautical aspects while suggesting that political considerations 'rightly belong to the forum of the United Nations.' Simultaneously, the Nigerians urged US authorities to withdraw naval vessels from the Gulf or suspend military activities, and Iranian authorities to cease attacks on neutral shipping and halt mine planting.[88] The last argument was clearly political, although at the same time balanced in the sense that it referred to both American and Iranian deeds.

Importantly from the perspective of this study, numerous speakers besides the already mentioned representative of Nigeria referred to the non-political character of the organization and the need not to engage in political issues. The representative of Egypt said the accident was a 'by-product' of the war between Iran and Iraq, urging all concerned to end the conflict or such accidents may happen again, called for strengthening military and civil coordination, and reminded about the technical character of ICAO. The representative of Canada said that the political context of the incident would be addressed in the UN Security Council on the following day and expected the Council to focus on the technical aspects of the incident, such as the measures to be taken to avoid the reoccurrence of such incidents. The representative of Saudi Arabia offered readiness to work with all members so that

ICAO could exercise its role as a technical body. The representative of Japan said the incident was closely related to political conflicts, but the Council should focus on its technical aspects, arguing that it was inappropriate to address the political aspects of the incident, so the first action to be done should be to initiate an investigation to determine the its technical causes. The representative of France said that restoring peace in the region was essential, but it was not under the direct responsibility of ICAO, which should confine itself to the technical role.[89] The representative of Senegal said the Council should be concerned with the technical and legal aspects while the political aspect 'falls within the competence of other bodies,'[90] whereas the representative of Spain reminded that ICAO was a technical organization, saying that 'we must not, and from a legal point of view, we cannot go beyond this framework, and whatever we say or recommend here must be contained in the Convention and its Annexes.'[91] These interventions exemplify depoliticization commonly observed in the ICAO, characterized by a focus on the organization's statutory mission without apparent hidden intentions, one which bears the qualities of general depoliticization. They reflect most probably genuine efforts to sustain the organization's goals and seem not to favor any side of the conflict, although as we observed multiple times, sometimes such interventions might also reflect concealed defense.

Deliberations in the Council also featured direct argument between the United States and Iran. In response to earlier American intervention, the Iranian observer said the American mentioned points of political nature. He spoke about the United States trying to evade responsibility and find justification to downplay the effects of the crime. The Iranian underlined that he did not want to enter political debates in ICAO but felt obliged to respond. He said the attacks on merchant shipping were conducted by Iraq, and Iran has never attacked any neutral shipping. According to him, the warning (Notice to Airmen, NOTAM) mentioned by the US representative was illegal, and the Iranian Air aircraft was attacked from a further distance than the NOTAM requirements. He added that there was a risk of reoccurrence of such incidents as long as there were no rules of engagement for the US military forces in the Gulf. Responding, the US representative apologized for having to take the floor and said that Iran attempted to picture itself as the only law-abiding authority in the Gulf and denied the blame for the situation that led to the incident, reminded Iranian attacks on the US and other ships at the time of the incident, and expressed doubt whether Iran has never attacked neutral shipping.[92] This exchange demonstrates one of the typical ways of employing depoliticization in multilateral deliberations. Both sides of the conflict accused each other of making political points. Despite their declared opposition to the politicization of the ICAO, both representatives claimed they were compelled by their counterparts to respond and themselves discussed the political circumstances. Depoliticization rhetoric was manifested both in the position of a side guilty of the incident – the United States, but also in the Iranian position, probably in response to the American claims of some Iranian responsibility.

Following the discussion, the Council made a decision in the form of the President's statement approved by the Council, in which, among other things, it deplored the use of weapons against civil aircraft and directed the Secretary General to institute an immediate fact-finding investigation. The decision was thus not as severe as in the case of the KAL007 incident. Among other things, the Council used the less severe expression 'deplore' rather than 'condemn.' The Iranian observer, while commenting on the decision, spoke about Iran's will to cooperate, the political concerns and constraints involved in any matter discussed at the international level, and commented on the summary as being the best possible, which would allow the UN Security Council to make political decisions that would end the threats to civil aviation in the Persian Gulf. The representative of the United States appreciated that the Council rebuffed attempts to politicize the discussion.[93] The Iranian response might be considered unexpected since, as Sochor judged the Council's decision, it was 'surprisingly mild.'[94] These conclusions reveal higher readiness for cooperation in increasing the safety of civil aviation by both sides compared to the early deliberations on the KAL007 incident, which were much more confrontational. At this stage, references to depoliticization were visible in the speeches of both sides, but rather than accusing each other of politicizing the deliberations, the American and Iranian representatives appreciated the decision as successful in focusing on the technical subject matter.

ICAO Council's decision did not end the controversy. Shortly after its deliberations, the issue was to be dealt with by the UN Security Council at Iran's request. The UN SC adopted a resolution which, among other things, expressed its deep distress at the downing of the Iranian civil aircraft,[95] which is another example of a relatively mild phrasing of multilateral decisions regarding the incident. As to the ICAO, further deliberations resumed once the investigation was completed and the Air Navigation Commission studied the safety recommendations.[96] As a result, the issue was discussed during the 126th session of the Council in March 1989. The deliberation began following the presentation of the draft resolution by the British delegate. According to the document, the shooting down of the Iran Air Airbus A300 on flight IR655 'had not been intentional' and resulted from errors in identifying the aircraft. The observer from Iran responded that the proposed resolution and decision of the Council lacked certain elements. According to the Iranian, it should reflect a 'strong and impartial position against such violations, irrespective of political considerations,' which would prove that the Council 'would by no means compromise the safety and security of civil aviation with political considerations.' The shape of the resolution at the time, according to the Iranian delegation, 'would neither fulfil the aims and objectives of the Organization, nor satisfy by any means the expectations and demands' of the Iranian government and families of the victims.[97] It was another situation in the analyzed case when the depoliticizing argument was used in a reversed way than usually, not in an attempt to defend and soften the phrasing of the projected ICAO decision, but to argue that the draft resolution was too soft and thus politically biased.

Representatives from the Communist countries endorsed the Iranian position. Soviet and Czechoslovakian representatives proposed strengthening the resolution by including a reference to the American naval ship having shot down a civilian airliner and condemning the use of weapons against civil aircraft. The

British representative responded that the responsibility had been accepted and relevant actions to avoid such incidents in the future had been made, so sponsors of the draft resolution did not think condemnation was appropriate in the particular circumstances. Also, the US representative indicated his government's strong opposition to the proposed amendment because condemning the incident would be a greater risk to ICAO's credibility since not all uses of force against civil aviation equally deserve condemnation without regard to particular circumstances. The American argued that considering the circumstances with the Iranian F-14 operating against US units squawking only a civilian mode code, American cooperation with ICAO in the investigation and the compensations paid to the families of the victims, ICAO should not use the phrase condemnation with respect to this incident. The Iranian position was also endorsed by the Kenyan representative, who said that since the Council condemned such incidents in the past, it should do the same this time, which would mean acting in accordance with its mandate and not becoming influenced by political considerations. The representatives of Cuba and China also argued that the Council should condemn the incident.[98] Depoliticization rhetoric thus kept being used offensively in order to achieve a more severe phrasing of the resolution on the shootdown. Such offensive depoliticization as a diplomatic tactic might be the potential subject for future research of deliberations in international organizations.

Following the discussion, the Council adopted the resolution proposed by the United Kingdom with minor amendments to the original version, including a mild severance of several phrases, but without resorting to condemnation. In the final version, among other things, the Council deeply deplored 'the tragic incident which occurred as a consequence of events and errors in identification of the aircraft which resulted in the accidental destruction of an Iran Air airliner and the loss of 290 lives.'[99] The Iranian observer expressed his appreciation to the President for his efforts but said the resolution was not a proper answer to the incident and was not satisfactory to the Iranian government. The US representative thanked the Council for finding a solution 'in a fair manner.'[100] The American position revealed minor defensive depoliticization, implying that maintaining less severe phrasing reflected an objective rather than a politicized decision. Still, in the case of the IR655 shootdown, depoliticization was more straightforwardly used offensively.

Iranian dissatisfaction with the phrasing of the Council's resolution manifested itself on several subsequent occasions. On May 17, 1989, the Iranian government filed an application with the International Court of Justice against the US government, requesting that the decision of the ICAO Council be declared erroneous.[101] Apart from that, Iran voiced its disappointment during the 27th session of the Assembly in 1989. At the Executive Committee meeting, the Iranian delegate said that the Council's resolution was not acceptable, incompatible with the gravity of the incident, and contrary to decisions made concerning previous cases of shootdown of civil aircraft.[102] At the plenary meeting, the Iranian chief delegate called the occurrence 'the most outrageous and senseless crime' and described the Council's decision as not a just and decisive judgment, concluding that the Assembly was obliged to take the necessary actions for the prevention of such incidents. However, there were no further deliberations on the issue in the Assembly, as there was no such request by the Iranian delegation.

The developments occurring in ICAO after the shootdown of the Iranian Airbus by the US Navy led to several observations. Firstly, ICAO's reaction was much milder compared to how it reacted to the KAL007 incident, even though, according to American argumentation, the level of the American fault was different. The milder reaction might have been a result of a different power balance in the ICAO Council, with the United States having more allies than Iran. However, it should be admitted that the way the United States reacted was somehow different from, for example, the Soviet reaction after the KAL007 shootdown when it came to accepting responsibility. ICAO deliberations on the IR655 incident belong to politicized ones, which stems from the political circumstances surrounding the incident, the general tensions between the United States and Iran, and the context of the Cold War and the Iraq–Iran war. Representatives of each side of these conflicts were referring to political developments in attempts to support their respective positions. Besides that, both parties declared being against the politicization of the ICAO but claimed they were forced by their counterpart to respond, further engaging in political argumentation. Apart from that, Communist states that were not directly involved argued about the need for the United States to withdraw from the region to avoid repetition of such occurrences, claims which can be interpreted as attempts to improve Soviet strategic position in the Middle East.

The presence of politicization, as in all other cases analyzed in this book, also led to depoliticization. Numerous state representatives called for a focus on technical matters, advocating that political issues be left to the UN Security Council, in apparently genuine attempts to safeguard ICAO's politically neutral character. Apart from that, representatives of Iran and the United States accused each other of bringing political arguments to the ICAO while at the same time referring to political issues themselves. A characteristic feature of the IR655 case is that although depoliticization rhetoric was used for defense, it was used for offense on an even larger scale, with Iran and occasionally other states arguing that too mild phrasing of ICAO's decisions was politically biased. American representatives did not use such argument as often, but in a less straightforward way they also did, arguing the opposite – that milder phrasing of resolutions was fair.

Conclusions

The shootdowns of civil aircraft are among the most controversial and emotionally charged incidents in civil aviation. While primarily considered by ICAO, they are also often deliberated upon by the UN Security Council. The loss of many lives in such situations understandably makes deliberations emotional, with the intensity increasing if the shootdown is linked to international political estrangements or hostilities. In such situations, ICAO deliberations may turn into highly politicized debates, with the parties involved seeking to win political gains and hit their political adversaries on the occasion of tragic incidents, usually resulting from mistakes. This was the case of the two occurrences analyzed in this chapter – the downing of the Korean Air Lines Flight 007 by the Soviet Union, with the Cold War circumstances in the background, and the shootdown of the Iranian Air Lines Flight 655 by the United States, which corresponds with the US-Iran estrangement.

Both incidents occurred in different circumstances, so the specific course of the ICAO deliberations and the argumentation used by both sides differed substantially. In both cases, the main diplomatic tool of the accused ones was an attempt to shift responsibility to others. The Soviet Union underlined the illegal intrusion of the Korean airplane into its airspace, claimed it was on a spy mission, and highlighted the importance of protecting state sovereignty over its airspace. In contrast, the Americans, while claiming responsibility and being more cooperative regarding the investigation, argued that Iran bore some responsibility due to its involvement in the war with Iraq and attacks on merchant shipping. As a secondary argument, in the Soviet case used only when others did not work, both the United States and the Soviet Union employed defensive depoliticization. In the case of the KAL007 incident, the Soviet Union attempted to use depoliticization to downgrade the gravity of ICAO's decisions – through references to anti-Soviet hysteria and biased reports from the investigation. In turn, the United States employed depoliticization rhetoric to support its argument that the ICAO resolutions should be milder. The deliberations on the IR655 incident are particularly intriguing because both the accusing and defending sides employed depoliticization rhetoric, with Iran doing so even more frequently than the United States. This reveals the depoliticization's utility as an offensive tool in the diplomatic playbook. Besides that, both controversies also featured attempts by states not engaged in respective conflicts to focus deliberations on technical rather than aviation matters.

Notes

1 French commercial aircraft from West Germany to West Berlin shot down by the Soviet Union in 1952; Cathay Pacific aircraft en route from Bangkok to Hong Kong shot down by China in 1954, El Al flight en route from Vienna to Tel Aviv shot down by Bulgaria in 1955; Libyan Airlines plane shot down by Israel in 1973; Korean Air Lines aircraft en route from Paris to Seoul shot down by the USSR in 1978; Korean Air Lines aircraft en route from New York to Seoul shot down by the USSR in 1983; Iranian Airlines flight en route from Bandar Abbas to Dubai shot down by the United States in 1988; Brothers to the Rescue plane shot down by Cuba in 1996; flight from Naples to Johannesburg shot down by Ethiopia in 1999; Cessna 152 pilot school plane from Lebanon shot down by Israel in 2001; Tupolev Tu-154 en route from Tel Aviv to Novosibirsk shot down by Ukraine in 2001. Brian E. Foont, "Shooting Down Civilian Aircraft: Is There an International Law," *Journal of Air Law and Commerce* 72 (2007): 695–725.

2 See: Sascha-Dominik Bachmann, "Malaysia Airlines Flight MH17: The Day Russia Became a State Sponsor of Terrorism," *Amicus Curiae* 97 (2014): 14–28.

3 Eugene Sochor, *The Politics of International Aviation* (Basingstoke: Macmillan, 1991), 133–134.

4 See: Mateusz Osiecki, "Shooting Down Civil Aircraft in the Light of Sovereignty in the Airspace," *Sociology Study* 6, no. 6 (June 2016): 399, https://doi.org/10.17265/2159-5526/2016.06.005

5 Consolidated attendance list, 10th Session of the Assembly, June–July 1956, 77, A10-P/17, DOC 7708, ICAO Archival Documents; Minutes of the Second Plenary Meeting, Assembly – Eleventh Session, May 21, 1958, 24-25, A11-P/11, DOC 7886, ICAO Archival Documents; Minutes of the Second Plenary Meeting, Assembly – Tenth Session, June 20, 1956, 30, A10-P/17-2, DOC 7708-2, ICAO Archival Documents.

6 "Convention on International Civil Aviation." Signed at Chicago on 7 December 1944.

7 David MacKenzie, ICAO: A History of the International Civil Aviation Organization (Toronto: University of Toronto Press, 2010), 218, 278.

8 Annual Report of the Council to the Assembly for 1956, Supporting Documentation for the Eleventh Session of the Assembly, 1958, 49, A11-P/1, DOC 7788, ICAO Archival Documents.

9 Minutes of the Third Plenary Meeting, Assembly 24th Session, September 21, 1983, 36, A24-Min. P/3, DOC 9415, ICAO Archival Documents.

10 MacKenzie, *ICAO*, 302.

11 Craig A. Morgan, "The Downing of Korean Air Lines Flight 007," *Yale Journal of International Law* 11, no. 1 (Fall 1985): 231, 239.

12 MacKenzie, *ICAO*, 302.

13 Ibid., 303–304; Gerald F. FitzGerald, "The Use of Force against Civil Aircraft: The Aftermath of the KAL Flight 007 Incident," *Canadian Yearbook of International Law* 22 (1984): 293, https://doi.org/10.1017/S0069005800002733

14 Peter Svik, *Civil Aviation and the Globalization of the Cold War* (Cham: Palgrave Macmillan, 2020), 147, 150–153.

15 Ibid., 174.

16 Farrel Corcoran, "KAL 007 and the Evil Empire: Mediated Disaster and Forms of Rationalization," *Critical Studies in Mass Communication* 3, no. 3 (1986): 297, https://doi.org/10.1080/15295038609366656.

17 Marilyn J. Young, and Michael K. Launer, "Kal 007 and the Superpowers: An International Argument," *Quarterly Journal of Speech* 74, no. 3 (1988): 291, https://doi.org/10.1080/00335638809383842

18 2476th Meeting, United Nations Security Council Official Records, September 12, 1983, 12, S/PV.2476, available from https://documents.un.org/doc/undoc/gen/nl8/300/36/pdf/nl830036.pdf?token=YgmcyhrGsTSd0i3yEW&fe=true, accessed April 18, 2024.

19 MacKenzie, *ICAO*, 305–306.

20 Minutes of the First Meeting, Council – Extraordinary Session, September 15, 1983, 3-6, C-Min. EXTRAORDINARY (1983)/1, DOC 9416-C/1077, ICAO Archival Documents.

21 Ibid., 12–13.

22 Ibid., 16–17.

23 Ibid., 17.

24 Ibid., 22.

25 Ibid., 27.

26 Minutes of the Second Meeting, Council – Extraordinary Session, September 15, 1983, 36–37, C-Min. EXTRAORDINARY (1983)/2, DOC 9416-C/1077, ICAO Archival Documents.

27 Minutes of the First Meeting, Council – Extraordinary Session, September 15, 1983, 8, C-Min. EXTRAORDINARY (1983)/1, DOC 9416-C/1077, ICAO Archival Documents.

28 Ibid., 10–11, 16, 20, 29, 33.

29 Minutes of the Second Meeting, Council – Extraordinary Session, September 15, 1983, 38–42, C-Min. EXTRAORDINARY (1983)/2, DOC 9416-C/1077, ICAO Archival Documents.
30 W. W. Kulski, "Soviet Diplomatic Techniques," *The Russian Review* 19, no. 3 (1960): 221–224.
31 Minutes of the Second Meeting, Council – Extraordinary Session, September 15, 1983, 42–45, C-Min. EXTRAORDINARY (1983)/2, DOC 9416-C/1077, ICAO Archival Documents.
32 Minutes of the Third Meeting, Council – Extraordinary Session, September 16, 1983, 44, C-Min. EXTRAORDINARY (1983)/3, DOC 9416-C/1077, ICAO Archival Documents; Minutes of the Fourth Meeting, Council – Extraordinary Session, September 16, 1983, 49, C-Min. EXTRAORDINARY (1983)/4, DOC 9416-C/1077, ICAO Archival Documents.
33 Minutes of the Fourth Meeting, Council – Extraordinary Session, September 16, 1983, 49–51, C-Min. EXTRAORDINARY (1983)/4, DOC 9416-C/1077, ICAO Archival Documents.
34 Minutes of the Fourth Meeting, Council – Extraordinary Session, Appendix A, September 16, 1983, 59–60, C-Min. EXTRAORDINARY (1983)/4, DOC 9416-C/1077, ICAO Archival Documents.
35 Final Report of the Executive Committee, Assembly 24th Session, n.d., 11–14, A24-EX, DOC 9409, ICAO Archival Documents; Working Paper: Agenda Item 7: Annual Report of the Council to the Assembly for 1980, 1981 and 1982 and Work Programme for 1984-86, and their reference to the Executive Committee as a whole and to Commission as necessary, Draft Resolution, Executive Committee, Assembly – 24th Session, September 26, 1983, A24-WP/77 P/38 & EX/9, ICAO Archival Documents.
36 Minutes of the Second Plenary Meeting, Assembly 24th Session, September 20, 1983, 16–18, 22, 25, A24-Min. P/2, DOC 9415, ICAO Archival Documents.
37 Minutes of the Third Plenary Meeting, Assembly 24th Session, September 21, 1983, 39–41, A24-Min. P/3, DOC 9415, ICAO Archival Documents.
38 Minutes of the Seventh Plenary Meeting, Assembly 24th Session, September 23, 1983, 124, A24-Min. P/7, DOC 9415, ICAO Archival Documents.
39 Minutes of the Eighth Plenary Meeting, Assembly 24th Session, September 23, 1983, 128, A24-Min. P/8, DOC 9415, ICAO Archival Documents.
40 Minutes of the Second Plenary Meeting, Assembly 24th Session, September 20, 1983, 28–29, A24-Min. P/2, DOC 9415, ICAO Archival Documents.
41 Minutes of the Fifth Plenary Meeting, Assembly 24th Session, September 22, 1983, 78, A24-Min. P/5, DOC 9415, ICAO Archival Documents.
42 Minutes of the Eighth Plenary Meeting, Assembly 24th Session, September 23, 1983, 131, A24-Min. P/8, DOC 9415, ICAO Archival Documents.
43 Minutes of the Third Plenary Meeting, Assembly 24th Session, September 21, 1983, 36, A24-Min. P/3, DOC 9415, ICAO Archival Documents.
44 Minutes of the Fourth Plenary Meeting, Assembly 24th Session, September 21, 1983, 54–55, A24-Min. P/4, DOC 9415, ICAO Archival Documents.
45 Ibid., 64.

46 Minutes of the Fifth Plenary Meeting, Assembly 24th Session, September 22, 1983, 70, A24-Min. P/5, DOC 9415, ICAO Archival Documents.
47 Minutes of the Sixth Plenary Meeting, Assembly 24th Session, September 22, 1983, 103, A24-Min. P/6, DOC 9415, ICAO Archival Documents.
48 Minutes of the Seventh Plenary Meeting, Assembly 24th Session, September 23, 1983, 120–121, A24-Min. P/7, DOC 9415, ICAO Archival Documents.
49 Minutes of the Tenth Plenary Meeting, Assembly 24th Session, September 26, 1983, 138, A24-Min. P/10, DOC 9415, ICAO Archival Documents.
50 Minutes of the Twelfth Plenary Meeting, Assembly 24th Session, October 1, 1983, 160–161, A24-Min. P/12, DOC 9415, ICAO Archival Documents.
51 Ibid., 161–164, 167.
52 Minutes of the Sixth Meeting, Council – 111th Session, March 6, 1984, 83–84, 106, C-Min. 111/6, ICAO Archival Documents.
53 Ibid., 83–84.
54 Ibid., 84–90, 93, 96–97.
55 Ibid., 94–95, 100, 102.
56 Ibid., 99–100.
57 Ibid., 102–103.
58 Ibid., 104–105.
59 Annual Report of the Council – 1983, Documentation for the session of the Assembly in 1986, 145, DOC 9421, ICAO Archival Documents.
60 Minutes of the Second Plenary Meeting, Assembly 25th Session (Extraordinary), April 24, 1984, 25–26, A25-Min. P/2 DOC 9437, ICAO Archival Documents.
61 Minutes of the Third Plenary Meeting, Assembly 25th Session (Extraordinary), April 25, 1984, 46–48, A25-Min. P/3, DOC 9437, ICAO Archival Documents.
62 Minutes of the Second Plenary Meeting, Assembly 25th Session (Extraordinary), April 24, 1984, 33–38, A25-Min. P/2 DOC 9437, ICAO Archival Documents; Minutes of the Third Plenary Meeting, Assembly 25th Session (Extraordinary), April 25, 1984, 40–41, A25-Min. P/3, DOC 9437, ICAO Archival Documents.
63 Minutes of the Fourth Plenary Meeting, Assembly 25th Session (Extraordinary), April 25, 1984, 63, 72, A25-Min. P/4, DOC 9437, ICAO Archival Documents.
64 Minutes of the Fifth Plenary Meeting, Assembly 25th Session (Extraordinary), April 26, 1984, 84, A25-Min. P/5, DOC 9437, ICAO Archival Documents.
65 Minutes of the Second Plenary Meeting, Assembly 25th Session (Extraordinary), April 24, 1984, 27–30, A25-Min. P/2 DOC 9437, ICAO Archival Documents.
66 Ibid., 30–32; Minutes of the Third Plenary Meeting, Assembly 25th Session (Extraordinary), April 25, 1984, 43–44, 55–57, A25-Min. P/3, DOC 9437, ICAO Archival Documents; Minutes of the Fourth Plenary Meeting, Assembly 25th Session (Extraordinary), April 25, 1984, 59–61, 68–71, 73, 76–78, A25-Min. P/4, DOC 9437, ICAO Archival Documents.
67 Ibid., 65–66.
68 Working Paper, Report of the Executive Committee to the Plenary, Assembly – 25th Session (Extraordinary), May 10, 1984, A25-WP/20, ICAO Archival Documents.
69 Minutes of the Seventh Plenary Meeting, Assembly 25th Session (Extraordinary), May 10, 1984, 95, A25-Min. P/7 DOC 9437, ICAO Archival Documents.

70 Annual Report of the Council – 1984, Documentation for the session of the Assembly in 1986, 133, DOC 9451, ICAO Archival Documents.
71 Minutes of the Sixth Plenary Meeting, Assembly 26th Session, September 25, 1986, 109, A26-Min. P/6 DOC 9494, ICAO Archival Documents.
72 Nazir Hussain, "US-Iran Relations: Issues, Challenges and Prospects," *Policy Perspectives* 12, no. 2 (2015): 30–31, https://doi.org/10.13169/polipers.12.2.0029
73 Fakhreddin Soltani, and Reza Ekhtiari Amiri, "Foreign Policy of Iran after Islamic Revolution," *Journal of Politics and Law* 3, no. 2 (September 2010): 200.
74 Christian Emery, *US Foreign Policy and the Iranian Revolution: The Cold War Dynamics of Engagement and Strategic Alliance* (Basingstoke: Palgrave Macmillan, 2013), 46.
75 Adam Tarock, *The Superpowers' Involvement in the Iran-Iraq War* (Commack: Nova Science Publishers, 1998) 16–19.
76 James G. Blight, et al., *Becoming Enemies: U.S.-Iran Relations and the Iran-Iraq War, 1979–1988* (Lanham, Rowman and Littlefield, 2012), xi.
77 Michael Sterner, "The Iran-Iraq War," *Foreign Affairs* 63, no. 1 (Fall 1984): 129.
78 Blight, et al., 25–26.
79 Viola Vincze, "The USS Vincennes Incident: A case study involving Autonomous Weapon Systems," *HDR* 2 (2020): 94.
80 Sochor, *The Politics of International Aviation*, 138.
81 MacKenzie, *ICAO*, 317–318.
82 Vincze, "The USS Vincennes Incident," 95–97.
83 Minutes of the First Meeting, Council-Extraordinary Session, July 13, 1988, 4–7, C-Min. EXTRAORDINARY (1988)/1, DOC 9541-C/1106, ICAO Archival Documents.
84 Ibid., 8–14.
85 Ibid., 15–17.
86 Ibid., 26–30.
87 Minutes of the Second Meeting, Council-Extraordinary Session, July 14, 1988, 46, C-Min. EXTRAORDINARY (1988)/2, DOC 9541-C/1106, ICAO Archival Documents.
88 Minutes of the First Meeting, Council-Extraordinary Session, July 13, 1988, 22–25, 34–35, C-Min. EXTRAORDINARY (1988)/1, DOC 9541-C/1106, ICAO Archival Documents.
89 Ibid., 18–20, 22, 25–26, 32–33.
90 Minutes of the Second Meeting, Council-Extraordinary Session, July 14, 1988, 43, 45, C-Min. EXTRAORDINARY (1988)/2, DOC 9541-C/1106, ICAO Archival Documents.
91 Ibid., 45.
92 Minutes of the First Meeting, Council-Extraordinary Session, July 13, 1988, 36–40, C-Min. EXTRAORDINARY (1988)/1, DOC 9541-C/1106, ICAO Archival Documents.
93 Minutes of the Second Meeting, Council-Extraordinary Session, July 14, 1988, 47–52, C-Min. EXTRAORDINARY (1988)/2, DOC 9541-C/1106, ICAO Archival Documents.
94 Sochor, *The Politics of International Aviation*, 141.
95 UN Security Council resolution 616 (1988) of 20 July 1988, available from https://digitallibrary.un.org/record/42913, accessed February 5, 2024.
96 Annual Report of the Council – 1988, Documentation for the session of the Assembly in 1989, 119, DOC 9530, ICAO Archival Documents.

97 Minutes of the Twentieth Meeting, Council – 126th Session, March 17, 1989, 179–180, C-Min. 126/20, ICAO Archival Documents.
98 Ibid., 180–183.
99 Ibid., 186.
100 Ibid., 184.
101 Annual Report of the Council – 1989, Documentation for the Session of the Assembly in 1992, 108, DOC 9553, ICAO Archival Documents.
102 Report of the Executive Committee, Assembly 27th Session, 9, A27-EX, DOC 9545, ICAO Archival Documents.

6 Tensions between Russia and the West on the forum of ICAO

A more recent example of employing depoliticization as a defensive strategy involves the widely perceived tensions between Russia and its ally Belarus, and Western countries in the 21st century. Politicized debates connected to the estrangement have been taking place since the diversion of the Ryanair flight FR4978 to Minsk in 2021, followed by the Russian invasion of Ukraine in February 2022. Interestingly, despite more direct tensions emerging in 2014 with Russia's annexation of Crimea and the downing of Malaysia Airlines Flight MH17 over Eastern Ukraine, broader political tensions did not surface in International Civil Aviation Organization (ICAO) until 2021.

After the end of the Cold War, in the 1990s and 2000s, major attempts were made to build institutional ties between Russia and the West. However, since the beginning of the 2010s and, in particular, since the outbreak of the conflict over Ukraine in 2014, their relations have begun to deteriorate.[1] This period was marked by growing hostile rhetoric. For example, in 2012, Russian army chief General Nikolai Makarov threatened a pre-emptive strike on missile defense infrastructure in Europe.[2] Nevertheless, up until the early 2020s, despite escalating tensions, efforts to engage in dialogue and find common ground persisted. This was exemplified by events such as the Biden–Putin summit in Geneva in 2021.

The ultimate collapse of the Russia–West dialogue took place after the Russian invasion of Ukraine on February 24, 2022, pursued in cooperation with Belarus. The outbreak of the war marked another stage in the Russo-Ukrainian conflict, which began in 2014 with the annexation of Crimea and the subsequent outbreak of a hybrid war in Eastern Ukraine. This conflict was further complicated by an aviation-related crisis in July 2014, when Malaysia Airlines flight MH17 was downed over Eastern Ukraine. Investigations determined that a BUK-TELAR system, brought to the area from Russia and later returned, was used in the downing.[3]

As mentioned, international tensions between Russia and Western countries began to grow in the 2010s, particularly after the annexation of Crimea. However, such developments in international politics did not cause political tensions within the ICAO. No reference to the conflict in Ukraine was made during either the 201st session of the Council, held from February 24 to March 10, 2014, or the 202nd session, held from June 9 to 23, 2014. In the field of aviation, the mounting conflict

DOI: 10.4324/9781032695402-7

was exemplified by the already mentioned downing of the Malaysia Airlines flight MH17 over Eastern Ukraine by pro-Russian separatists. At its 203rd session, the Council undertook the loss of the MH17 flight, but the deliberations were not particularly politicized. In his speech, the Malaysian Minister of Transport did not accuse any state, focused on prevention, and only mentioned the geopolitical situation hindering the progress of the investigation. Russia, along with all other Council members, co-sponsored a resolution that, among other things, condemned the downing of MH17 in the strongest possible terms. Furthermore, during the subsequent discussion, no accusatory tones were observed in any of the interventions, including by the Ukrainian observer. Admittedly, Russia expressed a reservation about the Council's decision on risk assessment of operations over airspace affected by armed conflict, but the entire discussion was free from politicization and depoliticization.[4] Such a situation in the ICAO changed in 2021, following the incident concerning the Ryanair flight FR4978, even though it did not concern Russia directly.

Forced landing of Ryanair Flight 4978 in Minsk

Politicized deliberations in ICAO connected to the Russia–West estrangement occurred following two key events: the forced landing of Ryanair flight 4978 in Belarus in 2021 and the Russian invasion of Ukraine in 2022. The first event is somewhat associated with political developments in Belarus. Large-scale protests against Aleksandr Lukashenka's electoral victory in 2020 led to state terror and the subsequent virtual destruction of the free press and civil society,[5] demonstrating the dependence of the Belarusian regime on Russia's support.[6] Unlike many Western states, Russia recognized the legitimacy of Lukashenka.[7] This resulted in closer ties between Belarus and Russia, a deterioration of relations with the West, and Lukashenka's crackdown on opposition and free press. These circumstances are connected with the incident on May 23, 2021, when Ryanair flight 4978, traveling from Athens to Vilnius, was diverted to Minsk while passing through Belarusian airspace. Belarusian authorities claimed to have received emails stating that a bomb was planted on the aircraft, threatening to detonate over Vilnius.[8] After landing, Belarusian authorities detained journalist and activist Raman Pratasevich and his girlfriend Sofia Sapega. No evidence of a bomb was found, and the aircraft continued its journey without the detained passengers. Russia emerged as a staunch ally, consistently defending Belarus at ICAO forums, often associating criticisms of Belarus with broader political tensions with the West.

The first ICAO deliberations regarding the incident occurred in the Council four days after its occurrence. Depoliticization could be observed at the very beginning when the President of the Council reminded that the deliberations should remain within the scope of the Council, one of the few instances among all the analyzed cases when a representative of ICAO bureaucracy rather than a state representative called for keeping politics away. The discussion concerned letters from Lithuania (country of destination of the flight) and Poland (country of registration of the aircraft) requesting the Council to urgently launch an investigation. During the meeting, Belarus was represented by the Director of the Department of Aviation, who stated the aim was to prevent casualties or damage and emphasized that the pilot was merely advised to land in Minsk, asserting that the decision was made 'without any coercion from Belarus.' The director concluded that Belarus did not violate international air law and questioned the sanctions imposed on Belarus and its airline Belavia by the EU and several other states, arguing that similar incidents from the past, like the Belavia flight from Kyiv to Minsk, had not prompted such measures. The Belarusian also stressed the need for unbiased and objective investigation to avoid setting 'a worrying precedent' that could deter states from reacting to anonymous threats to civil aviation 'for fear of potential political and economic repercussions.'[9] Besides denying any infringement from the Belarusian side and overlooking the detainment of passengers, the director employed several diplomatic tactics. He attempted to show inconsistencies in ICAO's behavior by referring to different approaches adopted in the past in reference to, according to the Belarusian, comparable events. The director portrayed Belarus as the victim of the event, citing the imposition of sanctions, and subtly employed depoliticization by advocating for an impartial investigation and highlighting the risks of political repercussions. This is interesting because, at the time, Belarus had not faced criticism from anyone in the Council yet.

After the Belarusian director's statement, many speakers criticized the Belarusian action. The Polish Minister of Infrastructure spoke about several passengers who had not returned to the aircraft, the absence of evidence of explosives, and expressed doubts about the credibility of the information conveyed by the Belarusian Air Traffic Control to the crew of FR4978. The Minister for Environment, Climate & Communications and Transport of Ireland argued the landing was forced by the Belarusian authorities in order to detain a journalist aboard the aircraft. The Lithuanian Minister of Transport and Communications discussed the Belarusian authorities' arrest of two journalists and expressed doubts about Belarus's ability to ensure the safety of air navigation and referenced inconsistencies in the information provided by Belarus. The inconsistencies in the Belarusian version and the appearance that Belarusian authorities were more interested in arresting two specific passengers than searching the explosives were also mentioned by the representative of the United Kingdom, who suggested the only plausible explanation was that the action of the Belarusian authorities to divert the aircraft were aimed specifically to detain Mr. Raman Pratasevich and Ms. Sofia Sapega. Representatives of Germany, Canada, Japan, Australia, Greece, and Paraguay also expressed strong criticism of Belarus. Virtually all representatives intervening supported the need to investigate the incident. Out of those who presented a more moderate position, the representative of China spoke about refraining from rushing to conclusions and the need to exclude any external influence regarding extensive media reporting, while the representative of South Africa cautioned against prejudging the outcome. The representative of Nigeria additionally underlined the need to preserve the integrity of the Organization,[10] which can be interpreted as a subtle yet genuine attempt to avoid transferring international political conflicts into the ICAO, thus an example of general depoliticization in an international organization (IO).

Most of the deliberations on the forced landing of the Ryanair aircraft at the 223rd session of the Council should not be considered particularly politicized. Admittedly, several representatives were more critical of the Belarusian action, some referred to 'Belarusian regime,' but in principle, the interventions focused on the course of events and the concerns over the safety of civil aviation. This, however, did not prevent representatives from employing further depoliticization rhetoric. A particularly strong statement in this sense came from the representative of Russia, who vigorously defended Belarusian action. He said his government 'viewed with concern any attempts to utilize ICAO as a means to resolve political issues or engage in double standards,' expressed his country's surprise that the meeting had been convened so swiftly, and referred to the sanctions imposed against Belarus and its airlines by a number of states. Similarly to the Belarusian speaker, the Russian representative recalled past forced landings in Europe and the United States, resulting in the removal or detention of passengers, for which international response was not as quick or heavy-handed. The Russian concluded that 'ICAO had no remit with respect to the detention of passengers' and should not be used 'as a forum for pronouncements on this subject.'[11] The Russian statement revealed several defensive tactics, some of which were already used by the Belarusian director. The Russian spoke directly about the politicization of the ICAO through the debate, about double standards and different treatment of Western offenses, and questioned ICAO's competence over the detention of passengers. The Belarusian argumentation has been repeated, but defensive depoliticization was employed by the Russian representative in a more straightforward way. Russian and Belarusian depoliticizing moves were not responding directly to the interventions by other speakers. Rather, they were supposed to respond to the sanctions imposed against Belarus beyond ICAO and to avoid discussing the issue in ICAO.

The representatives of South Africa and China, already less critical toward the incident, also supported the Russian representative during the discussion on the draft decision. The three delegations opted to delete the word 'forced' regarding the diversion of the flight, whereas the representatives of France, the United Kingdom, Finland, the Netherlands, Germany, and the United States expressed the need to keep this phrase. During the discussion, the representative of South Africa questioned the political neutrality of the process of drafting the text of the decision, which was an evident depoliticizing move, though it cannot be unequivocally determined whether it was an attempt to defend Belarus or to protect ICAO from politicization. Following the discussion, the Council issued a decision expressing strong concern over the apparent forced diversion of Ryanair Flight FR4978 and initiating an investigation,[12] thus not including amendments advocated by Belarus, Russia, and several other delegations.

The FR4978 incident was debated during the 223rd session of the Council a couple more times, often featuring defensive depoliticization. When the Minister of Transport of Canada spoke about work related to conflict zones and the 'Safer Skies' initiative, he mentioned Belarus forcing 'the landing of Ryanair Flight FR4978, under false pretenses in order to arrest a journalist.'[13] In response, the representative of Russia once again noted the difference in the international community's reaction to a similar event involving the emergency landing of a Ryanair flight en-route from Dublin to Kraków in Berlin on May 30, 2021, due to an alleged security threat. The incident did not involve detaining passengers, as was reminded by the French representative,[14] but the statement by the Russian again revealed an attempt to defend Belarus by underlining alleged inconsistency in ICAO's actions.

The final chapter of the deliberation at the 223rd session of the Council on the landing of Ryanair flight 4978 in Minsk took place when the interim report of the Fact-Finding Investigation Team (FFIT) was being discussed. According to the report, the materials acquired by the FFIT at the time were insufficient to establish the facts, so further investigation was needed.[15] During the discussion, the Russian representative said that detainment of passengers traveling on the aircraft was 'a political issue that should be discussed separately at the United Nations Security Council in New York and not at ICAO, given the latter's role as a specialized technical body of the UN system.'[16] The Belarusian observer, among other things, spoke about sanctions against Belarus, saying that 'it was unclear to Belarus why ICAO had chosen to side with the United States, Europe, Ukraine, and other countries regarding this clear violation of the Chicago Convention.' The Belarusian repeated that the decision regarding the fact-finding investigation violated the Chicago Convention that the sanctions imposed by some states were 'politically motivated, discriminatory, and inconsistent given other comparable incidents' and mentioned two other incidents that did not bring similar reactions.[17] The representatives of Russia and Belarus once again utilized defensive depoliticization, directly accusing the Council of double standards and aligning with the West. They claimed that the issue was political and unsuitable for the ICAO.

Despite Russian and Belarusian argumentation, the vast majority of the Council members were in favor of continuing the investigation concerning missing information. The discussion turned more political, though. The representative of the United Kingdom responded to the Russian comment on the detained passengers that with no contrary evidence, the only plausible explanation was that it had been an operation designed by the Belarusian authorities to lead to the detention of Mr. Pratasevich and Ms. Sapega, and for this reason, the investigation should focus on this aspect. The Russian responded that if the Council wanted to discuss the aspect in greater detail, he could share the video showing the involvement of Mr. Pratasevich in military activities in Donbas, violating his country's laws and engaging in 'illegal and provocative activities.'[18] The exchange epitomizes a common scenario wherein the demarcation between advocating for the separation of politics and injecting political arguments becomes blurred. Within this context, the same speakers were trying to defend themselves or their allies by asserting the political nature of an issue while concurrently alluding to political matters themselves. Defensive depoliticization this time was employed with the intent of diverting the matter from the ICAO purview, notably with the aim of halting the investigation.

The incident was discussed again in the Council during two meetings of its subsequent 224th Session, although the investigation of the FFIT was not concluded and further evidence was still being gathered. During the third meeting, the

Chinese representative spoke about the need for the investigation to be transparent, open, and fair,[19] while the representative of Russia questioned several findings and stressed that 'the investigation should be objective and professional and based only on facts.'[20] During the eighth meeting, there was some discussion regarding the Belarusian request to the Council concerning sanctions imposed on its civil aviation and whether it should be considered before the final FFIT report is available.[21] At this stage, there was neither observable politicization nor depoliticization of the debate, with only subtle calls for objective investigation from the representatives of Russia and China.

The deliberations about the forced landing of the FR4978 were continued during the 225th session of the Council in January 2022, following the emergence of initial findings from the investigation. Notably, these debates occurred shortly before the escalation of tensions between Russia and the West, precipitated by the Russian invasion of Ukraine. The debates were more confrontational and, as a consequence, featured defensive depoliticization. According to the investigation report, the bomb threat had been deliberately false, but the FFIT was not able to determine any individual or state responsible. The report mentioned missing information, including the recordings from the Cockpit Voice Recorder that were not preserved and some information that was not provided by the Belarusian side. Regarding the arrested journalists, it was reported that according to Belarusian authorities, they found out about their presence when their phones were logged into the Belarusian network. The Council was also informed that additional evidence had been submitted after the report's publication.[22] The discussion featured some critical remarks against Belarusian authorities. The observer from Poland said diversion to Minsk was predicated on the instruction of the Minsk Area Control Centre (ACC) controller and that Polish authorities had obtained evidence that 'third parties engaged in an operation to detain a passenger on board Flight FR4978 were present in the Minsk ACC to ensure the flight was diverted for that purpose.'[23] The Minister of Transport and Communications of Lithuania spoke about the evidence that 'the Belarusian authorities had interfered in the Ryanair Flight FR4978 for the sole purpose of detaining a specific passenger.'[24] The representative of the United States said the report left little doubt that 'Belarus had manufactured a false bomb threat in order to forcefully divert Ryanair Flight FR4978 to land in Minsk for the purpose of detaining opposition journalist Raman Pratasevich and his companion, Sofia Sapega,' commenting that the incident 'constituted a direct affront to international norms, an egregious act of transnational repression, and a dangerous manipulation of the international civil aviation system by Belarus for domestic political purposes.'[25] The British representative said the only plausible explanation was that 'the events in question had been orchestrated by Belarus in order to detain two passengers on board the aircraft, in flagrant disregard for the safety and security of civil aviation.'[26] The Canadian representative said it appeared that 'Belarusian authorities had orchestrated the diversion and forced landing of a civilian aircraft for the sole purpose of arresting a political opponent, thus representing a blatant misuse of international civil aviation.'[27] The German representative commented that the entire incident had been fabricated in order to obtain the objective of arresting Pratasevich and Sapega. Apart from these examples, many representatives condemned the act, called for the continuation of the investigation and transferring the information to the UN, most being more or less critical of Belarus.[28] Consequently, Belarus faced substantial criticism for its actions, particularly from representatives of Western nations.

As before, Belarus was defended by the representative of Russia, who spoke about the ICAO's goals to promote cooperation and understanding among the nations. The representative criticized ICAO for the social media post from May 23, 2021,[29] claiming it demonstrated 'having taken a political position, and pre-emptive of the outcome of any investigation.' The Russian commented on the accusatory statements in the Council toward the government of Belarus and sanctions imposed by some states on Belarus as 'politically motivated and part of a collective effort to interfere in the domestic affairs of a sovereign State.' The representative argued that Belarusian authorities acted to preserve aviation safety, concluding that the Council should focus its attention on the sanctions imposed on Belarus or 'run the risk of international civil aviation being turned into a political tool.'[30] In his intervention, the representative employed defensive depoliticization in a very direct way. He referred to the ICAO's biased attitude and criticized the sanctions against Belarus as being political, suggesting the ICAO should first and foremost tackle them. In doing so, the representative appeared to have tried to redirect the Council's attention, employing defense through offense tactics.

Russia and Belarus received support from the representative of China, who argued there should be no discrimination or singling-out of any member state, particularly when information was still missing, and underlined that Belarus did not breach the Chicago Convention, according to the report. Apart from that, several representatives appeared to genuinely have sought the Council to focus on aviation issues in their interventions, with neither side being favored. For example, the representative of Brazil said the Council should address the issue from a strictly legal and technical perspective according to its competence, whereas the representative of Nigeria called for preserving the Council's neutrality on the matter and for cooperation.[31] Such statements naturally reflected many similar ones discussed earlier in the book. They demonstrated the attempts to depoliticize the deliberations of technical ICAO. At the same time, it cannot be ruled out that such statements were also meant to defend the attacked state, since even the interventions by the representative of China were rather balanced in their tone. This observation reveals a potential merit of defensive depoliticization. When used modestly, without political accusations against another side, and by a state not directly engaged in the conflict, it may be impossible to distinguish neutral from defensive depoliticization.

The discussion reemerged in reference to the wording of the summary. According to the original proposition drafted by the President, the Council, among other things, expressed concern at the gaps in information and the inconsistencies contained in the evidence provided by Belarus, referred to the deliberately false bomb threat, condemned the practices, and requested the FFIT to continue its work.[32] The representative of Russia, among other things, cautioned against taking 'a potentially hasty decision' and proposed that reference to inconsistencies in the evidence should refer to all states concerned. Regarding further investigation, the Russian said that 'given the political commitments of Member States, it would be important to ensure objectivity in considering any information received by the FFIT through these channels.'[33] In this statement, the Russian representative accused other states of injecting politics into the investigation, which can be interpreted as an attempt to question the credibility of the future report, another face of the defensive tactics through depoliticization.

During the subsequent discussion, the representative of South Africa agreed with the Russian that there were inconsistencies in information provided by various parties, whereas the representatives of Spain, Greece, France, Germany, the United Kingdom, and Finland expressed their support of the draft summary. Eventually, the text of the summary was slightly updated to refer to 'gaps in information provided by Belarus and the inconsistences in the evidence provided to the FFIT,' with objections to the final text being expressed by Russia and China.[34]

During the same meeting, the Council dealt with the sanctions imposed by some states against Belarus, another aspect of the FR4978 controversy. According to the Belarusian formal request, 21 'blockading states'[35] closed their airspace to aircraft registered in Belarus between May 28 and June 8, 2021, and imposed restrictions on the access of such aircraft to international airspace. The paper invited the Council to urge contracting states 'to refrain from using civil aviation for purposes incompatible with the objectives of the Convention' and to urge the blockading States to lift all restrictions.[36] While presenting the paper, the Belarusian Minister of Transport and Communications said that according to his government, the sanctions were 'of a discriminatory and political nature' and constituted an air blockade of Belarus. The Minister also complained about the negative campaign by the mass media, which had serious implications for Belarus and its people.[37] Like before the representative of Russia, the Belarusian attempted to picture the sanctions as political interference with aviation.

The Council first discussed whether the issue should be deferred until the final FFIT report is available, as proposed by the President of the Council. The representative of Russia, supported by the representative of China, asserted that the two issues were not related in any way and that the Council should consider the Belarusian request. Similarly, the South African representative failed to discern a clear connection between the FFIT report and the Belarusian request, while the Nigerian representative suggested the consideration of the request, proposing that if the deliberations reached an impasse necessitating the final report, it could be deferred for subsequent review. Several representatives argued for deferring the consideration until the FFIT final report was ready. In response, the representative of Russia remarked that states that imposed sanctions were now against proceeding with the consideration of the Belarusian request.[38] This part of the discussion did not feature explicit depoliticization rhetoric as a defensive tactic. In turn, it featured a typical depoliticization tool of endless postponing deliberations, in this case employed both by the President of the Council and by some delegations. Subtle depoliticization rhetoric could be seen in the Russian intervention that suggested those guilty of imposing sanctions were against considering the issue, a statement with some qualities of offensive depoliticization.

In the end, the Council discussed the Belarusian request. The representative of Russia expressed his delegation's solidarity with the government of Belarus, spoke about the sanctions violating international law and called for their immediate removal, and that member states should 'refrain from using international civil aviation for any purpose incompatible with the aims of the Chicago Convention,' a statement which can be interpreted as accusing Western states of politicizing civil aviation. The representative of China also spoke in favor of the Belarusian request, highlighting the Council's responsibility to give technical considerations to any issues brought before it 'free from political interference.'[39] In this instance, depoliticization rhetoric was used in a reversed way than normally. Calls for separating from politics were meant not to adjourn the inconvenient discussions but to introduce them as they were to confront the alleged politicization of civil aviation committed by the Western states. It should be kept in mind, though, that the discussion on sanctions against Belarus simultaneously can be considered as a backlash concerning the criticism against Belarus for the diversion of the FR4978 flight, thus another example of defense through offense.

Similarly as during the preliminary discussion on whether the Council should consider the issue, a number of delegations claimed the final FFIT report was needed to proceed. In accordance with the suggestion by the South African representative, the President proposed noting the Belarusian request and reconsidering the subject at a future meeting after the Secretariat assesses legal and procedural aspects.[40] The Russian representative responded by calling for condemnation of 'the use of international civil aviation for purposes incompatible with the objectives of the Chicago Convention,' otherwise the Council would have accepted what he considered 'the air blockade of Belarus.'[41] Although several representatives argued it was premature to refer the issue to the Secretariat, the President's proposition was accepted by the Council.[42] In a way typical for depoliticization in IOs, the sensitive decision was thus postponed, while the intervention of the Russian representative in a more glaring way demonstrates a diplomatic tactic of presenting Belarus as the victim of illegal Western sanctions, mirroring one of the classic Soviet diplomatic techniques.

The next stage of deliberations on the FR4978 controversy took place in July 2022 at the 226th session of the Council, already when the level of estrangement between Russia and the West had skyrocketed following the Russian invasion of Ukraine. Although other instances of politicization and depoliticization on the forum of the ICAO in regard to the Russia–West estrangement occurred earlier in 2022, for clarity, they will be introduced later. Regarding the FR4978 controversy, the FFIT final report was eventually ready in July 2022, concluding that the bomb threat was deliberately false. The report referred to the testimony of the Belarusian controller, which contradicted the Belarusian version and reflected the involvement of an unidentified individual who had been given access to the Minsk ACC.[43] According to the investigation, an unidentified individual had entered the ACC and had given the controller instructions that compelled the pilot to divert to Minsk while the controller was requested to cover this fact.[44]

A heated discussion followed the presentation of the report. The representative of the United Kingdom said it was then possible to attribute state responsibility for the incident to Belarus despite efforts to cover up their action and that Belarus 'clearly endangered an aircraft and its passengers for political purposes.'[45] In turn, the representative of Russia said the report 'appeared to represent a deliberate attempt to shape the main conclusions to match certain predetermined outcomes by which the Republic of Belarus would be blamed for everything.' The Russian underlined flaws in the investigation and called it 'one of those substandard action movies about Russian bad guys,' concluding by giving the example of a plane being forced to land at Vienna airport in 2013 to search if Edward Snowden was onboard when the ICAO Council took no action.[46] The Belarusian observer also spoke about some countries having 'a predetermined agenda of wishing to accuse Belarus' and recalled similar incidents in Germany a year after the FR4978 incident and more recently in Spain.[47] The defensive tactics thus focused on picturing the report and the ICAO as politically biased. Interestingly, even though the deliberations concerned Belarus, the Russian representative argued that criticism against Belarus stemmed from the negative Western approach toward Russia, further justifying the analysis of this controversy within the framework of the estrangement between Russia and the West. As previously, the Russian representative pictured the Belarusian government as the victim of the pro-Western politicization of ICAO.

Numerous representatives voiced criticism against Belarus and advocated for its condemnation. Among the most critical statements, the representative of Canada spoke about the 'blatant misuse of civil aviation for a purpose inconsistent with the aims of the Chicago Convention,' which 'represented an attack on media freedom.'[48] The United States alternate representative spoke about the false bomb alert manufactured 'for the benefit of the Lukashenko regime's own political agenda' and said ICAO should not allow 'civil aircraft in mid-flight to become instruments of political repression.'[49] In response, the representative of Russia reiterated that 'civil aviation should not be used for political means, which would be contrary to the principles of the Chicago Convention' and that Belarus was not given the opportunity to respond to some of the questions.[50] This statement can be interpreted as a very straightforward defensive depoliticization attempt, arguing that the accusations against Belarus were political and should not take place. Admittedly, the statements against Belarus were critical, confrontational, and sometimes featured political overtones, but at the same time were based on the offenses reported by the investigation.

Eventually, the Council noted that 'a number of senior officials of the Government of Belarus had knowingly participated or were involved in providing information about a false bomb threat to the flight leading to its diversion to land at Minsk Airport,' concluded endangering the safety of the Ryanair Flight FR4978 on the instructions of the senior government officials of Belarus, and condemned the actions of the government of Belarus. The conclusions were to be published on the ICAO website, while the Secretariat was to prepare a working paper to be submitted to the Assembly. The Russian representative conveyed the reservations of his delegation regarding the decision.[51] The Council's standpoint was critical of Belarus but did not refer to the detention of two passengers as was expected by several representatives. Still, defensive depoliticization once again proved unsuccessful.

Following the discussion that led to the condemnation of the Belarusian government, the Council once again undertook the Belarusian request regarding Western sanctions. Similarly as during the previous session of the Council, the working paper submitted by Belarus reported that certain states closed their airspace to aircraft registered in Belarus, that blockading states did not agree to hold consultations, and that the action violated a number of articles of the Chicago Convention and was intended to discriminate against Belarusian aviation. The proposal urged all contracting states to refrain from using civil aviation for purposes incompatible with the objectives of the Convention and urged the blockading States to lift all restrictions.[52] The working paper, presented by the Belarusian observer, was then endorsed by the Representative of Russia.[53] Bearing in mind a close link between the sanctions and the FR4978 incident, the bare bringing of the issue before ICAO exemplified the defense through offense tactics and picturing Belarus as the victim of the controversy.

The proceeding discussion in many ways resembled the earlier ones regarding the FR4978 controversy, with many representatives voicing strong accusations against Belarus. For example, the US alternate representative said that 'the Lukashenko regime of Belarus had taken actions that clearly undermined the safety of international civil aviation' and other states responded justifiably, while the paper was an attempt to 'redirect blame for its own violations of international civil aviation law.'[54] The representative of France said it was justified to impose restrictions since it was not possible 'to trust any state that invented false bomb threats for the sole purpose of arresting someone who was on board an aircraft.'[55] Similarly to previous instances, the representative of South Africa emphasized the importance of consistency in the actions of the Council and argued that aviation should not be used for political purposes and that the Council had determined the culpability of Belarus but not of the airline operators, concluding that punishing them was not justified. He also wondered if the reference to 'Lukashenko regime' by the representative of the United States was an appropriate language. The representatives of India and Zambia also spoke about the need for consistency in Council's actions.[56] Statements such as these appear to adopt a neutral stance concerning the tensions between Russia and the West, focusing instead on safeguarding the ICAO from politicization. However, particularly the South African intervention is difficult to definitely classify as neutral or supportive for Belarus, revealing proximity between defensive depoliticization and more general depoliticization moves which seek to keep politics away from the organization, with rhetorical arguments often being similar.

As before, the Belarusian standpoint was strongly supported by the representative of Russia, who argued that the discussion should not concern Belarus but the countries that unilaterally introduced measures against Belarus, which according to him warranted a criminal investigation. He also said the Council was engaging in double standards, with one item being claimed to be consistent with the aims of the Chicago Convention and the other not.[57] In this nuanced way, the Russian again accused the Council of lack of consistency and favoring the West, employing depoliticization for offensive purposes, with the main argument that not dealing with the issue would mean favoring Western countries, although the defensive character of the entire discussion of the sanctions against Belarus needs to be acknowledged as well.

In conclusion of the meeting, the President of the Council agreed that in the past, the Council did not always act consistently with the closing of the airspace and proposed referring the matter to the Legal Affairs and External Relations Bureau of the Secretariat to analyze past practices, suspending further consideration on the item.[58] A typical method of depoliticization by postponing of decision-making was thus used again within this controversy. As to the problem of Western sanctions against Belarus, despite the acknowledgment of inconsistencies in the Council's behavior, since the Council did not endorse the Belarusian request, this instance of defensive depoliticization should also be assessed as ineffective.

The Council considered the draft working paper on the infractions of the Chicago Convention by Belarus in connection to the incident with flight FR4978 during the subsequent 17th meeting of the 226th session. According to the document, the Council invited the Assembly to acknowledge and condemn the Belarusian infraction of its obligations under the Chicago Convention.[59] The atmosphere in the Council was already very tense since directly before proceeding with that item, the Council was dealing with the working paper on the infractions of the Convention by Russia, which will be discussed later in this chapter. At the beginning of the discussion, the representative of Russia delivered a statement, arguing that such papers 'undermine ICAO's longstanding impeccable reputation' and that President Emeritus Assad Kotaite would be terrified by it. The representative stated that the FFIT 'concocted an accusation against the government of a sovereign state under pressure from a number of states' and that the draft working paper was 'based on inaccurate information that goes beyond the mandate of the Organization and tarnished ICAO's longstanding impeccable reputation.' The Russian representative once again reminded the incident with the aircraft of the President of Bolivia forced to land in Vienna, which should be investigated.[60] In this exceptionally strong statement, though without using words 'politics' or 'political,' the representative accused ICAO of dealing with political issues which lied beyond its jurisdiction, deviating from political neutrality and lack of consistency, which in principle repeated its earlier arguments, though this using stronger words.

Despite Russian opposition, most of the speakers were in favor of the draft working paper and the Council approved it with only minor amendment proposed by the French delegation. The Russian representative once again opposed, claiming that, in his view, the Council 'had exceeded its mandate in taking this decision on this item,' and that it 'was not the UN Security Council, which would have been the more appropriate body to have held the preceding discussion.' The Russian also cautioned that by exceeding its mandate, the Council would meet the same fate as the League of Nations and expressed concern with 'the politicization of the Organization.'[61] In response, the representative of France said he disagreed with the Russian statement, commenting it was 'paradoxical that the Russian Federation would attempt to lecture the ICAO Council especially given the highly charged language and terminology that the Representative of the Russian Federation had just used.'[62] This exchange underscored several characteristic features of depoliticization perceived as a defensive diplomatic strategy. Notably, these include the accusations of introducing politics into the organization while concurrently employing political arguments. Additionally, it was asserted that the issue at hand should not fall under the purview of ICAO. The Council's decision did not mark the ultimate conclusion of deliberations in ICAO regarding the forced landing of the FR4978 flight. The issue was undertaken by the Assembly at its 41st session in 2022 but was discussed together with the issue of the Russian invasion of Ukraine, thus will be introduced later in this chapter. The issue was undertaken by the UN Security Council as well, but only after it was dealt with by the Assembly.

The Russian invasion of Ukraine

Russia, in cooperation with Belarus, invaded Ukraine on February 24, 2022, marking another stage of the Russo-Ukrainian conflict lasting since 2014, which featured the annexation of Crimea in 2014 and subsequent hybrid war connected with Russian support for the Ukrainian separatists in the Eastern oblasts of the country.[63] The Kremlin often accused the Ukrainian government of being extremist while persistently destabilizing the situation in the Eastern parts of Ukraine with the aim of restoring a regime that would align closely with Moscow's interests.[64] The conflict escalated again in late 2021 when Russia began deploying significant numbers of troops near the Ukrainian border.[65] On February 21, 2022, Russia recognized the self-proclaimed 'Donetsk People's Republic' and the 'Luhansk People's Republic,'[66] paving the way for sending Russian troops to the two regions as peacekeeping support and the subsequent full-scale invasion of Ukraine. Once it began on February 24, in a TV address, Russian President Vladimir Putin outlined a series of reasons for the so-called special military operation, including a threat to Russian security generated by territorial expansion of NATO in the 2000s and imposed by Ukrainian extremists and the Nazi government. Russia demanded, among other things, demilitarization, denazification, and denuclearization of Ukraine.[67] At the time of writing (April 2024), the ongoing war seems far from settled.

The Russian invasion of Ukraine became one of the most crucial developments in international relations of its time, leading to wide-scale international reactions, including the imposition of sanctions by the West. In the UN, the issue was being discussed already before the actual invasion. On February 23, 2022, an extraordinary meeting of the Security Council was held at Ukraine's request with regard to the anticipated Russian attack, which began when the meeting was underway. The UN Secretary-General unsuccessfully appealed to Putin to bring the troops back to

Russia. The UN General Assembly (GA) adopted resolutions regarding Ukraine. In the resolution from March 2, it demanded that 'the Russian Federation immediately, completely and unconditionally withdraw all its armed forces from the territory of Ukraine within its internationally recognized borders.' On March 24, 2022, in another resolution, the GA demanded that Russia immediately stop hostilities in Ukraine and end attacks on the civilian population and infrastructure. Only Russia, Belarus, North Korea, Syria, and Eritrea voted against both resolutions.[68] However, no decision was made by the Security Council, where Russia, as a permanent member, holds a veto power.

Besides being dealt with by the UN, the Russian invasion of Ukraine has also initiated a number of tense debates in ICAO, with strong political overtones and the use of defensive depoliticization rhetoric. The Council was the first to undertake the crisis, already one day after the invasion. The issue was introduced by the President of the Council, who said ICAO 'could not remain indifferent to events that were inconsistent with the principles laid out in the Charter of the United Nations, nor could it disregard its own charter, the Convention on International Civil Aviation.'[69] Such an active role of the President of the Council was extraordinary compared to the cases of politicized debates analyzed previously in this volume. Following the Secretary General's summary, which referenced the NOTAMs issued by Ukraine and Russia, indicating the closure of airspace over Ukraine and parts of adjacent airspace in Russia,[70] several representatives voiced criticism against the invasion, displaying varying degrees of assertiveness. For example, the representative of the United Kingdom called the invasion 'an unprovoked and premeditated act of aggression,' the representative of Finland spoke about ICAO's obligation to 'react to its fundamental tenets being violently and ruthlessly attacked,' while the representative of Colombia said the Russian attack 'not only jeopardized the safety of air travelers, but ignored the very principles of the Chicago Convention and its Annexes, and constituted a violation of the UN Charter.'[71]

A particularly strong statement was delivered by the alternate representative of Ukraine, who spoke, among other things, about 'the irony of having been brutally attacked by a permanent member of the UN Security Council.' He addressed the representative of Russia, saying that

> the world was witnessing war crimes being committed by the leadership of the Russian Federation, and would see to it that those responsible for these crimes, and the deaths of thousands of innocent people, were prosecuted at an international court of justice'

and solicited him 'to stop people's suffering and to stop people's tears.' Very critical was the representative of the United States, who referred to the words of the US President Joe Biden that 'Putin had chosen a premeditated war that would bring a catastrophic loss of life and human suffering.' The representative of the Netherlands called the invasion an 'indefensible act of war and a flagrant violation of international law.'[72] The representative of France spoke about 'paranoid revisionist line of the Russian Federation [that] could not be accepted.'[73] Basically, all the speakers, besides the Russian representative, were critical of the invasion, many calling for condemnation.[74] Regardless of the validity of these interventions, the confrontational nature of the remarks clearly signaled the politicization of the ICAO deliberations.

A few representatives did not attack Russia directly and instead focused on humanitarian problems and threats to aviation, calling for a diplomatic solution.[75] One of the less critical statements was delivered by the representative of South Africa, who, on the one hand, said that 'military invasion of one country by another would always be harmful, regardless of the century or the setting in which it occurred,' but on the other hand argued that the Council should 'eschew matters of politics to focus strictly on civil aviation matters related to safety, security and the environment,' and that there were no 'parameters that defined the circumstances under which condemnation should or should not be conferred.' Concluding, the South African cautioned against selectively determining the importance of conflicts and called to avoid the risk 'of politicizing this or other occurrences.'[76] This stance can be interpreted as an effort to shield the ICAO from politicization, while simultaneously potentially indicating sympathy toward Russia since, given the circumstances, direct defense of Russian actions in Ukraine would not have been feasible. A similar situation, with the South African position being possible to interpret either as neutral or defensive regarding the criticized side, was also visible regarding the FR4978 controversy discussed earlier, revealing close proximity between neutral and defensive depoliticization.

Depoliticization as a defensive tool in a very direct way was employed by Russia. Its representative said that he had consistently advocated that ICAO 'should not be a venue for discussing political agendas,' but since the subject was placed before the Council, he wished to deliver a speech. He spoke about Russian proposals to reach an agreement with NATO countries on the principles of security in Europe being 'met either with cynical deceit and lies, or attempts at pressure and blackmail' and about NATO expansion despite Russia's protests. He continued that the 'military machine' was coming close to Russia's borders, which was happening 'partly because the Russian Federation lost self-confidence after the collapse of the Soviet Union in the 1980s.' According to the representative, NATO lies and 'cheating behavior' contradicted the principles of international relations and the generally recognized norms of morality, 'demonstrating lies and hypocrisy rather than justice and truth.' He said that after the collapse of the USSR, the United States and other Western partners 'immediately tried to squeeze, finish off and destroy the Russian Federation completely,' referred to active support of separatism and mercenary gangs in southern Russia, and said that despite all this in December 2021 Russia 'once again made an attempt to agree with the United States and its allies on the principles of ensuring security in Europe and on not expanding NATO,' though with no effect. The representative mentioned NATO leadership openly speaking about the need to advance its infrastructure at the Russian border and claimed it would be irresponsible for Russia to continue only to observe such developments. He referred to hostile anti-Russian sentiment being created in the territories adjacent to the Russian Federation, which he called 'historical territories,' and added that 'NATO was only an instrument of United States' foreign policy,' that the '"policy of containment of Russia" had obvious geopolitical dividends' but for Russia, it was a matter of life and death, its existence and sovereignty. Regarding the situation in Ukraine, the Russian representative said that after the coup d'état in Ukraine in 2014, the forces that seized power had finally abandoned the peaceful settlement of the conflict regarding Donbas. Russia had been doing everything to resolve the situation with peaceful means, but it was necessary to 'immediately stop the genocide against the millions of people living in Donbas who rely only on Russia,' which was the main motive for recognizing the People's Republic of Donbas. Once the Republic asked Russia for assistance, it was decided to conduct a special military operation. According to the representative, the goal was 'to protect people who had been subjected to bullying and genocide by the Kyiv Regime for eight years.' The representative declared that Russia would stride to demilitarize and liberate Ukraine and remove Nazis and pro-Nazi ideologies, and that Russian plans did not include occupation or strikes on Ukrainian citizens or towns. Responding to the Ukrainian intervention, he expressed sympathy with those suffering, but hurting civilians could not be avoided because of force majeure. He concluded by asking why the death of people following the Minsk agreement did not attract attention.[77] The statement was overtly political, akin only to certain interventions observed in the context of the Arab–Israeli conflict within the ICAO, as detailed in Chapter 4. The Russian representative made no reference to aviation, contrary to other speakers who even when being very critical of Russia, drew more or less direct links to aviation, usually in the context of safety or infrastructure. The Russian began with an argument that such a political issue should not be discussed in ICAO, but in his intervention, we could see a characteristic declaration about not wanting to engage in a political debate but being forced to. The representative accused others, particularly NATO countries, of both injecting politics into the ICAO and being guilty of pushing Russia to invade Ukraine.

Further defensive depoliticization was employed by Russia during subsequent discussions on the Council's decision on the issue. The Russian representative inquired if the Secretariat 'would clarify to what extent the Council was authorized to examine issues related to the actions of member states,'[78] thus once again questioning ICAO's mandate to deal with issues he considered political. The representative of China said that since 'the Council was reviewing text containing politically sensitive vocabulary,' the conclusions should align with similar UN statements.[79] The South African representative also underscored the need to use words carefully in all the conclusions. Eventually, the Council, among other things, condemned 'the violation of the territorial integrity and sovereignty of a United Nations Member State, including sovereign airspace, which is inconsistent with the principles of the Charter of the United Nations and Article 1 of the Chicago Convention' and urged Russia to cease its unlawful activities,[80] a relatively strong statement for the ICAO. Defensive depoliticization employed by Russia once again proved unsuccessful, although criticism against Russia was omnipresent, and even voices neutrally calling for separation from politics were not particularly loud.

ICAO deliberations with a close link to the Russian invasion of Ukraine concerned dual registration of aircraft and were connected to the sanctions imposed by Western countries against Russia. Following the cancelation of the lease agreements for the aircraft, Russian authorities did not return them and attempted to register them in Russia, contrary to international aviation law. For the first time, the issue was brought before the ICAO Council on March 7, 2022, by the request of France, whose representative explained that according to recent information, Russia had requested its operators using leased aircraft registered in other countries to place them on its own register.[81] The representative of Russia responded that the Council should avoid discussions based on rumors and cited a statement by the Russian Federal Air Transport Agency from March 5, which stated that 'in conjunction with unfriendly decisions by several foreign States with respect to civil aviation of the Russian Federation, Russian airlines and passengers have become an instrument of and hostages to a political struggle.' The representative said that Russian actions related to civil aviation 'had always been in accordance with the Chicago Convention' and called upon the ICAO Council and Secretariat to avoid politicization by making insinuations or allegations that were not based on officially verified information, which would mean 'turning ICAO and civil aviation as a whole, into an instrument of political struggle.'[82] The representative of France responded that it was not his intention to try 'to politicize the work of the Organization' but to fulfill his role in ensuring aviation safety and security, underlining the dangers of flying without airworthiness certificates,[83] a statement bearing the hallmarks of discursive depoliticization. Besides these arguments, the discussion at this stage was not particularly confrontational compared to earlier ones. The Russian intervention was a typical example of depoliticization as a defensive tool. Besides mentioning unverified information, which later proved to be true, the Russian claimed discussing the issue would mean bringing politics to the ICAO and making it a political forum, hoping to terminate the inconvenient deliberations.

The Council made no decision regarding the problem of dual registration, which reemerged during its subsequent 226th session held in May and June 2022, this time in connection to other Western accusations against Russia, which led to heated debates on the working paper submitted by 19 Western states.[84] According to the paper, Russia had infringed several articles of the Chicago Convention by infringing the Ukrainian sovereign airspace, destroying civil aviation infrastructure, passing the law demanding Russian airlines re-register aircraft on the Russian Registry without the agreement of the current state of registry, and allowing its airlines to operate aircraft with revoked certificates of airworthiness. The paper requested the Council to report the infringements to the Contracting States and the Assembly and urge Russia to stop them.[85] At the beginning of the discussion, the representative of Finland said the paper was not supposed to be a political statement but to offer a technical and safety-oriented approach, called upon the Council to urge Russia to immediately stop all of its infractions and recalled a precedent from 1990 and the invasion of Kuwait by Iraq when the matter had been referred to the Assembly which condemned Iraqi actions.[86] From the beginning, we could thus observe attempts to defend the paper from accusations of politicization in a discursive way.

Responding, the representative of Russia first spoke about principles of unity and cooperation in the preamble of the Chicago Convention and wondered if 'any member of the Council now wanted to abandon the wisdom of the principles contained in this preamble' and 'whether members of the Council now believed the preamble to be outdated.'[87] He referred to hostile sentiments presented recently by the Director-General for Transport and Mobility of the European Commission, Mr. Henrik Hololei, who spoke about sanctions destroying Russian civil aviation. The representative said the paper suggested Russia violated article 1 and other provisions of the Chicago Convention, asking whether article 1 was not violated when NATO forces were bombing Yugoslavia, during military operations in Iraq in 2003, in Syria in 2014, and others. He noted that 'it was not the Russian Federation that had violated the provisions of the Chicago Convention when a number of countries had unilaterally imposed a ban on flights of Russian aircraft into their airspace' and that the closure of the national airspace by a number of states 'on the basis of national segregation' was followed by termination of leasing agreements and cancellation of aircraft certificates of airworthiness. He said that through such actions, states had deliberately violated fundamental human rights. The retaliatory actions taken by Russia were to be 'of an extremely forced nature and were taken exclusively in the interests of protecting the country's national security.' The Russian representative concluded by wondering if the Council believed Russia had no right to protect its national security in response to unfriendly actions and cautioned against 'the ICAO Council being used as an instrument of political pressure on individual States for the benefit of other States,' and expected that states which imposed sanctions on Russian civil aviation system and had presented the paper explain their legal position.[88] The Russian defense thus centered around being forced to act in response to Western sanctions, arguing ICAO's inconsistent reaction compared to the armed conflicts in which the West was engaged and suggesting that through such papers, the Council was being turned into a 'political instrument,' even though the entire discussion was not particularly confrontational. Defensive depoliticization resembled traditional Soviet diplomatic technique of picturing itself as a victim.

During the discussion, most speakers underlined the safety concerns connected to dual registration, but a few were more critical and, in their statements, also referred to the war in Ukraine. For example, the representative of Japan said his delegation 'condemned the violation of the territorial integrity and sovereignty of a Member State of the United Nations, including its sovereign airspace,' noted that Russia clearly violated various articles of the Chicago Convention and that the Council should bring the issue to the Assembly. The Spanish representative said that no action from the Council would damage ICAO's reputation. The representative of the United Kingdom said Russia kept breaching the Convention despite ample opportunities for corrective actions and responded to the calls for consistency, citing Iraq's invasion of Kuwait and ICAO's response at the time. The

Russian representative responded that contrary to other countries, Russia continued to place a high priority on aviation safety, but unfriendly actions against Russian civil aviation made it necessary first to consider these actions, concluding that all of them were taken only because of the actions against Russia. The Russian said that 'if the ICAO Council continued to politicize the issue of dual registration, then it would not be possible to make any progress,' whereas during the subsequent intervention contended that in order to address the Russian violations of the Chicago Convention, it was imperative for other violations to cease first, and that the Council should ensure that 'ICAO was not being used as an instrument of political pressure.' He concluded that Russia intended to rectify the situation, was not happy about its actions, and placed a high priority on safety, but his country's violation of the Chicago Convention was necessary in response to actions by other countries.[89] The representative thus repeated earlier arguments, underlining the guilt of other states and accusing the Council of falling victim to politicization by considering the item, but also expressed goodwill and readiness to solve the problem once the sanctions are removed.

Similarly as during previous discussions related to the Russia–West conflict, several delegations argued for the political neutrality of the ICAO. The representative of South Africa spoke about 'selective condemnation' and the need for the Council to act consistently, recalling similar cases that the Council had dismissed on the basis of the political character of the matter, and agreed with the Russian that before dealing with double registration which is not allowed, the Council should address the actions taken by other countries that made Russia to take action, while later urged the Council not to close the item definitively to allow Russian delegation to present its own working paper. The representative of China argued that the issue raised technical, legal, and political implications. The Council should avoid a decision that might give the impression of political interference, while dialogue between the parties should be encouraged. The representative of Zambia said it was important to condemn violations of the Convention. However, it seemed that the actions were taken in response to other violations triggering the Russian response, so the Council should consider all the violations. The representative of India said there were always two sides, and the Russian points also needed to be taken into account.[90] As before, it is impossible to unequivocally assess these statements as either reflecting the genuine will to defend ICAO from politicization or subtle attempts to defend Russia concerning the unambiguous circumstances of a military invasion that made direct defense more difficult. Admittedly, countries whose representatives argued for the political neutrality in ICAO belonged to those that voted similarly to Russia in the UN GA in 2022[91] which can speak of closer relationships, but such sentiments were not entirely clear in their representatives' statements.

The debate concluded with an exchange of positions between representatives of Ukraine and Russia. The observer from Ukraine said Russia had been violating fundamental principles of the Convention since 2014 and, in February 2022, 'had unleashed its full-scale barbaric war against Ukraine asserting itself as a persistent violator of the norms and principles of international law and a wide array of binding international treaties.' She said Russia had effectively stolen aircraft belonging to lessors and attempted to register them in Russia and that it was destroying civil aviation infrastructure in Ukraine. The Russian representative responded that the Ukrainian statement 'went beyond the bounds of the Chicago Convention' and that the UN Security Council 'was the appropriate venue for such statements and not the ICAO Council,' which constituted a very clear example of defensive depoliticization. Throughout the debate, the Russian delegation argued that the issue was political, that Russia was forced to act the way it acted by the Western sanctions, and that the Council was not acting neutrally and consistently. This did not work, though. With most delegations being in favor of the working paper, the Council requested the Secretary General to report the infractions to all contracting states and submit the matter for consideration at the Assembly.[92]

The subsequent phase of the estrangement between Russia and Western nations at the 226th session of the Council revolved around discussions regarding sanctions against Russia. According to the working paper presented by Russia, a number of ICAO member states[93] have breached several articles of the Chicago Convention through restrictions on flights in their airspace by civil aircraft of Russian operators, suspension of airworthiness certificates for aircraft operated by Russian airlines by Bermuda Civil Aviation Authority and Irish Aviation Authority, termination of lease agreements with Russian airlines by Aircraft Leasing Ireland, and denying spare parts and maintenance of aircraft. The working paper also referred to the sanctions against Belarus from the previous year, arguing that 'over recent years, the use of international civil aviation as an instrument of political pressure on "undesirable" States has become standard practice' which caused reputational damage to ICAO. The working paper, among other things, requested the Council to urge the immediate stop of all infractions, to enter into negotiations, and to take note of the Council's statement that 'any attempts to use ICAO and its Council as an instrument of political pressure on other countries are unacceptable and to refrain from any further attempts to politicize ICAO activities.'[94]

The working papers included explicit references to politics and politicization, which were to be tackled. This episode of the politicized Council debates regarding the Russian invasion of Ukraine differs slightly from others because it was Russia to have raised the issue. The working paper criticized the states that were critical of Russia and imposed sanctions against it. Aviation sanctions are undoubtedly connected to aviation, and ICAO appeared as an appropriate forum to discuss them, but the item directly corresponded with the Russian invasion, which would be reflected in the subsequent discussion. For this reason, the introduction of the working paper by Russia, criticizing other states for politicizing ICAO, should also be considered as an expression of defensive depoliticization, though executed in a more offensive manner.

Introducing the working paper, the Russian representative said its structure mirrored the one presented earlier by the EU countries to emphasize their infringements of the Chicago Convention and that its goal was to present reasons that had forced Russia to infringe Article 18 of the Chicago Convention,[95] which was the only violation. The representative reiterated his earlier question whether the 19 co-sponsors of the working paper against Russia had the intention to destroy Russian civil aviation, questioned the safety concerns against Russia, said that the infringements by the EU states and others 'posed a real threat to the future of ICAO,' declared Russia's readiness to remedy the violations if EU states did the same, and expressed hope the Council would avoid double standards.[96] The Russian intervention did not refer strongly to political issues except for a reference to double standards, while the entire statement was not as confrontational as earlier. The reference to mirroring the Western working paper clearly indicates the defensive purpose of the Russian proposal.

During the subsequent discussion, many representatives called for the rejection of the working paper, some being critical of Russia. The representative of the United States said Russia was attempting to 'justify its own illegal actions by creating a false equivalency with the conduct of other countries.' The British representative spoke about the 'unprovoked and illegal invasion of Ukrainian territory by Russia,' that the paper was designed to distract the Council, and that the reaction by the United Kingdom was proportional and lawful. The French representative also talked about an attempt to distract the Council and that it was Russian actions that prevented Ukraine from having normal air operations, not the EU sanctions to pose a threat to aviation safety. The Spanish representative said that current events in Ukraine constituted a break in the world order, and there could be no equivalence between the invasion of one country and the imposition of restrictions. The representatives of Greece, Finland, the Netherlands, Canada, Germany, and Mexico were also very critical of Russia, whereas a more neutral position was presented by the representative of China, who said that in regard to aviation safety, all ICAO member states should act prudently and avoid negative impact on international civil aviation system, that the Council should avoid political interference, and called to act in the spirit of the Convention and to look for solutions through negotiations and consultations.[97] The Chinese statement was, therefore, very balanced, attacking and defending neither side and calling for political neutrality in the ICAO, showcasing an attitude typical of neutral depoliticization.

The representative of Russia responded by saying that both this and the previous discussion 'had been beyond the mandate of the Organization' and that the 'ICAO Council should not seek to take on the function of the UN Security Council.' The Russian added that his country was not at war with Ukraine or its people, but such discussion should take place in the UN SC rather than in ICAO.[98] As argued elsewhere in the book, statements referring to political issues being beyond ICAO's mandate are characteristic of defensive depoliticization. Interestingly, in this particular case, they were used by the side that had introduced the item. Russian arguments were thus aimed at depreciating the critical statements and terminating the more general discussion on the war in Ukraine.

The discussion was followed by certain procedural difficulties after the Russian representative moved a motion to cease further consideration and hold a secret ballot, and concluded with the Council requesting the Secretariat to analyze the issues raised and the role of ICAO regarding the imposition of sanctions,[99] another instance of postponing decision-making on sensitive, politically related issues.

The Russian–Western conflict emerged again at the 226th session of the Council during the discussion on the draft Assembly working paper on the Russian infractions of the Chicago Convention, which was a consequence of Council's earlier decisions on submitting the matter for consideration to the Assembly. According to the document, Russia violated the exclusive sovereignty of the Ukrainian airspace, committed dual-registration of aircraft, and permitted them to fly without the required documents. The Assembly was also invited to condemn the infractions of its obligations by Russia.[100] The representative of Russia said the working paper did not present the real picture of events or offer realistic ways to resolve the crisis, expressed hope that neither President of the Council nor the 19 states aimed to destroy Russian civil aviation, and said his delegation did not understand what kind of violation of airspace sovereignty was referred to in the working paper. He then reiterated his earlier question about whether Article 1 of the Convention had been violated in Vietnam, Yugoslavia in 1999, Iraq in 2003, Syria in 2014, or during other military operations by the states presenting the working paper. He said he did not want to 'go beyond the organization's mandate, but the political demands included in the text of the draft working paper and the draft Assembly resolution' left him no choice. He then said that for eight years 'the regime in Ukraine, which came to power through a bloody coup d'état literally was wiping out the Russian-speaking population of Ukraine resulting in the deaths of more than 14,000 civilians,' mentioned children being killed by the nationalists with weapons supplied to Ukraine by Western countries, and accused Ukraine of several other crimes. The Russian asked if his European colleagues were not afraid of radioactive Europe, said the paper's aim was to vilify Russia, and that in the UN GA only Ukraine and the United States annually vote against the glorification of nazism. The representative added that Russia was ready to assist the Secretary General of ICAO in preparing a new version of the draft paper, which would present an objective picture, at the same time referring to 'the infringement of the Convention by the group of states.'[101] The statement featured several arguments typical for defensive depoliticization, including claims that the working paper and draft Assembly resolution were political and biased, and accusations that ICAO did not react similarly to the conflicts waged by Western states. In a characteristic manner, the Russian representative asserted a reluctance to engage in political discourse but highlighted the necessity to do so. Furthermore, he put forth several assertions regarding purported wrongdoings by Ukraine that ostensibly compelled Russia to intervene.

Several delegations argued in favor of the draft resolution, whereas this time, no representative attempted to defend Russia or call for ICAO's neutrality. When the Russian representative proposed a motion to withdraw and re-draft the working paper, it lapsed due to lack of a seconder. Eventually, the Council approved the working paper.[102] However, the decision was not the end of deliberating the Russian invasion of Ukraine in the ICAO Council. Another occasion occurred following the request from the International Coordinating Council of Aerospace Industries Associations (ICCAIA)[103] to be represented as an Observer at the closed meetings of the 227th Session of the Council. Russia objected because earlier, ICCAIA removed its Russian members. During a short discussion, the South African representative said he understood Russian objection, claimed it was a political matter, wondered 'whether the Council should permit an international organization that took political decisions to be then permitted to attend closed meetings of the Council' and questioned the value that ICCAIA would bring to the Council. The Russian representative added that experts from Russia that were excluded from being part of its membership were not associated with any government agency and that the only explanation was that ICCAIA made the decision based solely on political considerations. The Russian reminded that ICAO was a specialized agency of the United Nations with the mandate to focus on technical issues related to aviation and that all political issues were outside of its scope and should be left to the UN Security Council, a 'more appropriate forum for issues of a political nature.' The Observer from ICCAIA responded that its decisions were not based on political considerations but on the obligation to obey Canadian law, which forced ICCAIA to expel its Russian member UAI within the general sanction. The issue did not raise wider discussion and the Council, by majority decision, approved the request.[104] What is interesting is that the Russian representative, with some support from the South African representative, sought to achieve its objective through claims that an opposite decision would mean politicization of ICAO, which should focus on technical aspects, leaving politics to the UN. This case closely resembles one of the ICAO controversies being part of the Arab–Israeli conflict, when Israel opposed granting the PLO observer status in the Assembly.

Russia–West estrangement at the 41st Assembly

Deliberations regarding the forced landing of Ryanair flight 4978 and the controversies connected to the Russian invasion of Ukraine, according to respective decisions by the Council, were concluded during the 41st session of the Assembly in September and October 2022. In addition to the scheduled discussion of items concerning infringements by Belarus and Russia, the conflict emerged even earlier during the Council elections. As noted earlier, the Council elections are composed of three parts dependent on the respective state's position in international aviation. Since the Soviet Union's accession to ICAO, both the Soviet Union and subsequently Russia have consistently been elected to the Council, typically securing positions in part one of the elections. The 41st Assembly brought unprecedented developments in that matter.

Following the normal procedure, part one of the Council elections took place on October 1, 2022. A total of 11 member states participated in the election to occupy 11 seats in the Council reserved for the states of chief importance in air transport. Russia received 80 votes, falling short of the required 86, and was the only contender not to be elected. The unprecedented situation led to intense procedural debate. The South African President of the Assembly proposed proceeding to part two of the elections, whereas the delegate of Russia, with the support from the Chinese delegate, opted for another ballot to fill the remaining part one seat. The discussion that followed had a predominantly legal character, although it is noteworthy that some delegations opposing another part one vote were from the countries typically most critical of Russia. For instance, delegates from the United States and the United Kingdom asserted that the Assembly had previously decided not to endorse Russia's candidacy, a decision they insisted should be honored. Either way, the majority of delegations voted in favor of the President's ruling. The delegate of Russia stated that Russia would not stand for election under part two (states not otherwise included which make the largest contributions to the provision of facilities for international civil air navigation) and that 'his state viewed the outcome of the vote as a purely political step that had nothing to do with the Russian Federation's position in the field of civil aviation.' He added that he accepted the decision by Western countries and referred to the pressure exerted on others, 'forcing them to act in the same fashion.' The delegate concluded that he had hoped that dialogue with all the countries would soon re-occur.[105] In this case, the statement was obviously not aimed to change anything or in any way affect the shape of the Assembly's decision, but to undermine it as political, probably not without merit since it is hard to interpret this unprecedented Council election result in isolation from the global controversy raised by the Russian invasion of Ukraine.

The 41st Assembly was also dealing with the infractions of the Convention by Belarus in reference to the FR4978 flight and by Russia, both issues being discussed under the same item. A controversial debate started in the Executive Committee (EC), which considered two papers presented by the Council based on its decisions discussed earlier, as well as two papers presented by Belarus (regarding sanctions and unilateral measures, and about states refusing to provide information necessary for maintaining the continuing airworthiness and safe operation of the aircraft) and two by Russia (about unilateral restrictive measures imposed by a group of states which Russia asserted as infractions of Articles 4, 9, 22, 44, and 82 of the Convention, and about unilateral restrictive measures which according to Russia undermined the foundations of the Convention). Unfortunately, the format of the EC minutes did not allow tracing the entire debate. The main conclusion was that the EC supported the working papers presented by the Council and did not support Belarusian and Russian papers.[106] The discussion then moved to the plenary session, where the delegate of Russia spoke about 'the unprecedented politicization of the discussions that had occurred.' He added that 'the politicization of ICAO's work was subject to double standards' that was hindering the achievements of the system of international civil aviation and threatened ICAO's authority. The delegate said Russia had done everything 'to keep ICAO as a forum for strengthening friendship and mutual respect amongst the peoples and nations of the world.' In conclusion, the Russian delegate proposed a roll-call vote on the draft resolution presented by Russia in the EC which, among other things, called upon member states to end unilateral restrictions.[107] Russian interventions exhibited all the hallmark elements of defensive depoliticization while simultaneously conveying a sense of their last-resort nature. With other forms of argumentation having proven ineffective, all that was left was to depreciate the unfavorable decisions.

Several delegations took the floor to oppose the Russian proposition. A particularly strong statement was delivered by the delegate of the United States, who said that 'it was clear that the Russian Federation was merely attempting to distract the Assembly' from its unprovoked and premeditated act of aggression against Ukraine and its continued violations of various Articles of the Chicago Convention and the UN Charter.' In its final decision, the Assembly adopted resolutions regarding Belarus and Russia, condemning the actions of both countries, among other things.[108] The defensive depoliticization employed by Russia once again proved ineffective in preventing ICAO from adopting critical decisions against Russia and Belarus.

Subsequent ICAO meetings witnessed a notable reduction in political controversies linked to the estrangement between Russia and the West. Consequently, there were fewer instances, if any, of defensive depoliticization. In the subsequent 227th and 228th sessions of the Council (with the minutes of the 229th session not available at the time of writing), mentions of the estrangement between Russia and the West were limited to discussions concerning the MH17 flight and the dispute involving Australia, the Netherlands, and Russia, which feature Russian objection to the Council's jurisdiction over the matter.[109] The discussion naturally included accusations and a confrontational tone, with questioning of ICAO's jurisdiction being connected to depoliticization, but the deliberations were much less emotional. Further developments, though beyond ICAO, also featured UN interest in the FR4978 controversy. Following a request by UN SC members Albania, France, the United Kingdom, and the United States, the ICAO Council President briefed the Security Council about the ICAO fact-finding investigation on October 31, 2022, as requested in the resolutions of the ICAO Council and the ICAO Assembly,[110] but besides discussing the issue, the UN SC did not take action.

Conclusions

Even though tensions between Russia and the West started growing in the 2010s, it was not until the diversion of Ryanair flight 4978 to Minsk and the arrest of an oppositional journalist and his partner by the Belarusian authorities in 2021 that full-scale politicization and depoliticization was brought to the ICAO, further deepened in 2022 after the Russian invasion of Ukraine. Russia and Belarus were criticized for their behavior, both in connection to aviation-related misconduct and in response to international political developments. Some interventions critical against Russia or Belarus were admittedly confrontational and focused on political developments, but most of them were somehow connected to civil aviation matters. Both countries attempted to defend themselves or their ally through defensive depoliticization in order to end the inconvenient deliberations or avoid unfavorable decisions. Such depoliticization rhetoric had several faces, well-known from the previous chapters. They included accusations against ICAO and its Western member states of inconsistent behavior compared to similar events in the past, questioning the objectivity of various investigations, cautioning from turning ICAO into a political forum or arguing that it had already happened, and claiming that certain states were trying to use it to resolve political issues. Typically for this kind of debates, defending states argued that ICAO had no jurisdiction to consider such matters or that they should be considered by the UN. Similarly to the previously analyzed instances, representatives of Russia criticized others for injecting politics into the ICAO deliberations. However, simultaneously, they themselves addressed political matters directly in their interventions. Interestingly, on certain occasions, Belarus and Russia introduced items to be discussed, a tactic which could be described as defense through offense. This concerned the sanctions imposed against Belarus following the incident of flight FR4978 and against Russia after it invaded Ukraine. Such behavior can be interpreted as another defensive diplomatic tool, although both discussions also led to critical voices against Russia and Belarus and subsequent depoliticization attempts. In such a situation, contrary to most cases, depoliticization arguments were used in an attempt not to adjourn the items. Besides depoliticization rhetoric, representatives of Russia and Belarus attempted to picture their countries as the victims, a diplomatic technique borrowed from the Soviet playbook.

Developments concerning confrontational debates in the ICAO related to the estrangement between Russia and the West unveiled yet another parallel with earlier instances of defensive depoliticization within the ICAO. Certain representatives or delegates advocated for separation from politics, emphasizing a focus on aviation-related and technical aspects, or advocated for postponing decisions until specific investigations or studies were concluded. This argument was also echoed by representatives of the ICAO bureaucracy, constituting a typical technique for the general depoliticization of IOs. Among the state representatives, such arguments were particularly often used by representatives of China and South Africa, sometimes also of Nigeria, Zambia, Brazil, and India. Even though such interventions create an impression of reflecting genuine attempts to maintain politics away from the ICAO, at least some of them might also be perceived as subtle attempts to defend Russia and Belarus, concerning the fact that because of the general circumstances, more straightforward support could be difficult to defend. Such an argument can be supported by the voting coincidence of these states with Russia in the UN GA. In 2022, they belonged to countries voting most similarly to Russia, particularly if China is considered.[111] With this in mind, their representatives may have sought to prevent ICAO from politicization in a genuine way, but their interventions may also have reflected political vicinity. This observation highlights the proximity between neutral and defensive depoliticization, where rhetorical arguments often exhibit striking similarities despite differing underlying motivations.

Finally, similarly to previous cases, the Russian campaign of defensive depoliticization in ICAO after 2021 was not successful. Russia and Belarus lost all the votes, at best being able to postpone certain decisions. The culmination could be observed during the 41st Assembly, when, for the first time, Russia was not elected to the Council. All these developments in ICAO basically reflect the general international environment. Russian actions in international affairs led to the reorientation of many countries. For instance, numerous EU states opted to restrict or terminate the acquisition of Russian energy resources, thereby signaling a cessation of longstanding dependence on Russia. The Russia–West estrangements reached levels unseen since the Cold War and were waged on every possible forum, including technical ICAO. These observations connect with another quality of defensive depoliticization, which is also observable in other sections of this volume. In many cases, it can be considered a last-resort diplomatic technique. Besides objective arguments about the limited mandate of technical organizations and their declared political neutrality, defending states referred to depoliticization often only after other arguments proved ineffective. Amidst heightened emotions, Russia and Belarus found themselves with few remaining arguments, prompting them to resort to defensive depoliticization tactics from the outset.

Notes

1 Andrew Cottey, "The West, Russia and European security: Still the Long Peace?" *The British Journal of Politics and International Relations* 24, no. 2 (2022): 207, 10.1177/13691481211036381
2 Bartosz Cichocki, "Poland," in *National Perspectives on Russia: European Foreign Policy in the Making?* ed. Maxine David, Jackie Gower, and Hiski Haukkala (Routledge: Abigndon, 2013), 98.
3 Sebastiaan Rietjens, "Unraveling Disinformation: The Case of Malaysia Airlines Flight MH17," *The International Journal of Intelligence, Security, and Public Affairs* 21, no. 3 (2019): 196–198, https://doi.org/10.1080/23800992.2019.1695666
4 Summary Minutes of the First Meeting, Council – 203rd Session, October 27, 2014, 4–6, 8–27, C-Min. 203/1, DOC 10048-C/1179, ICAO Archival Documents.
5 Oleg Manaev, Natalie Rice, and Maureen Taylor, "The Evolution and Influence of Russian and Belarusian Propaganda during the Belarus Presidential Election and Ensuing Protests in 2020," *Canadian Slavonic Papers* 63, no. 3–4 (2021): 372, https://doi.org/10.1080/00085006.2021.1997285
6 Alla Leukavets, "Russia's Game in Belarus: 2020 Presidential Elections as a Checkmate for Lukashenka?" *New Perspectives* 21, no. 9 (2021): 98–99.
7 Manaev, Rice, and Taylor, "The Evolution," 376, 284.
8 Report of the ICAO Fact-Finding Investigation, Report into the Incident Involving Ryanair Flight FR4978 in Belarus Airspace on 23 May 2021, Appendix A, Event Involving Ryanair Flight FR4978 in Belarus Airspace on 23 May 2021, Council – 226th Session, 6, C-WP/15419, Appendix A, ICAO Archival Documents.
9 Summary Minutes of the Second Meeting, Council – 223rd Session, May 27, 2021, 23–25, C-Min. 223/2, DOC 10164-C/1199, ICAO Archival Documents.
10 Ibid., 25–35.
11 Ibid., 30–31.
12 Ibid., 36–39.
13 Summary Minutes of the Eighth Meeting, Council – 223rd Session, June 18, 2023, 120–121, C-Min. 223/8, DOC 10164-C/1199, ICAO Archival Documents.
14 Ibid., 126–127.
15 Interim Report into Incident Involving Ryanair Flight FR4978 in Belarus Airspace on 23 May 2021, Council – 223rd Session, June 21, 2021, 3–4, C-WP/15224, ICAO Archival Documents.
16 Summary Minutes of the Twelfth Meeting, Council – 223rd Session, June 28, 2021, 199–200, C-Min. 223/12, DOC 10164-C/1199, ICAO Archival Documents.
17 Ibid., 201.
18 Ibid., 201–202.

19 Summary Minutes of the Third Meeting, Council – 224th Session, October 25, 2021, 25, C-Min. 224/3, DOC 10173-C/1200, ICAO Archival Documents.
20 Ibid., 26.
21 Summary Minutes of the Eighth Meeting, Council – 224th Session, November 5, 2021, 107–108, C-Min. 224/8, DOC 10173-C/1200, ICAO Archival Documents.
22 Summary Minutes of the First Meeting, Council – 225th Session, January 31, 2022, 4–5, C-Min. 225/1, DOC 10188-C/1201, ICAO Archival Documents; Report of the ICAO Fact-Finding Investigation: Event Involving Ryanair Flight FR4978 in Belarus Airspace on 23 May 2021, January 2022, 36, 42, C-WP/15284, Appendix, ICAO Archival Documents.
23 Summary Minutes of the First Meeting, Council – 225th Session, January 31, 2022, 5, C-Min. 225/1, DOC 10188-C/1201, ICAO Archival Documents.
24 Ibid., 6.
25 Ibid., 6–7.
26 Ibid., 8.
27 Ibid.
28 Ibid., 9–15.
29 According to the ICAO Facebook post, ICAO was 'strongly concerned by the apparent forced landing of a Ryanair flight and its passengers, which could be in contravention of the Chicago Convention. We look forward to more information being officially confirmed by the countries and operators concerned.' International Civil Aviation Organization, Facebook post from May 23, 2021, www.facebook.com/InternationalCivilAviationOrganization/posts/pfbid02RS9j9LY6JhR4KSp3peSgne213LD9zfMdtpcf3zvebPmaunqNsqDL4DGe2dH2Hyv1l, accessed February 2, 2024.
30 Summary Minutes of the First Meeting, Council – 225th Session, January 31, 2022, 9–10, C-Min. 225/1, DOC 10188-C/1201, ICAO Archival Documents.
31 Ibid., 10, 12–13.
32 Ibid., 16.
33 Ibid., 16–17.
34 Ibid., 17–18.
35 Ukraine, Lithuania, Latvia, Poland, Spain, Estonia, UK, Malta, Germany, Austria, Romania, Cyprus, Bulgaria, Greece, Hungary, France, Czechia, Finland, the Netherlands, Belgium, and Luxembourg.
36 Working Paper, Request of the Republic of Belarus to the ICAO Council for Its Consideration Under Article 54 (j) of the Chicago Convention, December 26, 2021, 1, C-WP/15285, ICAO Archival Documents.
37 Summary Minutes of the First Meeting, Council – 225th Session, January 31, 2022, 19, C-Min. 225/1, DOC 10188-C/1201, ICAO Archival Documents.
38 Ibid., 19–20.
39 Ibid., 21.
40 Ibid.
41 Ibid., 22.
42 Ibid., 21–23.
43 Report of the ICAO Fact-Finding Investigation, Report into the Incident Involving Ryanair Flight FR4978 in Belarus Airspace on 23 May 2021, Appendix A, Event Involving Ryanair Flight FR4978 in Belarus Airspace on 23 May 2021, Council – 226th Session, 47, C-WP/15419, Appendix A, ICAO Archival Documents.
44 Summary Minutes of the Sixteenth Meeting, Council – 226th Session, July 18, 2022, 206, C-Min. 226/16, DOC 10192-C/1202, ICAO Archival Documents.

45 Ibid., 207.
46 Ibid., 208.
47 Ibid., 215.
48 Ibid., 211.
49 Ibid.
50 Ibid., 216–217.
51 Ibid., 217–218.
52 Working Paper, Request of the Republic of Belarus to the ICAO Council for Its Consideration under Article 45 (j) of the Chicago Convention, May 25, 2022, 1–4, C-WP/15418, ICAO Archival Documents.
53 Summary Minutes of the Sixteenth Meeting, Council – 226th Session, July 18, 2022, 219, C-Min. 226/16, DOC 10192-C/1202, ICAO Archival Documents.
54 Ibid., 219.
55 Ibid., 220.
56 Ibid., 220–221.
57 Ibid.
58 Ibid., 221–222.
59 Draft Assembly Working Paper, Infractions of the Convention of International Civil Aviation by the Republic of Belarus, August 15, 2022, 3, C-WP/15430, ICAO Archival Documents.
60 Summary Minutes of the Seventeenth Meeting, Council – 226th Session, August 24–25, 2022, 259, C-Min. 226/17, DOC 10192-C/1202, ICAO Archival Documents.
61 Ibid., 259–260.
62 Ibid., 260–261.
63 Robert G. Angevine, et al., *Learning Lessons from the Ukraine Conflict* (Alexandria: Institute for Defense Analyses, 2019), 1.
64 Tatyana Malyarenko and Stefan Wolff, "The Logic of Competitive Influence-Seeking: Russia, Ukraine, and the Conflict in Donbas," *Post-Soviet Affairs* 34, no. 4 (2018): 193, https://doi.org/10.1080/1060586X.2018.1425083
65 Paul Kirby, "Why Has Russia Invaded Ukraine and What Does Putin Want?" *BBC News*, accessed March 12, 2022, www.bbc.com/news/world-europe-56720589
66 Deutsche Welle, "Russia Recognizes Independence of Ukraine Separatist Regions," accessed March 1, 2022, www.dw.com/en/russia-recognizes-independence-of-ukraine-separatist-regions/a-60861963
67 President of Russia, "Address by the President of the Russian Federation," accessed December 1, 2022, http://en.kremlin.ru/events/president/news/67843
68 United Nations, "The UN and Ukraine: Year-Long War Spreads Global Fallout," accessed January 15, 2024, https://news.un.org/en/story/2023/03/1134122
69 Summary Minutes of the Fourth Meeting, Council – 225th Session, February 25, 2022, 65, C-Min. 225/4, DOC 10188-C/1201, ICAO Archival Documents.
70 Ibid., 65.
71 Ibid., 66–67.
72 Ibid., 67–69.
73 Ibid., 73.
74 Ibid., 68–73.
75 Such approach was presented by representatives of Malaysia, Brazil, Equatorial Guinea, United Arab Emirates, Saudi Arabia, China, Côte d'Ivoire, Nigeria, Zambia, South Africa. Ibid., 72–75.

76 Ibid., 75–76.
77 Ibid., 70–72.
78 Ibid., 76.
79 Ibid.
80 Ibid., 77–78.
81 Summary Minutes of the Eighth Meeting, Council – 225th Session, March 7, 2022, 147, C-Min. 225/8, DOC 10188-C/1201, ICAO Archival Documents.
82 Ibid., 148.
83 Ibid., 150.
84 Australia, Canada, Colombia, Costa Rica, Dominican Republic, Finland, France, Germany, Greece, Italy, Japan, Republic of Korea, Mexico, Kingdom of the Netherlands, Paraguay, Peru, Spain, UK, and US.
85 Working Paper, Infractions of the Convention under Article 54(j) of the Chicago Convention by the Russian Federation, Council – 226th Session, June 14, 2022, Revision No. 1 from June 16, 2022, 2–4, C-WP/15425, ICAO Archival Documents.
86 Summary Minutes of the Fourteenth Meeting, Council – 226th Session, June 24, 2022, 181–182, C-Min. 226/14, DOC 10192-C/1202, ICAO Archival Documents.
87 Ibid., 182.
88 Ibid., 183–184.
89 Ibid., 184–189.
90 Ibid., 186–190.
91 See: Pardee Centre for International Futures, UNGA Coincidence Score, February 20, 2024, available from https://public.tableau.com/app/profile/pardeecenterifs/viz/VotesterTableauDashboard_16529835337750/UNGACoincidenceScores?publish=yes, accessed April 17, 2024.
92 Summary Minutes of the Fourteenth Meeting, Council – 226th Session, June 24, 2022, 190–191, C-Min. 226/14, DOC 10192-C/1202, ICAO Archival Documents.
93 Albania, Aruba, Austria, Belgium, Bulgaria, Canada, Croatia, Cyprus, Czech Republic, Denmark (including Greenland, Faroe Islands and the territorial sea), Dominican Republic, Estonia, Finland, France, Germany, Greece, Hungary, Iceland, Ireland, Italy, Latvia, Lithuania, Luxembourg, Malta, Mexico, Moldova, Monaco, Montenegro, the Netherlands (including Bonaire, Saba, Saint Eustatius), North Macedonia, Norway, Poland, Portugal, Romania, Saint Maarten, Slovenia, Spain, Sweden, Switzerland, UK (including the overseas territories of Anguilla, Bermuda, Gibraltar, Jersey, the British Virgin Islands, Cayman Islands, Montserrat, Isle of Man, Turks and Caicos Islands), US.
94 Working Paper, Information Pursuant to Article 54(J) of the Chicago Convention on Infractions of the Convention by a Group of ICAO Member States, Council – 226th Session, July 11, 2022, Revision No. 1 from July 15, 2022, 1–5, C-WP/15429, ICAO Archival Documents.
95 The article prohibits registration of an aircraft in more than one state.
96 Summary Minutes of the Seventeenth Meeting, Council – 226th Session, August 24–25, 2022, 247–248, C-Min. 226/17, DOC 10192-C/1202, ICAO Archival Documents.
97 Ibid., 248–251.
98 Ibid., 251.
99 Ibid., 251–255.

100 Draft Assembly Working Paper, Infractions of the Convention on International Civil Aviation by the Russian Federation, Council – 226th Session, July 7, 2022, 1–4, C-WP/15427, ICAO Archival Documents.

101 Summary Minutes of the Seventeenth Meeting, Council – 226th Session, August 24–25, 2022, 256–257, C-Min. 226/17, DOC 10192-C/1202, ICAO Archival Documents.

102 Ibid., 257–258.

103 ICAO, "The Postal History of ICAO: Organization Promoting Technological Advancements in Civil Aviation," accessed February 6, 2024, https://applications.icao.int/postalhistory/iccaia_international_coordinating_council_of_aerospace_industries_associations.htm

104 Summary Minutes of the Seventeenth Meeting, Council – 226th Session, August 24–25, 2022, 261–262, C-Min. 226/17, DOC 10192-C/1202, ICAO Archival Documents.

105 Minutes of the Fourth Plenary Meeting, Assembly – 41st Session, October 1, 2022, 23–26, A41-Min. P/4, DOC 10182, ICAO Archival Documents.

106 Executive Committee Report, Assembly – 41st Session, n.d., 170–176, A41-EX, DOC 10183, ICAO Archival Documents.

107 Minutes of the Ninth Plenary Meeting, Assembly – 41st Session, October 7, 2022, 56, A41-Min. P/9, DOC 10182, ICAO Archival Documents. See: Working Paper, The Incompatibility of Unilateral Restrictive Measures Impacting International Civil Aviation Activities with the Provisions of the Convention of International Aviation, Assembly – 41st Session, August 1, 2022, 1–3, A41-WP/456, EX/210, ICAO Archival Documents.

108 Minutes of the Ninth Plenary Meeting, Assembly – 41st Session, October 7, 2022, 56–57, 59, A41-Min. P/9, DOC 10182, ICAO Archival Documents.

109 Summary Minutes of the Third Meeting, Council – 228th Session, March 17, 2023, 36–43, C-Min. 228/3, DOC 10196, ICAO Archival Documents.

110 ICAO, "Council President Presents Briefing to UN Security Council on the Forced Landing of Ryanair Flight FR4978 by Belarus," accessed January 16, 2024, www.icao.int/Newsroom/Pages/Council-President-presents-briefing-to-UN-Security-Council-on-the-forced-landing-of-Ryanair-Flight-FR4978-by-Belarus.aspx

111 Pardee Centre for International Futures, UNGA Coincidence Score, February 20, 2024, available from https://public.tableau.com/app/profile/pardeecenterifs/viz/VotesterTableauDashboard_16529835337750/UNGACoincidenceScores?publish=yes, accessed April 17, 2024.

Conclusions

The research presented in this book was dedicated to the politicized debates occurring on the forum of the International Civil Aviation Organization (ICAO), which stemmed from various types of international conflicts and estrangements, featuring the engagement of representatives of a number of states. Particular focus was directed toward the strategies employed by the representatives and delegates defending their states and their allies against verbal attacks stemming from or linked to political conflicts. In addition to presenting substantive arguments, they often asserted that the issues under discussion were inherently political, a tactic termed in the book as defensive depoliticization. As argued throughout the text, participants of the politicized debates on the forum of ICAO have been employing depoliticization rhetoric in order to defend themselves from ostracism on the multilateral forum.

Before reviewing the empirical observations made throughout the volume, it was necessary to briefly discuss ICAO as the diplomatic forum and an arena for politicized multilateral deliberations. According to all the theoretical assumptions regarding international organizations (IOs), intergovernmental organizations (IGOs) such as ICAO should belong to the least politicized. With strictly technical preoccupation and limited authority, ICAO should be falling victim to external conflicts resonating on its forum to a lesser extent. However, as demonstrated in the empirical part of the study, politics frequently infiltrated the proceedings of the ICAO, although the design of this research did not allow for a comparison of the level of politicization of the ICAO with other IOs.

The first group of politicized ICAO deliberations that led to the use of defensive depoliticization roughly fell into the category of membership controversies, featuring the debates over several states' right to be represented in ICAO. Each of the instances originated from various international conflicts: in the case of Spain as a spin-off of the World War II alliances; in the case of China as one of the many consequences of the Chinese civil war and the establishment of two centers of power; in the case of South Africa as a result of the African states' pursuit to oppose the discriminatory apartheid policy; in the case of Cyprus as a result of its conflict with Turkey.

Debates regarding Spain's post-war ICAO membership were not particularly fierce and confrontational and were connected virtually exclusively with the UN expectations rather than any state's hostility against Spain. Axis states were ostracized after the end of World War II. For example, they did not become UN members or were not invited to compete in the Olympic Games. Still, Spain was not actively engaged in the war, so in ICAO, it was not subject to direct verbal attacks, while the need to expel it from the organization was only argued in reference to the need to enter into a relationship with the UN. Still, depoliticization was present, both in the statements of delegations arguing that technical ICAO should not be subject to political decisions and in the statements of the delegations from Spain and several other countries, which attempted to defend Spanish membership and claimed it was more important to keep Spain in ICAO than to follow political expectations of the UN.

The debates surrounding the Taiwanese presence in the ICAO were notably more confrontational, even though they did not involve representatives from the People's Republic of China (PRC), which for various reasons, including the initial lack of interest, for many years was absent from ICAO. In the ICAO, the developments concerning the so-called Chinese question between 1950 and the early 1970s reflected the situation in other IGOs and international non-governmental organizations (INGOs). For a long time, Taiwan managed to secure its presence within such organizations, mostly owing to American support. However, there were many countries that consequently argued in favor of the membership of Communist China, which, as a result of the character of the mutual relationship between the PRC and Taiwan, would mean the expulsion of the latter. On the forum of the ICAO Assembly, several countries spoke against the presence of the delegation of the Republic of China (RoC), often by commenting or expressing reservations about the reports of the Credentials Committee. Interestingly, such views were expressed not only by delegates from the Communist countries who argued that the PRC should be represented in ICAO rather than RoC but also by delegates from several developing and Western states, such as the United Kingdom and France. Other delegations sometimes defended the Taiwanese presence, but in most cases, it was RoC's delegates who attempted to defend their presence. In doing so, they employed various techniques. They argued about their government's legal standing, the UN membership, and diplomatic relations with many countries in the world. Among these defensive techniques, they also used depoliticization rhetoric, within which they argued ICAO was not a proper place for political debates and declarations. Besides pure defense, Taiwanese delegates on many occasions have also attacked and criticized the government in Beijing, referring to its illegitimate character or various misconducts, thus they were arguing against referring to politics and doing this at the same time.

One of the recurring multilateral controversies, which also surfaced in the ICAO proceedings, pertains to African states' objections to the participation of South African representatives, occasionally linked to decisions made within the UN framework. African states' delegates were using various tools of isolating South Africa in ICAO, ranging from demanding expulsion, through monitoring its isolation in the field of aviation, to declaratory decisions without further political and diplomatic implications. The deliberations frequently revolved around the proposal to exclude South Africa from participating in ICAO activities. However, the broader objective seems to have been to ensure that the issue of apartheid in South Africa remained on the ICAO agenda, mirroring the situation in the UN General Assembly and other IOs. It is noteworthy that the relatively democratic nature of the ICAO rendered it an ideal platform for newly independent African nations and other states to advance their political agendas, since some Western states that at the time often lent support to South African governments had less privileged positions than in some other IOs. Depoliticization rhetoric became the dominant technique used by those against the isolation of South Africa in ICAO and by the South African delegates themselves. Those against South African ICAO's presence defended bringing the issue of apartheid by attempting to draw a link between South African policy and aviation. However, there were also situations when they openly acknowledged that the issues raised went beyond technical matters, arguing that they were justified by the gravity of the abuse, which was rather extraordinary compared to other cases analyzed in this book. On several occasions, there were also voices that seemed to have sought to genuinely prevent ICAO from politicization, but they could well also conceal attempts to defend South Africa. In the last case, certain objections to the politicization of the ICAO could be construed as an endeavor to rationalize non-support for resolutions targeting South Africa. Given the objective challenge posed by the issue of racial discrimination in South Africa, openly opposing condemnation of apartheid might have been viewed unfavorably by the international public. Such an observation originates from the oft-repeated statements of the representatives of predominantly Western states, who claimed that their position (not supporting anti-South Africa decisions) did not mean their approval of apartheid.

The South African issue in ICAO led to multiple instances of using defensive depoliticization. During the initial years of the controversy, South African delegates, enjoying unrestricted participation in the ICAO, and delegates from certain predominantly Western nations often invoked the political nature of the topics under discussion, contrasting them with the technical mandate of the ICAO. This argument was used to discourage debates or endorsements of measures such as condemnation, expulsion, or other limitations on South Africa's involvement in the organization. It appeared to be one of few arguments available since it was difficult to defend apartheid policy on a multilateral forum, which corresponds with the argument about the last-resort character of defensive depoliticization that will be discussed below.

The last of the ICAO controversies connected with the membership in the organization stemmed from the conflict between Cyprus and Turkey, although it featured not only situations when Turkish delegates questioned the presence of the delegations of the Republic of Cyprus but also often unrelated to the above Cypriot accusations against Turkey in relations to its invasion of the island, occupation of its northern part, and aviation services that the Cypriot delegates described as illegal. In the former instance, Turkish delegates adopted a comparable strategy akin to the approach used against the presence of Taiwan at ICAO meetings, namely by voicing reservations or commenting on reports from the Credentials Committees. The Turks, in principle, were claiming that the Cypriot delegation only represented the Greek Cypriot community of the island. Both parties naturally sought to defend themselves against such accusations, with Cyprus frequently receiving support from Greek delegations. They referred to substantive arguments, but during some of the exchanges, delegates of the attacked side also referred to the depoliticization argument in an attempt to defend their countries, using typical claims about the political character of the statements of the other side. There were even meetings at which both sides simultaneously used political arguments against the adversary, depoliticization rhetoric in defense, and accused each other of politicizing ICAO, which corresponds with the pejorative perception of politics in technical organizations.

As noted already in the introduction, the Arab–Israeli conflict was one of the most preoccupying for IOs throughout the 20th century. The UN is believed to have devoted more attention to this issue than to any other matter.[1] The politicization associated with the Arab–Israeli conflict occurred in multiple IOs, including ICAO. Regarding the depth and scope of the conflict within ICAO, an entire chapter has been dedicated to its examination. Among the six instances of the Arab–Israeli conflict on the forum of ICAO analyzed within this research, defensive depoliticization was employed by the Arab states solely in the first case, in response to Israeli complaints regarding Arab aviation practices. Even though it only concerned verbal complaints, without expecting any formal action from ICAO, Arab states responded by attempting to depreciate the accusation through highlighting their political character, unfit for ICAO, with politics pictured as something highly pejorative. Arab defensive depoliticization aimed to terminate the discussion even though their delegations admitted committing some of the activities Israel accused them of. It should also be noted that the activities had a certain link to the aviation matters and that Israeli delegates did not claim that the issues discussed were not political.

Further controversies featuring Israel and the Arab states in ICAO had a reversed direction, with the Arab states criticizing Israel, using ICAO as a convenient, cheap, and visible ground to hit their political adversary. Israel, in turn, defended itself, among other things with depoliticization rhetoric. Many of the controversies were connected to the actual aviation-related offenses committed by Israel. The first of a kind were the deliberations regarding the Israeli attack on the Beirut airport in 1968. Israel at first employed defense through offense tactics by unsuccessfully attempting to introduce into the deliberations a motion against Lebanon in connection to the bombing of El Al airliner at Athens airport from December 1968, to which the attack on the airport was supposed to respond. Besides that, the Israeli representative accused Lebanon of tolerating terrorism, spoke about the political character of the accusations against Israel, and argued that the issue was beyond ICAO's jurisdiction because of its political character. According to the Israeli standpoint, it was a belligerent situation beyond the scope of the organization and a response to the Lebanese offenses, whereas the Lebanese standpoint was that an attack on a civil airport was making the matter aviation-related and that it should not be held responsible for the actions of non-state actors. The discussions also featured two sides accusing each other of politicizing the deliberations and, at the same time, raising arguments with more or less direct political overtones. In addition, similarly to most cases examined, depoliticization rhetoric was invoked by representatives not directly involved in the controversy, which can be interpreted as a potentially genuine attempt to limit the Council's activity to aviation matters. This rhetoric often coincided with expressions of support for Israel's defense, despite nearly every speaker criticizing the Israeli attack on the Beirut airport.

Discussions regarding the Israeli shootdown of the Libyan civil aircraft over Sinai in 1973 did not lead to defensive depoliticization, probably as a result of the unequivocal guilt of Israel combined with its clear link to civil aviation. In turn, defensive depoliticization was extensively used in the same year with regard to the interception of the Lebanese civil aircraft by the Israeli Air Force. Despite the dominant ostracism against Israel, its delegate used depoliticization to argue against discussing the issue, but also made a very strong and confrontational statement against the Arab states, claiming he did not want to engage in the political debates but was forced to do so. Unlike the instances of Arab–Israeli conflict discussed earlier, defensive depoliticization proved ineffective, with the Assembly adopting a resolution in which it 'strongly condemned' the Israeli act.

ICAO deliberations also included accusations against Israeli behavior regarding the operation of the Jerusalem airport, which, according to the Arab states, was situated on occupied Arab territories. Although the subject matter of this dispute was entirely different from those discussed above, the argumentation used by Israel did not change much and was built around defensive depoliticization and claims that political issues should have no place in ICAO. According to Israel, the issue of the Jerusalem airport was political since it concerned territorial sovereignty. Despite criticizing the politicization of the deliberations, the Israeli delegate did not avoid political statements to support his argument either. At the time, the voting distribution in the Assembly shifted in favor of the Arab states after new states have joined the organization following decolonization and increased engagement of the Communist states, rendering it more challenging for Israel to evade the adoption of critical decisions and resolutions. This trend was also evident in relation to the Jerusalem airport, underscoring the limited effectiveness of depoliticization tactics.

Within the general attempt to hit their political adversary, though without a direct criticism, Arab states have also attempted to grant the Palestine Liberation Organization (PLO) the right to send observers to the ICAO meetings. Israel opposed, like in the previous instances, claiming the issue was political and should not be discussed and arguing that PLO was responsible for terrorism. According to the Israelis, PLO's observer would be turning the ICAO Assembly into a political forum. The Israeli argumentation proved ineffective again, and PLO received the right to send observers to ICAO meetings.

The final instance of the Arab–Israeli conflict analyzed in this volume pertained to the deliberations surrounding the interception of a Libyan Arab Airlines flight by Israel in 1986. This time held in the Council, the debate featured a predominantly legal discussion regarding ICAO jurisdiction concerning the uncertain status of the said aircraft. However, there were also statements referring to the possible political character of the matter that was making it unfit for ICAO, whereas those arguing against proceeding with the issue were accused of trying to divert the Council's attention. Defensive depoliticization based on the legal argument that it was a state aircraft was also employed by the Israeli observer. Besides that, the Israeli representative has also attacked Libya, requesting the Council to consider Libyan threats to civil aviation, thus employing defense through offense tactics. In general, both sides engaged in mutual attacks, often resorting to political arguments. Simultaneously, each side contended that motions against them should not be considered due to their inherently political nature.

It was characteristic of the Arab–Israeli conflict on the forum of ICAO that states directly engaged in particular deliberations were often receiving support from their political allies. Arab states usually spoke in each other's favor, whereas the United States was among the countries that most actively defended Israel, except in instances when its guilt was most obvious. Besides that, the general pattern was that one of the sides complained about the actions perpetrated by the other, but there were also instances that should rather be interpreted as attempts to simply hit the political opponent on another of the multilateral forums. They were all leading to highly confrontational debates featuring political overtones. Although the accusations had at least some reference to aviation in most cases, political aspects were never omitted. Specific defensive tactics featured arguments about the political character of the accusations and the legal constraints regarding ICAO's jurisdiction that did not encompass political matters, although the defending parties often equally eagerly attacked their adversary. Besides the two sides of the conflict and their allies, the need to separate from politics was also raised in a more neutral manner, which can be interpreted as an attempt to protect ICAO genuinely from politicization, although they could well have been examples of more concealed defensive depoliticization. Generally, though, the Arab–Israeli conflict on the forum of ICAO demonstrated glaringly the link between politicization and depoliticization, with depoliticization in most cases being used not to remove politics but for self-defense.

Shootdowns of civil aircraft, one of the most controversial and tragic types of incidents that can occur in civil aviation, were analyzed with regard to two occurrences associated with international tensions. The first of these incidents, the tragic downing of Korean Air Lines Flight 007 by the Soviet Union, occurred within the context of the Cold War, sparking emotional debates in numerous international forums. In the ICAO, it was debated both in the Council and in the Assembly. The Soviet Union was criticized in an emotional manner by multiple speakers, many of whom described it as a brutal force, irrespective of human lives. Still, the deliberations also featured calls for distancing the deliberations from politics by the speakers not representing either of the countries engaged in the crisis, reflecting an apparently sincere will to keep politics away from ICAO or at least framed this way. In response, the Soviet Union and its allies built their defense around the offensive argumentation, primarily accusing the United States of employing the aircraft for a spy mission and seeking to emphasize the violation of their airspace as the central aspect of the deliberations. In the early stages of the controversy, depoliticization as a defensive tool was used modestly, mostly through references to the anti-Soviet hysteria, aggravation of the international situation, and complaints about sanctions imposed against Soviet aviation. Calls for refraining from referring to politics in the deliberations were present, but rather not in the defensive context.

More straightforward defensive depoliticization was employed at a later stage of deliberations. Representatives of the Soviet Union and its allies criticized the wording of ICAO resolutions, decisions, or reports as politically tendentious and spoke about political attacks on the Soviet Union. The use of defensive depoliticization became more prevalent only after earlier arguments centered around a spy mission and airspace violation proved unsuccessful. This suggests that defensive depoliticization was viewed as a last-resort tool. In other words, if other arguments do not work or are not available, diplomats on a forum of a technical organization may refer to depoliticization in an attempt to protect their states from ostracism.

The final stage of the ICAO deliberations initiated by the shootdown of the KAL007 flight, which concerned the amendment of the Chicago Convention concerning the refraining from the use of force against civil aviation, had an entirely different character compared to the previous ones. It was much less confrontational and generally oriented toward seeking a common solution. Despite their differing standpoints, Communist and Western countries were able to achieve a compromise. With less confrontational tones, the need for defense through depoliticization arguments diminished. However, to some extent, these arguments were still present in the statements of Communist delegations, who claimed that the amendment of the Convention was driven more by political considerations than by actual necessity.

The KAL007 controversy, besides typical defensive depoliticization arguments and instances of neutral depoliticization visible also in reference to other controversies discussed throughout this volume, also featured evidence of a method of depoliticization studied in the literature on general depoliticization of IOs – postponing the decisions. Interestingly, while this technique is typically employed by an organization's bureaucracy, in this instance, it was advocated by speakers aiming to defend the Union of Soviet Socialist Republics (USSR) in the early stages of the controversy. Consequently, it also bore the hallmarks of defensive depoliticization in this particular case. In addition, the controversy highlighted the more active role of ICAO as both a diplomatic actor and a facilitator of diplomacy. Despite tensions, the incident led to direct contact between the countries concerned, contributing to the increased safety of civil aviation. Still, the KAL007 controversy was also a glaring example of the use of ICAO as a forum of confrontational diplomatic deliberations with political overtones, clear Cold War divisions, and the use of depoliticization rhetoric to defend the Soviet Union and to protect ICAO from politicization.

The shootdown of the Iran Air Flight 655 by the US Navy in 1988 also led to politicized ICAO deliberations, this time in connection to the tensions between the United States and Iran. Besides that, the incident was connected with the American presence in the Persian Gulf, which was a response to attacks on civilian ships during the war between Iraq and Iran. At the forum of ICAO, the United States was naturally attacked by the Iranian observers and delegates. Although admitting their responsibility, the Americans claimed that the incident was partly caused by the political circumstances for which Iran was responsible. Besides that, representatives of predominantly Communist states called for the US withdrawal from the Gulf, apparently attempting to achieve certain geopolitical gains with the use of the political context of the shootdown, an argumentation also embraced by the Iranian side. Both the pro- and anti-American speakers declared being against the politicization of the ICAO but claimed they were forced by their counterparts to respond, further engaging in political argumentation.

ICAO deliberations regarding the IR655 flight, besides some instances of potentially neutral depoliticization arguments, featured depoliticization used in a reversed way, not in an attempt to defend the state under criticism, but more offensively. From the Iranian perspective, it was connected with the attempt to achieve a more severe phrasing of the decisions regarding the shootdown. The Iranians claimed that the use of overly soft language was influenced by political considerations. The Americans also employed depoliticization arguments, with the opposite goal of softening the phrasing, but offensive depoliticization was used more actively throughout the deliberations.

The most recent conflict that resonated within the ICAO, leading to highly politicized debates featuring defensive depoliticization, concerns the ongoing tension between Russia and Western countries. This was exemplified by the deliberations on the forced landing of Ryanair Flight 4978 in Minsk in 2021 and the subsequent arresting of an oppositionist and his partner, as well as in response to the Russian invasion of Ukraine in 2022. While the first case did not directly involve Russia, the close ties between Belarus and Russia led to predominantly Russian representatives and delegates defending Minsk on the forum of ICAO. Consequently, it was assumed that the incident and subsequent controversies also pertained to the estrangement between Russia and the West.

The Russian/Belarusian line of defense during the ICAO deliberations regarding the forced landing of the Ryanair flight in Minsk centered around denying any infringements, highlighting ICAO's inconsistency in dealing with similar occurrences in the past, and picturing Belarus as the victim of Western sanctions. Defensive depoliticization at the early stage appeared mainly in the calls for unbiased investigation and warnings about political repercussions. Russian and Belarusian representatives have also used depoliticization rhetoric in response to the imposition of Western sanctions, speaking about the politicization of the ICAO, about double standards and different treatment of Western offenses, and questioning the ICAO's competence regarding the detention of passengers. In general, they argued that the ICAO was biased toward the West and contended that the entire issue was political and unsuitable for the ICAO's involvement. Similar to many previous cases, Russian and Belarusian representatives have also accused others of injecting politics into the ICAO, while simultaneously referring to political issues themselves. Besides that, deliberations featured attempts to use depoliticization by Russia and Belarus more offensively, arguing that ICAO should deal with the sanctions against Belarus and that not doing so would only mean politicization of ICAO, another example of defense through offense tactics. Besides that, there were also attempts to postpone the sensitive decision, a typical general depoliticization tool.

During the latter stages of the ICAO deliberations concerning the forced landing of Flight FR4978 in Minsk, the primary defensive argument that emerged was that Belarus was the victim. This echoes one of the classic Soviet diplomatic techniques. When the ICAO report was available, it was described as politically biased. Besides that, there were also claims about the political character of the accusations against Belarus. Naturally, there were also more neutral interventions advocating for the separation of politics from the deliberations. However, in this particular case, many of them were difficult to unequivocally classify as defensive or neutral – on the one hand, they seemed not to favor any of the sides, but on the other, they were repeatedly raised by representatives of states open to collaboration with Russia. This reveals the proximity between defensive depoliticization and more general depoliticization efforts aimed at keeping politics away from the organization. Rhetorical arguments often exhibited similarities in both approaches.

The final and still ongoing politicized controversy in ICAO concerns the Russian invasion of Ukraine in February 2022. The occurrence led to versatile international reactions, including the imposition of sanctions, also in the field of aviation. In ICAO, it led to many critical remarks against Russia. Some statements cautioned against discussing political issues, potentially with a neutral stance. However, the most crucial aspect from the perspective of the research goals was the defensive argumentation put forth by Russia. During the first discussion on the issue at the 225th session of the Council, the Russian representative attempted to justify the intervention, claimed that such a political issue should not be discussed in ICAO, and argued about being forced to engage in a political debate. Besides that, the Russians accused others, particularly North Atlantic Treaty Organization (NATO) countries, of both bringing politics to the ICAO and being guilty of pushing Russia to invade Ukraine.

In addition to addressing the invasion directly, ICAO also tackled the associated problem of dual registration of aircraft. This was in response to Russia's nationalization of civil aircraft following the imposition of sanctions and demands to return leased machines. Apart from that, the Assembly made a controversial and unprecedented decision when it did not elect Russia to the Council. The Russian line of defense featured arguments about Western hostility, violation of human rights through the imposition of aviation sanctions, and simply responding to Western sanctions. Russian representatives also argued that ICAO was being politicized and turned into a political instrument. They claimed that the organization's reactions were inconsistent with its handling of armed conflicts initiated by Western countries and asserted that its decisions were politically motivated. Overall, they portrayed Russia as a victim in the situation. In several interventions, Russian representatives and delegates also underlined the issues under discussion as being beyond ICAO's jurisdiction. There were also several offensive attempts, predominantly when

Russia sought to initiate the discussion on the Western sanctions. Despite undertaking several specific depoliticizing arguments, ICAO's decisions in general were unfavorable toward Russia, supporting the argument of the ineffectiveness of defensive depoliticization.

The ICAO deliberations discussed throughout the book demonstrate that politics has been injected into the organization on multiple occasions and in various ways. There are diverse reasons for the politicization of this organization. Compared to many other IGOs, it has a relatively democratic character, with comparatively limited influence of world powers, allowing states the opportunity to seek the realization of their non-aviation foreign policy goals, including hitting political adversaries, without the risk of having their motions vetoed by world powers. In addition, despite its technical focus, ICAO's affiliation with the UN system can entangle it in broader political controversies, such as the Arab–Israeli conflict or the issue of South African apartheid. As the case of Spanish expulsion demonstrates, there were even situations when being or seeking to become a UN agency was the main reason for politicization. ICAO's limited authority naturally renders most potential political gains on its forum merely symbolic. However, even symbolic losses to political adversaries are something few states can afford, paving the ground for often emotional debates featuring depoliticization rhetoric.

ICAO's potential for holding politicized debates also lies elsewhere. If the Assembly is considered, chief delegates in addition to technical expertise are expected to possess diplomatic skills, qualifying them to speak about issues beyond aviation matters. When considering the Council, member states have the right to bring issues under its consideration, and decisions are made by a majority of Council members. This potentially makes it easier than, for example, in the UN, to achieve desirable decisions, such as condemning or isolating political adversaries. Such a situation makes potential politicization of ICAO deliberations possible and reveals its qualities of a forum organization, despite theoretically not being assumed as one.

Throughout this volume, we have analyzed several international controversies with clear political overtones that unfolded on the forum of ICAO. All of them originated from international conflicts and estrangements, but not all of them directly corresponded with matters related to civil aviation, even though the technical character of ICAO and its precisely defined scope suggest it should deal exclusively with civil aviation. The civil aviation-related controversies were usually connected to various examples of state offenses with regard to aviation, such as establishing illegal aviation services (Turkey–Cyprus), withholding flight information, attacking civil airports, intercepting civil aircraft, operating an airport on occupied territory (Arab states–Israel), shootdown of civil aircraft (USSR–West, US–Iran), forced landing of civil aircraft, seizure of aircraft (Russia–West). In general, representatives and delegates from states aiming to target their political adversaries on the ICAO forum sought out aviation-related issues as a foundation for their attacks. Still, there were also situations when politicized deliberations concerned issues with little or no civil aviation context. This was particularly glaring in the cases of questioning states' right to be present at ICAO meetings, but also in some instances of the Arab–Israeli conflict or in the recent tensions between Russia and the collective West. Still, it appears that in most cases, one of the main goals of introducing controversial issues was to hit political adversaries in the first place, with civil aviation matters being instrumentally used for this purpose.

The instrumental nature of using civil aviation matters to initiate attacks on political adversaries on the ICAO forum is linked to the fact that all politicized debates stemmed from conflicts and estrangements reaching far beyond the scope of ICAO. In other words, each of the controversial deliberations was part of a much wider problem, deliberated on many other multilateral forums. While specific issues, such as reports on the credentials of contested delegations, were clearly addressed uniquely within the ICAO, each of the conflicts was also being waged elsewhere. These disputes extended to various arenas, including the UN Security Council, the UN General Assembly, other UN specialized agencies, and international non-governmental organizations. Naturally, some deliberations were connected with clear aviation-related offenses, such as shootdowns or interceptions of civil aircraft. However, the fact that all were part of wider international controversies provides additional support for the argument about the often-instrumental character of aviation-related matters used to initiate politicized deliberations in ICAO.

A common feature of all the politicized deliberations analyzed throughout the book was that representatives or delegates of one state (or a group of states) verbally attacked another state, sometimes in an emotional manner. As noted above, such attacks sometimes originated from actually culpable behaviors like shootdowns or interceptions of civil aircraft, sometimes in connection with more vague accusations like questioning the statehood of other countries or seeking to punish them for their domestic (like in the case of South Africa) or international (like in the case of 21st-century Russia) policies and actions. Regardless of the actual guilt of the criticized state or states, criticism against them on the forum of ICAO was leading to backlashes. Responses to verbal attacks assumed several forms. They included, for example, denying the behavior to be accused of, explaining why they have been committed, and arguing that accusations and criticism had no merit. More confrontational responses assumed verbally attacking the other side, claiming that others were guilty of specific occurrences, or criticizing their political system. Another group of responses included attempts to divert attention, for example, through trying to include into the agenda matters like sanctions imposed against such a state in response to the offense under discussion or asking ICAO to deal with alleged offenses of the attacking state, which were to be the reason for occurrences under discussion. The playbook of diplomatic responses to criticism on the forum of ICAO also included depoliticization rhetoric, a diplomatic technique that this research has been dedicated to exploring.

The main argument of this research was that participants of the politicized debates in the ICAO have been employing depoliticization rhetoric to defend themselves from criticism and attacks. It has been the case for the delegations defending their countries or those attempting to defend their political allies or states with which they sympathized. By claiming an issue as political and thus unfit for the ICAO, they tried to get away from an inconvenient situation and avoid international ostracism on the forum of a UN agency, and when this was not possible, to mitigate such ostracism.

Depoliticization analyzed in this volume differs from how it has traditionally been studied, both generally and with regard to IOs. Depoliticization is most typically considered in reference to processes, tactics, strategies, and tools used to protect decision-makers from political temptations, public pressure, media storms, etc. With regard to IOs, depoliticization is about removing the potentially political character of decision-making, according to the assumption that distancing an organization from politics increases effectiveness and reduces controversies. Depoliticization understood this way on multiple occasions was observed throughout the study, but it focused on depoliticization rhetoric as another type of response to the verbal attacks.

Depoliticization rhetoric is based on the argument typical for specialized IOs, according to which their scope lies beyond the sphere of politics. The argument posits that certain issues are inherently political in nature and, consequently, should not be deliberated within the purview of a technical organization like ICAO. Depoliticization rhetoric in the ICAO covered two types of behavior. Firstly, it was used by representatives or delegates of states not directly engaged in the political conflicts waged in ICAO. Their primary contention revolved around the assertion that ICAO, being a technical organization, ought to abstain from engaging in political endeavors and instead concentrate on the technical dimensions of the events. Depoliticization rhetoric employed within such a context may also be interpreted as an illustration of the broader conception of depoliticization. However, in the instances examined, it was predominantly state representatives rather than ICAO bureaucrats who sought to shield the organization from politicization. It should be highlighted, though, that at least some of the interventions interpreted as such neutral depoliticization could well have been concealed attempts to defend the criticized states. The second type of behavior entails employing depoliticization rhetoric to defend the state or states under attack, utilized either by the targeted delegation itself or by its allies or sympathetic states. For the purpose of this study, such use of depoliticization rhetoric has been termed 'defensive depoliticization' and has been assumed principally as a diplomatic technique, alongside neutral and offensive depoliticization.

The focal point of the study was defensive depoliticization as a response to verbal attacks within the ICAO forum. Regardless of the legitimacy of the subject of the attacks, representatives of the targeted states and their sympathizers contended that the topics under discussion were unsuitable for ICAO due to their inherently political nature. Such an argument was employed to realize several specific goals. Firstly, it was used in an attempt to terminate inconvenient deliberations based on the assumption that there is no place whatsoever for political matters in the ICAO. Thus, it was very often used already at the stage of adopting the agenda. Secondly, defensive depoliticization was utilized in an endeavor to circumvent the adoption of unfavorable decisions, such as critical resolutions, the initiation of investigations, expulsions, and similar measures. Thirdly, it was used in attempts to postpone decisions that could have been unfavorable. Fourthly, when it was not possible to avoid the undesirable decision, defensive depoliticization was used to mitigate provisions of ICAO's decisions in an attempt to make them less critical or so that they also featured offenses committed by the adversary. Fifthly, defensive depoliticization served as a means to simply counter critical remarks made by political adversaries. This particular objective was most evident in situations when the politicization of ICAO deliberations was not connected to a particular expectation from ICAO but was simply about using its forum to verbally attack another country, like in the cases of reservation regarding credentials of the contested delegation. In such situations, depoliticization was used merely as a reactive measure in alignment with the prevailing negative approach to politics in IOs.

As mentioned above, one of the purposes of defensive depoliticization was to amend the phrasing of ICAO decisions into more favorable ones. The wording of decisions made by IOs, including resolutions, frequently holds a symbolic yet significant character from the viewpoint of states. Those conflicted with the state that is subject to such a decision, or those affected by its offenses, seek to phrase such documents as severely as possible, contrary to the ostracized states. Such deliberations often refer to emotive and instructive words. Giuseppina Scotto di Carlo presented a classification of such words, from weakest to strongest. For emotive words, it is as follows: concerned, grieved, deplored, condemned, alarmed, shocked, indignant, and censured. For instructive words, they are as follows: decide, call upon, recommend, request, urge, warn, and demand. As to emotive words, IOs rarely use stronger ones than condemn. For example, it was the strongest phrasing used by the UN Security Council with regard to North Korea.[2] In general, the phrase 'calls upon' is commonly utilized to request an entity to comply, whereas stronger terms such as 'condemns' and 'deplores' are typically employed to denounce direct violations of past resolutions and international law.[3] Despite the presence of general guidelines, the wording of decisions within ICAO was a recurrent topic of deliberation, particularly concerning the emotive and instructive language used, as well as the consideration of whether specific states should be explicitly mentioned (stronger expression) or if the decisions should adopt a more general approach (weaker expression). Depoliticization rhetoric was primarily deployed in a defensive manner, with the contention that the wording was overly forceful due to its perceived alignment with political motives. However, there were also examples of reversed situations when representatives of states seeking to make decisions stronger claimed they were too weak for political reasons.

Defensive depoliticization on the forum of ICAO very often was accompanied by making political arguments. Representatives and delegates, in their attempts to shield their states, contended that the criticism directed toward them was politically motivated and therefore unsuitable for consideration within a technical organization. However, in the course of making these assertions, they themselves frequently introduced political arguments into the discussion. An oft-repeated statement used in many such situations was that 'I did not want to engage in the political debates, but was forced to,' followed by attacks against the adversary with the use of political arguments, often without any link to aviation matters. This, in turn, reinforces the argument about the highly political character of depoliticization.[4]

Defensive depoliticization has an unequivocally defensive character. It does not aim to remove politics from the IO but principally to avoid ostracism, which is why while arguing against discussing political issues, the same delegates often were ready to discuss them with regard to the offenses of the other side. On the other hand, though, examples of potentially neutral depoliticization rhetoric expressed by representatives and delegates of the states not engaged in such conflicts appear to reflect a genuine will to sustain the political neutrality of specialized agencies such as ICAO, which is supposed to increase their effectiveness and prestige. Still, besides its defensive character, defensive and neutral depoliticization rhetorics does not differ much with regard to the actual arguments used, which speaks about the proximity between defensive depoliticization and more general depoliticization moves that seek to keep politics away from the organization. What is more, in several situations, it was impossible to conclusively interpret if a particular depoliticizing move was neutral or defensive. This situation pertained to instances where representatives of states not directly involved in the conflict advocated against politicizing deliberations. However, they refrained from levying political accusations against either side or directly defending the criticized state. Such situations reveal a potential merit of defensive depoliticization, which when used modestly can conceal its instrumental character.

Both defensive and neutral depoliticization rhetoric stem from explicitly pejorative perceptions of politics and politicization on the forum of IOs. It connects with the so-called ideology of depoliticization and the functionalist argument, which assumes politics and politicization as something clearly negative. The explicit pejorative connotation of 'politics' within the ostensibly 'technical' ICAO has made accusing others of bringing political issues before ICAO a convenient means of demeaning their claims and arguments. This occurs irrespective of the gravity and context of the alleged offenses or whether any aviation-related transgression was involved initially. The unequivocally negative perception of politics sometimes even led to situations when two sides of the debate were accusing each other of making political arguments. Thus, the pejorative connotation of politics and politicization appears to have been a foundational assumption for the defensive use of depoliticization, which speaks in favor of the second detailed hypothesis.

In addition to the ideologically negative associations with politics, defensive depoliticization was sometimes utilized within the context of legal deliberations arising from the constrained jurisdictional scope of ICAO, as defined in its founding document – the Chicago Convention. The Convention made several clear restrictions, for example, that it applies to civil aircraft only, putting state aircraft beyond its jurisdiction.[5] As a result, some of the politicized debates featured legal arguments that ICAO has no jurisdiction over a certain matter, for example, with regard to one of the flights intercepted by the Israeli Air Force, when the discussion focused on deciding whether it was a state aircraft beyond ICAO jurisdiction or a civil aircraft. Such legal deliberations could merge with defensive depoliticization, with those being criticized claiming ICAO did not have jurisdiction and competence over an issue. Such claims were often associated with the arguments that political bodies such as the UN should deal with the issue or that they had already done so and there was no need to repeat the discussion in technical ICAO.

Some of the analyzed politicized deliberations suggest the last-resort character of depoliticization, perceived as a defensive diplomatic technique. In other words, state representatives and delegates have frequently resorted to employing defensive depoliticization when other arguments were either unavailable or proved ineffective. This was particularly evident in the lasting controversies in which the position of the defending side was evolving, like in the case of the shootdown of the KAL007 flight by the Soviet Union or the 21st-century Russia–West estrangement. In both cases, when substantive arguments did not work, state representatives resorted to the argument about the political character of the issue.

In addition to the depoliticization rhetoric employed by state representatives and delegates, it is important to underscore the role of the ICAO bureaucracy, particularly the President of the Council. As argued in Chapter 1, the President holds a special position within the organizational structure of ICAO. This raises the question of whether such a person can be an intermediary when there is a conflict, whether technical or political. Even though that was not the direct subject of the study, in many cases and contexts, an active role of the President of the Council could be observed. Although not always similarly active, Council Presidents sometimes acted as intermediaries in the conflicts waged on the forum of ICAO. They did not necessarily oppose political arguments, however, in their decisions and proposals, a consistent pursuit of compromise and decisions reached by consensus was evident. Moreover, even though it was often not visible directly in the analyzed minutes of the proceedings, on many occasions, the two sides of the conflict thanked the Presidents of the Council for their active role.

An aspect of depoliticization as a diplomatic technique in a multilateral organization that was not the primary subject of the research but was still observed refers to 'offensive depoliticization.' Offensive depoliticization, just as defensive depoliticization, is about utilizing depoliticization rhetoric within the politicized deliberations, but in order to hit political adversaries rather than in self-defense. Such rhetoric was used predominantly to make decisions against adversaries more severe, arguing that too weak phrasing meant politicization. Offensive depoliticization was employed, for example, by Iran concerning the resolution regarding the shootdown of its civilian aircraft by the US Navy, and by Russia, which aimed to persuade ICAO to address the issue of sanctions imposed by Western countries against Belarus in response to the forced landing of the Ryanair aircraft. Their representatives argued that the failure to address the issue, or using too weak phrasing of the ICAO decisions, was motivated by political interests. Offensive depoliticization, like its defensive cousin, capitalizes on the inherently negative ideological connotation of politics within IOs.

Depoliticization studied in this research differs slightly from the mainstream depoliticization literature regarding the focus, pushing this volume toward the strand of diplomatic studies. However, some of the observations connect and contribute to the depoliticization theory. For example, politicized deliberations in ICAO featured many instances of discursive depoliticization defined by Wood and Flinders as speech acts 'that make certain issues appear to be "normal" or "natural".'[6] In this study, such speech acts were sometimes used by delegates or representatives seeking to include controversial issues into the deliberation in ICAO, for example, through argumentation that an issue was in fact connected to aviation even when such link was in fact minor or non-existent, or through direct mentions about the non-political character of the issue. Such discursive depoliticization was factually contributing to the politicization of the deliberations.

Depoliticization as a diplomatic technique used in a multilateral environment also connects to preference-shaping and agenda-setting depoliticization, one of the types of depoliticization occurring in IOs. Such depoliticization assumes establishing a 'dominant rationality' and non-decision-making dynamics in order to delete certain issues or problems from the debate or consideration[7] and involves 'ideological, discursive or rhetorical claims in order to justify a political position that a certain issue or function does, or should, lie beyond the scope of politics.'[8] Examples of such depoliticization were most glaringly visible in the instances of neutral depoliticization, but defensive depoliticization was also built on its ideological premises, although in a rather instrumental way.

The negative connotation associated with politics, which underpins depoliticization efforts, whether defensive, offensive, or neutral, is closely linked to the functional theory of international relations. Functionalist approaches emphasized that solutions to common international problems would occur 'through joint application of technical expertise by various national participants' and that such activities crucially were to be 'noncontroversial politically.' Early functionalist theory has been reformulated to include political processes, leading to an increase in the controversial component,[9] although in general, politicization is considered by functionalism as something bad for the realization of functions of IOs. As observed by Jarvis, 'functionalists saw "politics" as an anathema, increasingly obsolescent.'[10] The reasonable consequence of this sort of thinking is that politically driven arguments and waging political conflicts can only hamper the functioning of an organization such as ICAO, which is purely technical with clearly defined aviation-related functions. The argument that political issues should not be injected into ICAO directly reflected the functional theory. However, such arguments echoed the desire to protect ICAO from politicization predominantly in the case of representatives of states that were not engaged in the particular conflict and possibly in the words of the organization's bureaucrats, although such cases were not particularly common among the analyzed politicized debates. When utilized defensively, the argumentation against politicization seemed to be driven more by considerations of state interests, a perspective corroborated by instances where countering political claims was accompanied by the introduction of political arguments. Acting in accordance with state interests on the forum of specialized agency would be best described by more realist approaches to international relations, although we should also not forget that politicized debates were still rather rare in ICAO, which in general proved effective in the realization of its statutory mission. What is more, some of the instances show that despite conflictual circumstances, on the forum of ICAO states often managed to collaborate for the sake of safer aviation, like in the case of the KAL007 incident when after very confrontational debates featuring political overtones and defensive depoliticization, in the end both sides agreed on the amendment of the Chicago Convention. Instances of politicized deliberations on the forum of such organizations shall be considered their temporal dysfunctions, although from another perspective, they might also be considered attempts to use IOs as arenas for the realization of state interests, specifically hitting political opponents.

In addition to employing qualitative content analysis as the primary research method, instances of political controversies observed on the ICAO forum, characterized by the defensive deployment of depoliticization rhetoric, were further investigated. This inquiry involved the examination of several variables with the aim of elucidating additional generalizations and validating the first specific hypothesis, according to which defensive depoliticization is relatively ineffective. Although thematically divided into four chapters, 15 political controversies were identified: expulsion of Spain, membership of the Republic of China, apartheid in South Africa, representation of Cyprus, Turkish invasion in Cyprus (featuring Turkish occupation, providing illegal air navigation services), aviation-related difficulties caused by Arab states against Israel, the Israeli attack on Beirut airport, interception of the Lebanese civil aircraft by Israel, Jerusalem airport, PLO's observer status, interception of Libyan Arab Airlines flight by Israel, KAL007 shootdown, IR655 shootdown, forced landing of Ryanair FR4978 (featuring also Western sanctions), the Russian invasion of Ukraine (featuring also the problem of dual registration of aircraft by Russia and Western sanctions). Because some of the controversies had a persistent character and were waged during more than one ICAO meeting, the 15 controversies led to 46 politicized deliberations that featured defensive depoliticization, with one of the deliberations dealing with two controversies simultaneously. For clarity, we only used controversies in which the attacked party defended itself, with the exception of several discussions on the forced landing of Ryanair flight in Minsk, in which Belarus was often defended solely by the Russian representative. All the controversies stemmed from seven international conflicts: World War II allies and Axis, the People's Republic of China and Taiwan (Republic of China), African states and South Africa, Cyprus and Turkey, Arab states and Israel, Russia (featuring the Soviet Union during the Cold War, Russia in the 21st century, Belarus with regard to the forced landing of Ryanair flight in 2021) and Western states, Iran and the United States. Details regarding the deliberations under study are presented in Table C.1.

As indicated in Table C.2, politicized deliberations featuring defensive depoliticization were held in the Assembly (26 times) and the Council (20 times). In several situations during the same ICAO meeting more than one controversial debate was held – they were coded like this if they were discussed separately and concerned different specific issues. Most observations have been made for the conflict between Russia and the West (including criticism against the USSR during the Cold War and Belarus) (19), followed by Arab states–Israel (9), PRC–RoC (8), Cyprus–Turkey (4), African states–South Africa (3), US–Iran (2), and World War II allies–Axis (1). Twelve states employed defensive depoliticization: Soviet

Table C.1 Politicized deliberations in ICAO featuring defensive depoliticization

Controversy	*Conflict*	*Defending state*	*Objective of the criticism in ICAO*	*Purpose of depoliticization*	*ICAO forum (body – meeting number – year)*
Expulsion of Spain	World War II allies–Axis	Spain	Isolation	Avoiding isolation	Assembly – 1 – 1947
Membership of RoC	PRC–RoC	RoC	Verbal	Response to verbal attack	Assembly – 11 – 1958
Membership of RoC		RoC	Verbal	Response to verbal attack	Assembly – 12 – 1959
Membership of RoC		RoC	Verbal	Response to verbal attack	Assembly – 13 – 1961
Membership of RoC		RoC	Verbal	Response to verbal attack	Assembly – 14 – 1962
Membership of RoC		RoC	Verbal	Response to verbal attack	Assembly – 15 – 1965
Membership of RoC		RoC	Verbal	Response to verbal attack	Assembly – 16 – 1968
Membership of RoC		RoC	Verbal	Response to verbal attack	Assembly – 17 – 1970
Membership of RoC		RoC	Verbal	Response to verbal attack	Assembly – 17A – 1971
Apartheid in SA	African states–South Africa	South Africa	Isolation	Avoiding isolation	Assembly – 15 – 1965
Apartheid in SA		South Africa	Critical decision	Terminating deliberations	Assembly – 15 – 1965
Apartheid in SA		South Africa	Isolation	Avoiding isolation	Assembly – 18 – 1971
Turkish intervention in Cyprus	Turkey–Cyprus	Turkey	Verbal	Response to verbal attacks	Assembly – 22 – 1977
Turkish intervention in Cyprus		Turkey	Verbal	Response to verbal attacks	Assembly – 24 – 1983
Turkish intervention in Cyprus		Turkey	Verbal	Response to verbal attacks	Assembly – 26 – 1986
Representation of Cyprus		Cyprus	Verbal	Response to verbal attacks	Assembly – 26 – 1986
Aviation-related difficulties against Israel	Arab states -Israel	Egypt/Arab states	Verbal	Response to verbal attacks	Assembly – 9 – 1955
Aviation-related difficulties against Israel		Lebanon/Arab states	Verbal	Terminating deliberations	Assembly – 10 – 1956
Israeli attack on Beirut airport		Israel	Critical decision	Preventing the decision	Council – Extraordinary – 1969
Interception of the Lebanese civil aircraft		Israel	Critical decision	Preventing the decision	Assembly – 20- Extraordinary – 1973
Jerusalem airport controversy		Israel	Critical decision	Preventing the decision	Assembly – 21 – 1974
Jerusalem airport controversy		Israel	Critical decision	Preventing the decision	Assembly – 23 – 1980

PLO's observer status		Israel	Observer status to an adversary	Preventing the decision	Assembly – 21 – 1974
PLO's observer status		Israel	Observer status to an adversary	Preventing the decision	Assembly – 22 – 1977
Interception of Libyan Arab Airlines flight by Israel		Israel	Critical decision	Preventing the decision	Council – 117 – 1986
KAL007 shootdown by the USSR	Russia–West	Soviet Union	Critical decision	Postponing decision	Council – Extraordinary – 1983
KAL007 shootdown by the USSR		Soviet Union	Critical decision	More favorable phrasing	Assembly – 24 – 1983
KAL007 shootdown by the USSR		Russia	Critical decision	More favorable phrasing	Council – 111 – 1984
IR655 shootdown by the United States	Iran–United States	United States	Critical decision	More favorable phrasing	Council – Extraordinary – 1988
IR655 shootdown by the United States		United States	Critical decision	More favorable phrasing	Council – 126 – 1989
Forced landing of FR4978 in Belarus	Russia–West	Belarus	Critical decision	More favorable phrasing	Council – 223 – 2021
Forced landing of FR4978 in Belarus		Belarus	Verbal	Response to verbal attacks	Council – 223 – 2021
Forced landing of FR4978 in Belarus		Belarus	Further investigation	Terminating deliberations	Council – 223 – 2021
Forced landing of FR4978 in Belarus		Belarus	Critical decision	More favorable phrasing	Council – 225 – 2022
Forced landing of FR4978 in Belarus		Belarus	N/A	Revocation of sanctions	Council – 225 – 2022
Forced landing of FR4978 in Belarus		Belarus	Critical note of the investigation	More favorable phrasing	Council – 226 – 2022
Forced landing of FR4978 in Belarus		Belarus	N/A	Revocation of sanctions	Council – 226 – 2022

(*Continued*)

Table C.1 (Continued)

Controversy	*Conflict*	*Defending state*	*Objective of the criticism in ICAO*	*Purpose of depoliticization*	*ICAO forum (body – meeting number – year)*
Forced landing of FR4978 in Belarus		Belarus	Critical decision	Avoiding critical decision	Council – 226 – 2022
Russian invasion of Ukraine		Russia	Critical decision	Avoiding critical decision	Council – 225 – 2022
Russian invasion of Ukraine		Russia	Taking action	Terminating deliberations	Council – 225 – 2022
Russian invasion of Ukraine		Russia	Critical decision	Terminating deliberations	Council – 226 – 2022
Russian invasion of Ukraine		Russia	N/A	Revocation of sanctions	Council – 226 – 2022
Russian invasion of Ukraine		Russia	Critical decision	More favorable phrasing	Council – 226 – 2022
Russian invasion of Ukraine		Russia	Observer status of the adversary	Preventing the decision	Council – 226 – 2022
Russian invasion of Ukraine		Russia	N/A	Responding to not being elected to the Council	Assembly – 41 – 2022
Russian invasion of Ukraine/ Forced landing of FR4978		Russia	Critical decision	More favorable phrasing	Assembly – 41 – 2022

Source: Own study

Table C.2 Defending states' characteristics

Defending state	*Political bloc*	*GPI*	*Power status*
Spain	Other	0.007012896726	Lesser power
RoC	Western	0.002431482097–0.002748236353	Lesser power
South Africa	Other	0.003147672749–0.003158268788	Lesser power
Cyprus	Other	0.0001281287531	Lesser power
Turkey	Western	0.003430236528–0.003699119439	Lesser power
Egypt	Arab states	0.001992559667	Lesser power
Lebanon	Arab states	0.005963048904	Lesser power
Israel	Western	0.009402538334–0.01327612991	Lesser power
Soviet Union	Russian	0.1025560317–0.1035642768	World power
United States	Western	0.2593800537	World power
Belarus	Russian	0.0004975653615–0.0005447354059	Lesser power
Russia	Russian	0.03262996684	Middle power

Source: Own study partly based on Frederick S. Pardee Center for International Futures Global Power Index.

Union (3), Russia (8), Belarus (8) (in this particular case, more often it was Russia to defend her ally using defensive depoliticization), Taiwan (8), Israel (7), Turkey (3), South Africa (3), Cyprus (2), United States (2), Spain (1), Egypt (1), Lebanon (1). It is essential to clarify that the aforementioned figures should not be construed as indicative of the degree of politicization within individual ICAO bodies, the extent of political controversy arising from particular conflicts, or the propensity of specific states to utilize defensive depoliticization tactics. Instead, these figures are contingent upon data accessibility and the unique contextual factors at play.

Each of the controversies was further studied with regard to independent and dependent variables. Independent variables were connected to some of the qualities of the defending states, and of the specific controversy, featuring the political bloc of the defending state, its power status, and whether the controversy was related to aviation-related misconduct. The variable regarding political blocs was connected to the fact that political allies tend not only to vote in favor of each other but also to defend their allies verbally. Belonging to a particular political bloc was determined based on military and political alliances and other forms of close collaboration. Drawing upon the historical framework of Cold War blocs and contemporary tensions between Russia and Western nations in the 21st century, we have posited the formation of two distinct blocs: the Western bloc featuring the United States, Israel, Turkey, and Taiwan, and the Russian bloc encompassing Russia, the former Soviet Union, and Belarus. In addition, Egypt and Lebanon were classified as Arab states, while Spain, South Africa, and Cyprus were categorized as 'Others.' This classification was based on the absence of direct association with the key group of states during the period of controversy. However, it is acknowledged that this approach has limitations, such as overlooking periodic instances of close collaboration between South Africa and certain Western states, as well as the geographical and historical proximity between Cyprus and Greece. The power status of the defending state was assessed based on the Global Power Index (GPI) for the year of the controversy in ICAO. Following the framework proposed by the Frederick S. Pardee Center for International Futures, we have classified certain states as either global, middle, or lesser powers. The specifics of the independent variables connected to the characteristics of the defending state are delineated in Table C.2. In instances of enduring controversy, a spectrum encompassing the lowest and highest GPI values was presented.

The last independent variable was connected to the specific character of the circumstances leading to the politicized deliberations in ICAO, specifically whether the defending state actually committed a civil aviation offense, such as illegal interception of an aircraft or a shootdown. This variable was to some extent subjective since the countries criticizing another state often sought to draw a link to aviation. There were also several other difficulties in unambiguous determination of the character of some controversies, for example when ICAO jurisdiction was unclear or when the misconduct was related to military aviation rather than civil aviation. For such reasons, in several situations, an ambiguous coding of 'partly yes' was used.

Dependent variables assumed whether representatives or delegates of other states defended the attacked state, whether neutral depoliticization was used, and whether the defense was successful. The initial two variables pertain to the trajectory of the deliberations, while the final variable is associated with their outcomes. Several of the observations were subject to minor limitations. For example, it was sometimes difficult to unequivocally determine whether depoliticization rhetoric used by a third-country representative was neutral or defensive. The effectiveness of defense could not be determined in the cases of verbal criticism without expectation of direct ICAO action – situations marked as N/A.

All politicized deliberations characterized by defensive depoliticization, concerning both independent and dependent variables, have been consolidated in Table C.3.

Our research shows that defensive depoliticization is a relatively unsuccessful diplomatic tool. Of the 30 observations where effectiveness could be assessed, defense succeeded in only six instances, constituting 20 percent of the total. These findings lend support to the specific hypothesis positing that depoliticization serves as a relatively ineffective mechanism for circumventing undesirable decisions within a multilateral organization. Even though in some cases the arguments of the delegations defending their countries were at least to some extent valid, usually they were not able to terminate the debates, with bloc voting prevailing over argumentation. Most probably, such results connect to the last-resort character of defensive depoliticization as a diplomatic tool. As argued above, in many cases, state representatives resorted to defensive depoliticization only when no other diplomatic methods were available, and in such a difficult situation it is hard to expect effective persuasion. The few instances of effective defensive depoliticization feature the defense from the first attempt to expel South Africa from ICAO, one instance when Arab states were defending against Israeli accusations of aviation-related difficulties, one instance when Israel sought to avoid critical decision after

Table C.3 Comparison of conflicts waged in ICAO

Controversy	*Meeting when controversy was deliberated*	*Conflict*	*Defending state*	*Independent variables*			*Dependent variables*		
				Political block of defending state	*Power status of defending state*	*Controversy related to an aviation-related misconduct*	*Defense by other delegations*	*Neutral depoliticization*	*Successful defense*
Expulsion of Spain	Assembly – 1 – 1947	World War II allies–Axis	Spain	Other	Lesser power	No	Yes	Yes	No
Membership of RoC	Assembly – 11 – 1958	PRC–RoC	RoC	Western	Lesser power	No	No	No	N/A
Membership of RoC	Assembly – 12 – 1959	PRC–RoC	RoC	Western	Lesser power	No	Yes	No	N/A
Membership of RoC	Assembly – 13 – 1961	PRC–RoC	RoC	Western	Lesser power	No	No	No	N/A
Membership of RoC	Assembly – 14 – 1962	PRC–RoC	RoC	Western	Lesser power	No	Yes	No	N/A
Membership of RoC	Assembly – 15 – 1965	PRC–RoC	RoC	Western	Lesser power	No	Yes	No	N/A
Membership of RoC	Assembly – 16 – 1968	PRC–RoC	RoC	Western	Lesser power	No	Yes	No	N/A
Membership of RoC	Assembly – 17 – 1970	PRC–RoC	RoC	Western	Lesser power	No	No	No	N/A
Membership of RoC	Assembly – 17A – 1971	PRC–RoC	RoC	Western	Lesser power	No	No	No	N/A
Apartheid in SA	Assembly – 15 – 1965	African states–South Africa	South Africa	Other	Lesser power	No	Yes	Yes	Yes
Apartheid in SA	Assembly – 15 – 1965	African states–South Africa	South Africa	Other	Lesser power	No	No	Yes	No
Apartheid in SA	Assembly – 18 – 1971	African states–South Africa	South Africa	Other	Lesser power	No	Yes	Yes	No

(*Continued*)

Table C.3 (Continued)

Controversy	*Meeting when controversy was deliberated*	*Conflict*	*Defending state*	*Independent variables*			*Dependent variables*		
				Political block of defending state	*Power status of defending state*	*Controversy related to an aviation-related misconduct*	*Defense by other delegations*	*Neutral depoliticization*	*Successful defense*
Turkish intervention in Cyprus	Assembly – 22 – 1977	Cyprus–Turkey	Turkey	Western	Lesser power	Partly yes	No	No	N/A
Turkish intervention in Cyprus	Assembly – 24 – 1983	Cyprus–Turkey	Turkey	Western	Lesser power	Yes	No	No	N/A
Turkish intervention in Cyprus	Assembly – 26 – 1986	Cyprus–Turkey	Turkey	Western	Lesser power	Partly yes	No	No	N/A
Representation of Cyprus	Assembly – 26 – 1986	Cyprus–Turkey	Cyprus	Other	Lesser power	No	No	No	N/A
Aviation-related difficulties against Israel	Assembly – 9 – 1955	Arab states–Israel	Egypt/Arab states	Arab states	Lesser power	Yes	No	No	N/A
Aviation-related difficulties against Israel	Assembly – 10 – 1956	Arab states–Israel	Lebanon/ Arab states	Arab states	Lesser power	Yes	Yes	Yes	Yes
Israeli attack on Beirut airport	Council – Extraordinary – 1969	Arab states–Israel	Israel	Western	Lesser power	Yes	No	Yes	Yes
Interception of the Lebanese civil aircraft	Assembly – 20- Extraordinary – 1973	Arab states–Israel	Israel	Western	Lesser power	Yes	No	Yes	No
Jerusalem airport controversy	Assembly – 21 – 1974	Arab states –Israel	Israel	Western	Lesser power	Partly yes	No	Yes	No

Jerusalem airport controversy	Assembly – 23 – 1980	Arab states –Israel	Israel	Western	Lesser power	Partly yes	No	No	No
PLO's observer status	Assembly – 21 – 1974	Arab states–Israel	Israel	Western	Lesser power	No	No	No	No
PLO's observer status	Assembly – 22 – 1977	Arab states–Israel	Israel	Western	Lesser power	No	No	No	No
Interception of Libyan Arab Airlines flight by Israel	Council – 117 – 1986	Arab states–Israel	Israel	Western	Lesser power	Yes	Yes	Yes	No
KAL007 shootdown by the USSR	Council – Extraordinary – 1983	Russia–West	Soviet Union	Russian	World power	Yes	Yes	Yes	No
KAL007 shootdown by the USSR	Assembly – 24 – 1983	Russia–West	Soviet Union	Russian	World power	Yes	Yes	Yes	No
KAL007 shootdown by the USSR	Council – 111 – 1984	Russia–West	Soviet Union	Russian	World power	Yes	Yes	Yes	No
IR655 shootdown by the United States	Council – Extraordinary – 1988	Iran–US	United States	Western	World power	Yes	No	Yes	Yes
IR655 shootdown by the United States	Council – 126 – 1989	Iran–US	United States	Western	World power	Yes	Yes	No	Yes
Forced landing of FR4978 in Belarus	Council – 223 – 2021	Russia–West	Belarus	Russian	Lesser power	Yes	Yes	Yes	No
Forced landing of FR4978 in Belarus	Council – 223 – 2021	Russia–West	Belarus	Russian	Lesser power	Yes	Yes	No	N/A

(Continued)

Table C.3 (Continued)

Controversy	*Meeting when controversy was deliberated*	*Conflict*	*Defending state*	*Independent variables*			*Dependent variables*		
				Political block of defending state	*Power status of defending state*	*Controversy related to an aviation-related misconduct*	*Defense by other delegations*	*Neutral depoliticization*	*Successful defense*
Forced landing of FR4978 in Belarus	Council – 223 – 2021	Russia–West	Belarus	Russian	Lesser power	Yes	Yes	No	No
Forced landing of FR4978 in Belarus	Council – 225 – 2022	Russia–West	Belarus	Russian	Lesser power	Yes	Yes	Yes	No
Forced landing of FR4978 in Belarus	Council – 225 – 2022	Russia–West	Belarus	Russian	Lesser power	Yes	Yes	Yes	No
Forced landing of FR4978 in Belarus	Council – 226 – 2022	Russia–West	Belarus	Russian	Lesser power	Yes	Yes	No	No
Forced landing of FR4978 in Belarus	Council – 226 – 2022	Russia–West	Belarus	Russian	Lesser power	Yes	Yes	Yes	No
Forced landing of FR4978 in Belarus	Council – 226 – 2022	Russia–West	Belarus	Russian	Lesser power	Yes	Yes	No	No
Russian invasion of Ukraine	Council – 225 – 2022	Russia–West	Russia	Russian	Middle power	No	Yes/no	Yes	No
Russian invasion of Ukraine	Council – 225 – 2022	Russia–West	Russia	Russian	Middle power	Yes	No	No	Yes
Russian invasion of Ukraine	Council – 226 – 2022	Russia–West	Russia	Russian	Middle power	Partly yes	Yes/no	Yes	No

Russian invasion of Ukraine	Council – 226 – 2022	Russia–West	Russia	Russian	Middle power	Partly yes	No	Yes	N/A
Russian invasion of Ukraine	Council – 226 – 2022	Russia–West	Russia	Russian	Middle power	Partly yes	No	No	No
Russian invasion of Ukraine	Council – 226 – 2022	Russia–West	Russia	Russian	Middle power	No	Yes	No	No
Russian invasion of Ukraine	Assembly – 41 – 2022	Russia–West	Russia	Russian	Middle power	No	Yes	No	N/A
Russian invasion of Ukraine / Forced landing of FR4978	Assembly – 41 – 2022	Russia–West	Russia	Russian	Middle power	Partly yes	No	No	No

Source: Own study.

its attack on Beirut airport, two instances when the United States was seeking to achieve more favorable phrasing of the ICAO decisions after the shootdown of Iranian civil aircraft, and one Russian attempt to prevent ICAO Council from taking action after its invasion of Ukraine.

The United States demonstrated the highest success rate in deflecting criticism within ICAO through defensive depoliticization, achieving a success rate of 100 percent. Similarly, the collective Arab states also achieved a success rate of 100 percent. However, it is worth noting that the limited number of measurements may somewhat attenuate the robustness of these findings. Regarding the respective independent variables, it is challenging to draw definitive conclusions about their impact on the efficacy of depoliticization. The highest efficacy rate, observed at 40 percent, was associated with world powers. A higher percentage for world powers could have been anticipated, with many authors arguing that the most powerful states will dictate the outcomes in the IO.[11] It is important to note, however, that the high score attributed to world powers is predominantly influenced by the effectiveness of the United States. A detailed breakdown of the effectiveness of defense into specific levels of power is presented in Figure C.1.

In terms of the impact of political blocs on the efficacy of defense (see Figure C.2), states affiliated with the Russian bloc exhibited notably low effectiveness at 6 percent, in contrast to the 33 percent observed for Western states. A high percentage was observed for the Arab states, but few instances of the Arab states being ostracized make this measurement inconclusive, whereas Others (25 percent) should be considered a control group. We should seek explanations for factors such as bloc voting potential and the gravity of the offenses from which the controversies originated.

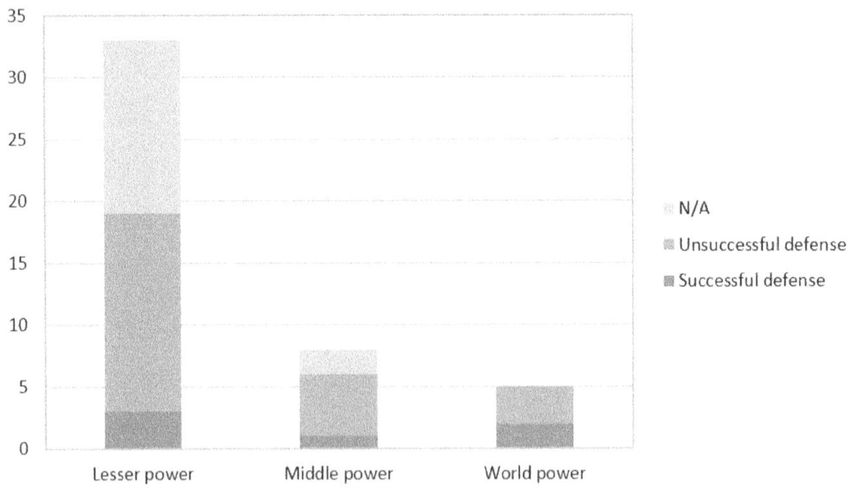

Figure C.1 Effectiveness of defense according to the power of the defending state.

Source: Own study.

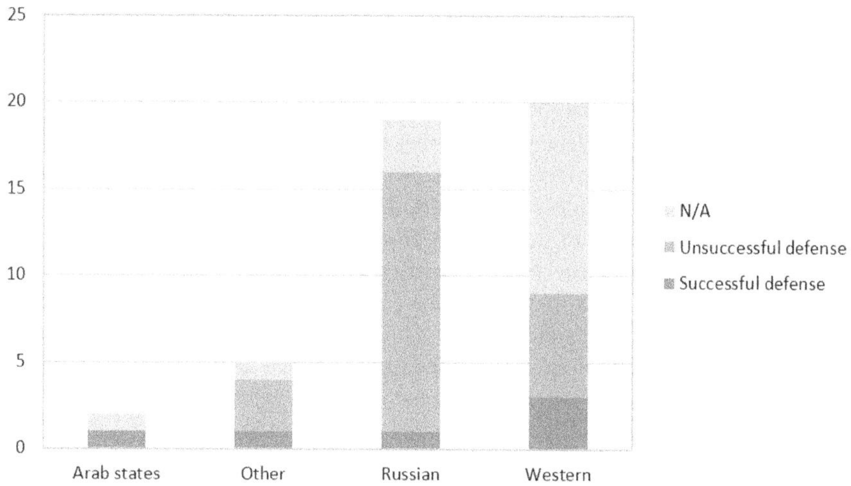

Figure C.2 Effectiveness of defense according to the political bloc of the defending state.

Source: Own study.

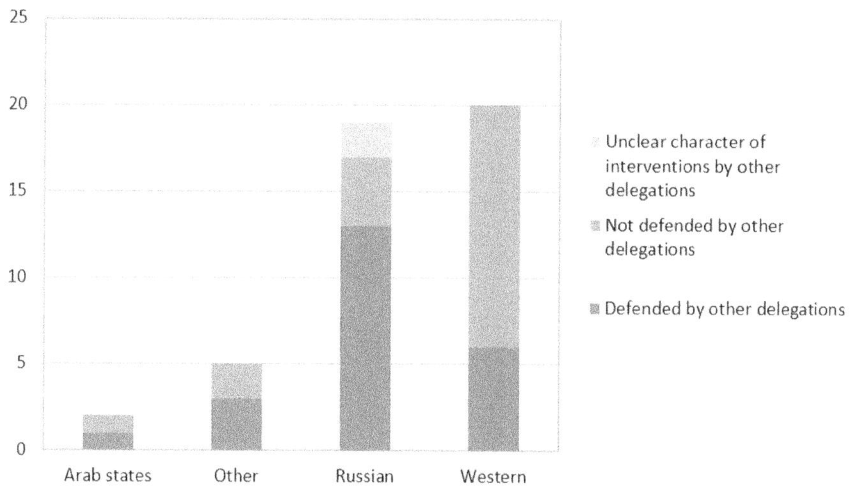

Figure C.3 Defense by other delegations according to the political bloc of the defending state.

Source: Own study.

Conversely, nations within the Russian bloc exhibited the highest likelihood of being defended by other delegations, with a percentage of 76 percent (see Figure C.3), which further increases when considering ambiguous statements as indicative of defensive support. On the other side of the spectrum, Western countries were defended by other delegations only in 30 percent of cases. These observations suggest the presence of a robust collective solidarity among states aligned with Russia. Qualitative results seem to confirm this estimation. The Soviet Union was always defended by other Communist countries, similarly as Belarus, which was sometimes exclusively defended by Russia. In turn, a low result for Western states is aligned with the controversies concerning Israel, which often were the result of clear offenses that were difficult to defend. Western states did not consistently demonstrate unanimity in mutual defense in ICAO, but they often constituted a solid voting bloc, just as the Arab states. Both groups exhibited a high degree of unanimity particularly when criticizing adversaries such as Russia or Israel.

Consideration was given to whether the occurrences of neutral depoliticization and defense by other delegations were influenced by the fact that deliberations stemmed from an aviation-related misconduct. The two dependent variables are interlinked because even though many statements categorized as evidence of neutral depoliticization explicitly demonstrated genuine efforts to safeguard ICAO from politicization or to steer its attention toward the technical aspects of the issues under discussion, some of them could also have represented covert defensive depoliticization. This analysis was predicated on the assumption that in the absence of clear violations within the realm of aviation, other states would endeavor to shield the organization from politicization and lend support to the criticized state. Twenty-eight of the deliberations were clearly or somehow clearly connected with aviation-related misconduct by the criticized state. Surprisingly, neutral depoliticization occurred more frequently in situations where the defending state was implicated in an offense related to civil aviation, accounting for 56 percent of cases, as opposed to 28 percent (see Figure C.4). Regarding the relationship between aviation-related misconduct and being defended by other delegations, states were also defended

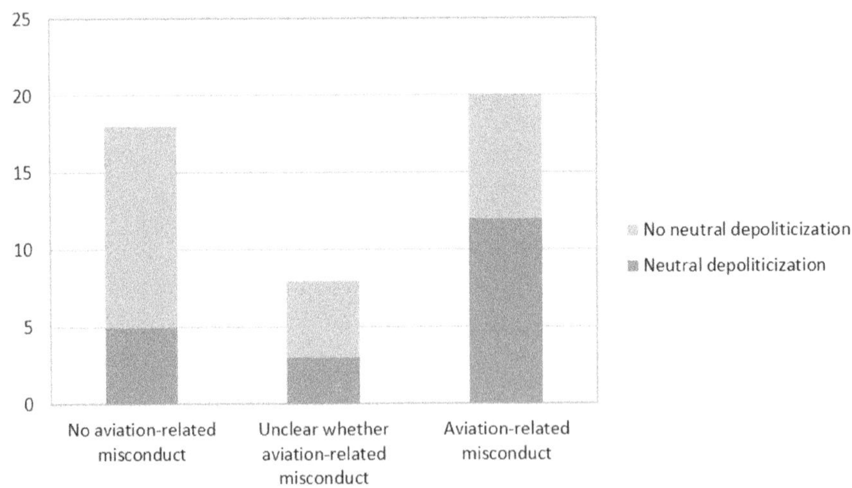

Figure C.4 Neutral depoliticization according to aviation-related misconduct.

Source: Own study.

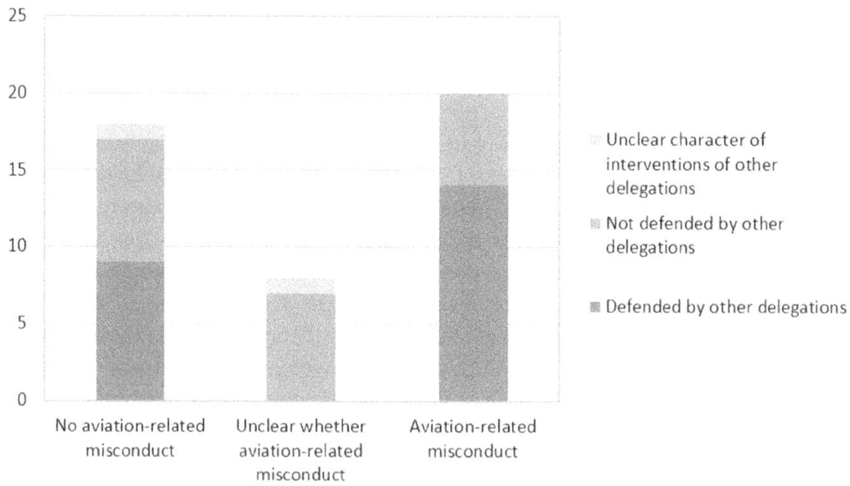

Figure C.5 Defense by other delegations according to aviation-related misconduct.

Source: Own study.

more frequently following the aviation-related misconduct – in 70 percent of cases, as opposed to 53 percent (see Figure C.5). These findings clearly indicate that there is no link between the prior behavior of the ostracized state and other delegations' engagement in the forum of ICAO. Secondly, it appears that criticism of a state on the forum of ICAO for behavior that is not directly under ICAO's jurisdiction does not lead member state representatives to argue against the ostracism, which in turn suggests that in such situations member states rather than seeking to maximize the efficiency and neutrality of ICAO seek to realize foreign policy goals in the first place, although of course the judgment concerning the aviation-related misconduct was to some extent subjective.

This book is dedicated to the politicized debates conducted on the forum of the ICAO. They all originated from international conflicts and were brought to ICAO by states aiming to utilize its forum to target their political adversaries. These politicized debates involved mutual accusations and attacks, frequently characterized by emotional statements. As argued throughout this volume, claims that specific issues were political were used as a diplomatic technique, either to defend the criticized state or alternatively to speak against the politicization of the ICAO proceedings in general. Despite its generally ineffective nature, defensive depoliticization has been employed since the inception of ICAO and continues to be utilized to this day. Rooted in the functionalist perspective that assigns a negative connotation to politics and politicization within specialized IOs, it is unlikely that such tactics will be eradicated from the diplomatic repertoire in the near future. For this reason, besides academic contribution, the findings of this book offer some practical recommendations to the practitioners of international relations in a multilateral environment.

Even though defensive depoliticization appears to be a natural diplomatic move in the multilateral environment, it has not received adequate attention within the field of diplomatic studies. Most crucially, defensive depoliticization could be studied in reference to other IGOs, particularly other specialized agencies, where the use of such a tool is expected in conflictual situations. An interesting prospective research area concerns defensive depoliticization in non-governmental organizations. Organizations such as the International Olympic Committee have traditionally attempted to distance themselves from politics, although as many studies show, they are inherently embedded into the world of politics. They can, therefore, offer another potential arena for defensive depoliticization. Furthermore, this study only indicated offensive depoliticization which concerns depoliticization rhetoric but with a reversed purpose of hitting political adversaries but building on the similar assumption of negative connotations of politics, which surely deserves further theoretical and empirical consideration.

Notes

1 David P. Forsythe, "The UN and the Arab-Israeli Conflict: What Has Been Learned in 25 Years," *International Organization* 26, no. 4 (1972): 705.

2 Giuseppina Scotto di Carlo, "Analysis of UN Resolutions Relating to North Korea: A Comparison with Resolutions Relating to the Second Gulf War," *International Journal for the Semiotics of Law* 27, no. 4 (2013): 7, 13.

3 Benjamin Habib, "The Enforcement Problem in Resolution 2094 and the United Nations Security Council Sanctions Regime: Sanctioning North Korea," *Australian Journal of International Affairs* 70, no. 1 (2016): 54, https://doi.org/10.1080/10357718.2015.1095278

4 See: Peter Burnham, "Globalization, Depoliticization and 'Modern' Economic Management," in *The Politics of Change*, ed. Werner Bonefeld and Kosmas Psychopedis (London: Palgrave Macmillan, 2002), 22, https://doi.org/10.1057/9780333993798_2

5 "Convention on International Civil Aviation." Signed at Chicago on December 7, 1944: 2.

6 Matt Wood and Matthew Flinders, "Rethinking Depoliticisation: Beyond the Governmental," *Policy & Politics* 42, no. 2 (2014): 152, https://doi.org/10.1332/030557312X655909

7 Diane Stone, "Global Governance Depoliticized: Knowledge Networks, Scientization, and Anti-Policy," in *Anti-Politics, Depoliticization, & Governance*, ed. Paul Fawcett, Matthew Flinders, Colin Hay, and Matthew Wood (Oxford: Oxford University Press, 2017), 93–94.

8 Matthew Flinders and Jim Buller, "Depoliticisation: Principles, Tactics and Tools," *British Politics* 1 (2006): 307, https://doi.org/10.1057/palgrave.bp.4200016

9 Peter Wolf, "International Organization and Attitude Change: A Re–Examination of the Functionalist Approach," *International Organization* 27 (1973): 349–350, https://doi.org/10.1017/S0020818300003544

10 D. S. L. Jarvis, "Integration Theory Revisited: Haas, Neo-Functionalism, and the Problematics of European Integration, Policy," *Organisation and Society* 7, no. 1 (1994): 20, https://doi.org/10.1080/10349952.1994.11876793

11 Mona M. Lyne, Daniel L. Nielson, and Michael J. Tierney, "Who Delegates? Alternative Models of Principals in Development Aid," in *Delegation and Agency in International Organization*, ed. Darren G. Hawkins, David A. Lake, Daniel L. Nielson, and Michael J. Tierney (Cambridge: Cambridge University Press, 2009), 45.

Bibliography

Primary sources

Archival documents

Annual Report of the Council – 1970. Documentation for the session of the Assembly in 1974. A19-P/1, DOC 8982. ICAO Archival Documents.

Annual Report of the Council – 1973. Documentation for the session of the Assembly in 1974. DOC 9085. ICAO Archival Documents.

Annual Report of the Council – 1983. Documentation for the session of the Assembly in 1986. DOC 9421. ICAO Archival Documents.

Annual Report of the Council – 1984. Documentation for the session of the Assembly in 1986. DOC 9451. ICAO Archival Documents.

Annual Report of the Council – 1988. Documentation for the session of the Assembly in 1989. DOC 9530. ICAO Archival Documents.

Annual Report of the Council – 1989. Documentation for the session of the Assembly in 1992. DOC 9553. ICAO Archival Documents.

Annual Report of the Council – 1993. Documentation for the session of the Assembly in 1995. DOC 9622. ICAO Archival Documents.

Annual Report of the Council – 1994. Documentation for the session of the Assembly in 1995. DOC 9637. ICAO Archival Documents.

Annual Report of the Council. 2007. DOC 9898. ICAO Archival Documents.

Annual Report of the Council to the Assembly for 1956. Supporting Documentation for the Eleventh Session of the Assembly, 1958. A11-P/1, DOC 7788. ICAO Archival Documents.

Annual Report of the Council to the Assembly for 1957. Supporting Documentation for the Eleventh Session of the Assembly. May 1958. A11-P/3, DOC 7866. ICAO Archival Documents.

Annual Report of the Council to the Assembly for 1960. Supporting Documentation for the Fourteenth Session of the Assembly. April 15, 1961. A14-P/3, DOC 8140. ICAO Archival Documents.

Consolidated attendance list, 10th Session of the Assembly. June–July 1956. A10-P/17, DOC 7708. ICAO Archival Documents.

Decisions Taken by the Assembly at Its Fifth and Sixth Meetings, Assembly – Nineteenth Session (Extraordinary). March 1, 1973. A19-Decisions 5&6. ICAO Archival Documents.

Draft Assembly Working Paper. Infractions of the Convention of International Civil Aviation by the Republic of Belarus. August 15, 2022. C-WP/15430. ICAO Archival Documents.

Draft Assembly Working Paper. Infractions of the Convention on International Civil Aviation by the Russian Federation, Council – 226th Session. July 7, 2022. C-WP/15427. ICAO Archival Documents.

Draft Resolution. Agenda Item 41: The question of South Africa's continued membership in ICAO, Executive Committee, Assembly – Fifteenth Session. July 8, 1965. A15-WP/183. ICAO Archival Documents.

Executive Committee Minutes of the Eighth Meeting, Assembly – Fourth Session. June 8, 1950. A4-WP/213, EX-Approved Min. 8. ICAO Archival Documents.

Executive Committee Minutes of the Sixteenth Meeting, 10th Session of the Assembly. July 11, 1956. A10-WP/150, Min. Ex-16. ICAO Archival Documents.

Executive Committee Report, Assembly – 41st Session, n.d. A41-EX, DOC 10183. ICAO Archival Documents.

Final Report of the Executive Committee, Assembly 24th Session. n.d. A24-EX, DOC 9409. ICAO Archival Documents.

Interim Report into Incident Involving Ryanair Flight FR4978 in Belarus Airspace on 23 May 2021. Council – 223rd Session. June 21, 2021. C-WP/15224. ICAO Archival Documents.

Minutes of 1st Meeting Held in Council Chamber on Thursday. First Assembly, Commission No. 1 – Constitutional and General Policy Questions. May 8, 1947. A1-CP/32, DOC 4232. ICAO Archival Documents.

Minutes of the Eighth Meeting, Council – 117th Session. February 28, 1986. C-Min. 117/8. ICAO Archival Documents.

Minutes of the Eighth Plenary Meeting, Assembly 24th Session. September 23, 1983. A24-Min. P/8, DOC 9415. ICAO Archival Documents.

Minutes of the Eighth Plenary Meeting, Assembly 26th Session. September 26, 1986. A26-Min. P/8 DOC 9491. ICAO Archival Documents.

Minutes of the Eighth Plenary Meeting, Assembly 29th Session. September 25, 1992. A29-Min. P/8 DOC 9601. ICAO Archival Documents.

Minutes of the Eleventh Plenary Meeting, Assembly – 21st Session. October 15, 1974. A21 Min. P/11, DOC 9119. ICAO Archival Documents.

Minutes of the Eleventh Plenary Meeting, Assembly – Fifteenth Session. July 16, 1965. A15-P/5, DOC 8516. ICAO Archival Documents.

Minutes of the Eleventh Plenary Meeting, Assembly 23rd Session. October 3, 1980. A23 Min. P/11, DOC 9317. ICAO Archival Documents.

Minutes of the Fifth Plenary Meeting, Assembly – 31st Session. September 21, 1995, 22, DRAFT A31-Min. P/5, ICAO Archival Documents.

Minutes of the Fifth Plenary Meeting, Assembly – 31st Session. September 21, 1995. DRAFT A31-Min. ICAO Archival Documents.

Minutes of the Fifth Plenary Meeting, Assembly – Twentieth Session (Extraordinary). August 30, 1973. A20-Min. P/5, DOC 9087. ICAO Archival Documents.

Minutes of the Fifth Plenary Meeting, Assembly 24th Session. September 22, 1983. A24-Min. P/5, DOC 9415. ICAO Archival Documents.

Minutes of the Fifth Plenary Meeting, Assembly 25th Session (Extraordinary). April 26, 1984. A25-Min. P/5, DOC 9437. ICAO Archival Documents.

Minutes of the First Meeting, Council – Extraordinary Session. January 20, 1969. C/982-1 C-Min. EXTRAORDINARY/1, DOC 8793-1. ICAO Archival Documents.

Minutes of the First Meeting, Council – Extraordinary Session. September 15, 1983. C-Min. EXTRAORDINARY (1983)/1, DOC 9416-C/1077. ICAO Archival Documents.

Minutes of the First Meeting, Council – Extraordinary Session. July 13, 1988. C-Min. EXTRAORDINARY (1988)/1, DOC 9541-C/1106. ICAO Archival Documents.
Minutes of the First Plenary Meeting, Assembly – Fifth Session. June 5, 1951. A5-P/2-1, DOC 7168-1. ICAO Archival Documents.
Minutes of the First Plenary Meeting, Assembly – Twelfth Session. June 16, 1959. A12-P/2, DOC 7996. ICAO Archival Documents.
Minutes of the First Plenary Meeting, Assembly – Twentieth Session (Extraordinary). August 28, 1973. A20-Min. P/1, DOC 9087. ICAO Archival Documents.
Minutes of the First Plenary Meeting, First Assembly. May 6, 1947. A1-P/18 6/5/47, DOC 4102. ICAO Archival Documents.
Minutes of the First Plenary Meeting, Interim Assembly – Plenary Meetings, May 21, 1946. A/29 21/5/46, DOC 1686. ICAO Archival Documents.
Minutes of the First Plenary Meeting, Third Assembly. June 7, 1949. A3-P/25, DOC 6456. ICAO Archival Documents.
Minutes of the Fourteenth Plenary Meeting, Assembly – Eighteenth Session. July 6, 1971. A18 Min. P/14, DOC 8963. ICAO Archival Documents.
Minutes of the Fourteenth Plenary Meeting, Assembly 24th Session. October 7, 1983. A24-Min. P/14 DOC 9415. ICAO Archival Documents.
Minutes of the Fourteenth Plenary Meeting, Assembly 27th Session. October 6, 1989. A27-Min. P/14 DOC 9550. ICAO Archival Documents.
Minutes of the Fourth Meeting, Council – Extraordinary Session, Appendix A. September 16, 1983. C-Min. EXTRAORDINARY (1983)/4, DOC 9416-C/1077. ICAO Archival Documents.
Minutes of the Fourth Meeting, Council – Extraordinary Session. September 16, 1983. C-Min. EXTRAORDINARY (1983)/4, DOC 9416-C/1077. ICAO Archival Documents.
Minutes of the Fourth Plenary Meeting, Assembly – 22nd Session. September 14, 1977. A22 Min. P/4, DOC 9216. ICAO Archival Documents.
Minutes of the Fourth Plenary Meeting, Assembly – 41st Session. October 1, 2022. A41-Min. P/4, DOC 10182, Corrigendum No. 1 from April 5, 2023. ICAO Archival Documents.
Minutes of the Fourth Plenary Meeting, Assembly – 41st Session. October 1, 2022. A41-Min. P/4, DOC 10182. ICAO Archival Documents.
Minutes of the Fourth Plenary Meeting, Assembly – Eleventh Session. June 2, 1958. A11-P/11, DOC 7886. ICAO Archival Documents.
Minutes of the Fourth Plenary Meeting, Assembly – Fifth Session. June 18, 1951. A5-P/2-4, DOC 7168-4. ICAO Archival Documents.
Minutes of the Fourth Plenary Meeting, Assembly – Nineteenth Session (Extraordinary). February 28, 1973. A19-Res., Min., DOC 9061. ICAO Archival Documents.
Minutes of the Fourth Plenary Meeting, Assembly 23rd Session. September 17, 1980. A23 Min. P/4, DOC 9317. ICAO Archival Documents.
Minutes of the Fourth Plenary Meeting, Assembly 24th Session. September 21, 1983. A24-Min. P/4, DOC 9415, ICAO Archival Documents.
Minutes of the Fourth Plenary Meeting, Assembly 25th Session (Extraordinary). April 25, 1984. A25-Min. P/4, DOC 9437. ICAO Archival Documents.
Minutes of the Ninth Plenary Meeting, Assembly – 21st Session. October 11, 1974. A21 Min. P/9, DOC 9119. ICAO Archival Documents.
Minutes of the Ninth Plenary Meeting, Assembly – 41st Session. October 7, 2022. A41-Min. P/9, DOC 10182. ICAO Archival Documents.
Minutes of the Ninth Plenary Meeting, Assembly 29th Session. September 26, 1992. A29-Min. P/9 DOC 9601, ICAO Archival Documents.

Minutes of the Second Meeting, Council – Extraordinary Session. January 21, 1969. C/982-2 C-Min. EXTRAORDINARY/2, DOC 8793-2. ICAO Archival Documents.
Minutes of the Second Meeting, Council – Extraordinary Session. September 15, 1983. C-Min. EXTRAORDINARY (1983)/2, DOC 9416-C/1077. ICAO Archival Documents.
Minutes of the Second Meeting, Council-Extraordinary Session. July 14, 1988. C-Min. EXTRAORDINARY (1988)/2, DOC 9541-C/1106. ICAO Archival Documents.
Minutes of the Second Plenary Meeting (Draft), Assembly – Thirteenth Session (Extraordinary). June 19, 1961. A13-Draft Min. P/2. ICAO Archival Documents.
Minutes of the Second Plenary Meeting, Assembly – 21st Session. September 24, 1974. A21 Min. P/2, DOC 9119. ICAO Archival Documents.
Minutes of the Second Plenary Meeting, Assembly – 22nd Session. September 13, 1977. A22 Min. P/2, DOC 9216. ICAO Archival Documents.
Minutes of the Second Plenary Meeting, Assembly – Eighteenth Session. June 15, 1971. A18 Min. P/2, DOC 8963. ICAO Archival Documents.
Minutes of the Second Plenary Meeting, Assembly – Eleventh Session. May 21, 1958. A11-P/11, DOC 7886, ICAO Archival Documents.
Minutes of the Second Plenary Meeting, Assembly – Fifteenth Session. June 23, 1965. A15-P/5, DOC 8516. ICAO Archival Documents.
Minutes of the Second Plenary Meeting, Assembly – Fourteenth Session. August 22, 1962. A14-P/21, DOC 8269. ICAO Archival Documents.
Minutes of the Second Plenary Meeting, Assembly – Ninth Session. June 1, 1955. A9-P/13-2, DOC 7596-2. ICAO Archival Documents.
Minutes of the Second Plenary Meeting, Assembly – Seventeenth Session (A). March 11, 1971. A17 A-P/7, DOC 8931. ICAO Archival Documents.
Minutes of the Second Plenary Meeting, Assembly – Seventh Session. June 17, 1953. A7-P/2, DOC 7409. ICAO Archival Documents.
Minutes of the Second Plenary Meeting, Assembly – Sixteenth Session. September 3, 1968. A16-Min. P/2, DOC 8775. ICAO Archival Documents.
Minutes of the Second Plenary Meeting, Assembly – Tenth Session. June 20, 1956. A10-P/17-2, DOC 7708-2. ICAO Archival Documents.
Minutes of the Second Plenary Meeting, Assembly – Twelfth Session. June 17, 1959. A12-P/2, DOC 7996. ICAO Archival Documents.
Minutes of the Second Plenary Meeting, Assembly 24th Session. September 20, 1983. A24-Min. P/2, DOC 9415. ICAO Archival Documents.
Minutes of the Second Plenary Meeting, Assembly 25th Session (Extraordinary). April 24, 1984. A25-Min. P/2 DOC 9437. ICAO Archival Documents.
Minutes of the Second Plenary Meeting, First Assembly. May 7, 1947. A1-P/21, DOC 4155. ICAO Archival Documents.
Minutes of the Second Plenary Meeting, Third Assembly. June 8, 1949. A3-P/26, DOC 6457, ICAO Archival Documents.
Minutes of the Seventh Meeting, Council – 117th Session. February 27, 1986. C-Min. 117/7. ICAO Archival Documents.
Minutes of the Seventh Plenary Meeting, Assembly – Fourteenth Session. September 14, 1962. A14-P/21, DOC 8269, ICAO Archival Documents.
Minutes of the Seventh Plenary Meeting, Assembly – Sixteenth Session. September 24, 1986. A16-Min. P/7, DOC 8775. ICAO Archival Documents.
Minutes of the Seventh Plenary Meeting, Assembly 23rd Session. September 19, 1980. A23 Min. P/7, DOC 9317. ICAO Archival Documents.

Minutes of the Seventh Plenary Meeting, Assembly 24th Session. September 23, 1983. A24-Min. P/7, DOC 9415. ICAO Archival Documents.
Minutes of the Seventh Plenary Meeting, Assembly 25th Session (Extraordinary). May 10, 1984. A25-Min. P/7 DOC 9437. ICAO Archival Documents.
Minutes of the Seventh Plenary Meeting, Assembly 26th Session. September 26, 1986. A26-Min. P/7 DOC 9494. ICAO Archival Documents.
Minutes of the Seventh Plenary Meeting, Assembly 27th Session. September 22, 1989. A27-Min. P/7, DOC 9550. ICAO Archival Documents.
Minutes of the Sixth Meeting, Council – 111th Session. March 6, 1984. C-Min. 111/6. ICAO Archival Documents.
Minutes of the Sixth Meeting, Council – 117th Session. February 26, 1986. C-Min. 117/6. ICAO Archival Documents.
Minutes of the Sixth Plenary Meeting, Assembly – 22nd Session. September 15, 1977. A22 Min. P/6, DOC 9216. ICAO Archival Documents.
Minutes of the Sixth Plenary Meeting, Assembly – Twentieth Session (Extraordinary). August 30, 1973. A20-Min. P/6, DOC 9087. ICAO Archival Documents.
Minutes of the Sixth Plenary Meeting, Assembly 24th Session. September 22, 1983. A24-Min. P/6, DOC 9415. ICAO Archival Documents.
Minutes of the Sixth Plenary Meeting, Assembly 26th Session. September 25, 1986. A26-Min. P/6 DOC 9494. ICAO Archival Documents.
Minutes of the Tenth Plenary Meeting, Assembly – Fifteenth Session. July 14, 1965. A15-P/5, DOC 8516, ICAO Archival Documents.
Minutes of the Tenth Plenary Meeting, Assembly 23rd Session. October 3, 1980. A23 Min. P/10, DOC 9317. ICAO Archival Documents.
Minutes of the Tenth Plenary Meeting, Assembly 24th Session. September 26, 1983. A24-Min. P/10, DOC 9415. ICAO Archival Documents.
Minutes of the Tenth Plenary Meeting, Assembly 27th Session. September 23, 1989. A27-Min. P/10 DOC 9550. ICAO Archival Documents.
Minutes of the Third Meeting, Council – Extraordinary Session, September 16, 1983. C-Min. EXTRAORDINARY (1983)/3. DOC 9416-C/1077. ICAO Archival Documents.
Minutes of the Third Meeting, Council – Extraordinary Session. January 23, 1969. C/982-3 C-Min. EXTRAORDINARY/3, DOC 8793-3. ICAO Archival Documents.
Minutes of the Third Plenary Meeting, Assembly – 21st Session. September 25, 1974. A21 Min. P/3, DOC 9119. ICAO Archival Documents.
Minutes of the Third Plenary Meeting, Assembly – 31st Session. September 20, 1995. DRAFT A31-Min. P/3. ICAO Archival Documents.
Minutes of the Third Plenary Meeting, Assembly – Eighteenth Session. June 16, 1971. A18 Min. P/3, DOC 8963. ICAO Archival Documents.
Minutes of the Third Plenary Meeting, Assembly – Fifteenth Session. June 23, 1965. A15-P/5, DOC 8516. ICAO Archival Documents.
Minutes of the Third Plenary Meeting, Assembly – Seventeenth Session. June 18, 1970. A17-Min. P/3, DOC 8893, ICAO Archival Documents.
Minutes of the Third Plenary Meeting, Assembly 24th Session. September 21, 1983. A24-Min. P/3, DOC 9415. ICAO Archival Documents.
Minutes of the Third Plenary Meeting, Assembly 25th Session (Extraordinary). April 25, 1984. A25-Min. P/3, DOC 9437. ICAO Archival Documents.
Minutes of the Third Plenary Meeting, Assembly 26th Session. September 24, 1986. A26-Min. P/3 DOC 9494. ICAO Archival Documents.

Minutes of the Third Plenary Meeting, First Assembly. May 13, 1947. A1-P/24, DOC 4184. ICAO Archival Documents.
Minutes of the Thirteenth Plenary Meeting, Assembly – Eighteenth Session. July 6, 1971. A18 Min. P/13, DOC 8963. ICAO Archival Documents.
Minutes of the Thirteenth Plenary Meeting, Assembly 23rd Session. October 6, 1980, A23 Min. P/13, DOC 9317. ICAO Archival Documents.
Minutes of the Thirteenth Plenary Meeting, Assembly 26th Session. October 10, 1986. A26-Min. P/13 DOC 9494. ICAO Archival Documents.
Minutes of the Twelfth Plenary Meeting, Assembly – 21st Session. October 15, 1974. A21 Min. P/12, DOC 9119. ICAO Archival Documents.
Minutes of the Twelfth Plenary Meeting, Assembly – 22nd Session. October 3, 1977. A22 Min. P/12, DOC 9216. ICAO Archival Documents.
Minutes of the Twelfth Plenary Meeting, Assembly – Fifteenth Session. July 16, 1965. A15-P/5, DOC 8516. ICAO Archival Documents.
Minutes of the Twelfth Plenary Meeting, Assembly 24th Session. October 1, 1983. A24-Min. P/12, DOC 9415. ICAO Archival Documents.
Minutes of the Twentieth Meeting, Council – 126th Session. March 17, 1989. C-Min. 126/20. ICAO Archival Documents.
Provisional Verbatim Record of the 2655 Meeting, UN Security Council. February 6, 1986. S/PV.2655. Accessed February 2, 2024. https://digitallibrary.un.org/record/112779.
Report of the Council to the Assembly of the Activities of the Organization in 1950, Supporting documentation for the 5th Session of the Assembly. June 1951. A5-P/1, DOC 7148. ICAO Archival Documents.
Report of the Council to the Assembly on the Activities of the Organization, June 1, 1947-March 1, 1948, 8, A2-P/5, DOC 5221. ICAO Archival Documents.
Report of the Council to the Assembly on the Activities of the Organization in 1949, Supporting Documentation for the 4th Session of the Assembly. March 23, 1950. A4-P/1, DOC 6969. ICAO Archival Documents.
Report of the Council to the Assembly on the Activities of the Organization in 1951, Supporting Documentation for the 6th Session of the Assembly. May 1952. A6-P/1, DOC 7270. ICAO Archival Documents.
Report of the Council to the Assembly on the Activities of the Organization in 1953, Supporting Documentation for the 8th Session of the Assembly. June 1954. A8-P/2, DOC 7456. ICAO Archival Documents.
Report of the Council to the Assembly, vol. I, Supporting Documentation for the 3rd Assembly. June 1949. DOC 6433. ICAO Archival Documents.
Report of the Executive Committee on Agenda Item 39, Assembly – Eighteenth Session. July 5, 1971. A18-WP/177, P/55. ICAO Archival Documents.
Report of the Executive Committee on Agenda Item 41, Assembly – Fifteenth Session. July 12, 1965. A15-WP/212, P/43 – Item 41. ICAO Archival Documents.
Report of the Executive Committee, Assembly – 21st Session. A21-EX, DOC 9113. ICAO Archival Documents.
Report of the Executive Committee, Assembly 26th Session. A26-EX, DOC 9489. ICAO Archival Documents.
Report of the Executive Committee, Assembly 27th Session. A27-EX, DOC 9545. ICAO Archival Documents.
Report of the ICAO Fact-Finding Investigation, Report into the Incident Involving Ryanair Flight FR4978 in Belarus Airspace on 23 May 2021, Appendix A, Event Involving

Ryanair Flight FR4978 in Belarus Airspace on 23 May 2021, Council – 226th Session. C-WP/15419, Appendix A. ICAO Archival Documents.

Report of the ICAO Fact-Finding Investigation: Event Involving Ryanair Flight FR4978 in Belarus Airspace on 23 May 2021. January 2022. C-WP/15284, Appendix, ICAO Archival Documents.

Resolutions and Minutes, Assembly – Nineteenth Session (Extraordinary). February 27–March 2, 1973. A19-Res., Min., DOC 9061, ICAO Archival Documents.

Resolutions of the Assembly. A23-5: The airport of Jerusalem. Assembly Resolutions in Force (as of 8 October 1992). ICAO Archival Documents.

Summary Minutes of the Eighth Meeting, Council – 223rd Session. June 18, 2023. 126–127, C-Min. 223/8, DOC 10164– C/1199. ICAO Archival Documents.

Summary Minutes of the Eighth Meeting, Council – 224th Session. November 5, 2021. C-Min. 224/8, DOC 10173- C/1200. ICAO Archival Documents.

Summary Minutes of the Eighth Meeting, Council – 225th Session. March 7, 2022. C-Min. 225/8, DOC 10188– C/1201. ICAO Archival Documents.

Summary Minutes of the First Meeting, Council – 203rd Session. October 27, 2014. C-Min. 203/1, DOC 10048-C/1179. ICAO Archival Documents.

Summary Minutes of the First Meeting, Council – 225th Session. January 31, 2022. C-Min. 225/1, DOC 10188– C/1201. ICAO Archival Documents.

Summary Minutes of the Fourteenth Meeting, Council – 226th Session. June 24, 2022. Min. 226/14, DOC 10192- C/1202, ICAO Archival Documents.

Summary Minutes of the Fourth Meeting, Council – 225th Session. February 25, 2022. C-Min. 225/4, DOC 10188– C/1201. ICAO Archival Documents.

Summary Minutes of the Second Meeting, Council – 223rd Session. May 27, 2021. C-Min. 223/2, DOC 10164– C/1199. ICAO Archival Documents.

Summary Minutes of the Seventeenth Meeting, Council – 226th Session. August 24-25, 2022. C-Min. 226/17, DOC 10192- C/1202 ICAO Archival Documents.

Summary Minutes of the Sixteenth Meeting, Council – 226th Session. July 18, 2022. C-Min. 226/16, Doc 10192- C/1202. ICAO Archival Documents.

Summary Minutes of the Third Meeting, Council – 228th Session. March 17, 2023. C-Min. 228/3, DOC 10196. ICAO Archival Documents.

Summary Minutes of the Third Meeting. Council – 224th Session. October 25, 2021. C-Min. 224/3, DOC 10173- C/1200. ICAO Archival Documents.

Summary Minutes of the Twelfth Meeting, Council – 223rd Session. June 28, 2021. C-Min. 223/12, DOC 10164– C/1199. ICAO Archival Documents.

Working Paper, Agenda Item 17: Resolutions of the United Nations concerning invitations to liberation movements to attend meetings of the Specialized Agencies, Appendix A, Assembly – 21st Session. May 23, 1974. A21-WP/36 EX/9, ICAO Archival Documents.

Working Paper, Agenda Item 2: Diversion and seizure by Israeli military aircraft of a civil aircraft. Assembly – 20th Session (Extraordinary). August 29, 1973. A20-WP/12. ICAO Archival Documents.

Working Paper, Agenda Item 4: Completion of the consideration of the United Nations General Assembly Resolutions 2555 and 2704, Assembly – Nineteenth Session (Extraordinary). February 28, 1973. A19-WP/7. ICAO Archival Documents.

Working Paper, Agenda Item 5: Adoption of the Agenda (Presented by Iraq and Jordan), Assembly – 21st Session. October 14, 1974. A21-WP/191, P/63. ICAO Archival Documents.

Working Paper, Agenda Item 5: Adoption of the Agenda. September 26, 1980. A23-WP/97, P/42. ICAO Archival Documents.

Working Paper, Agenda Item 7: Annual Report of the Council to the Assembly for 1980, 1981 and 1982 and Work Programme for 1984–1986, and their reference to the Executive Committee as a whole and to Commission as necessary, Draft Resolution, Executive Committee, Assembly – 24th Session. September 26, 1983. A24-WP/77 P/38 & EX/9, ICAO Archival Documents.

Working Paper, Information Pursuant to Article 54(J) of the Chicago Convention on Infractions of the Convention by a Group of ICAO Member States, Council – 226th Session. July 11, 2022, Revision No. 1 from July 15, 2022. C-WP/15429. ICAO Archival Documents.

Working Paper, Infractions of the Convention under Article 54(j) of the Chicago Convention by the Russian Federation, Council – 226th Session, June 14, 2022, Revision No. 1 from June 16, 2022, 2–4, C-WP/15425, ICAO Archival Documents.

Working Paper, Report of the Executive Committee to the Plenary, Assembly – 25th Session (Extraordinary), May 10, 1984, A25-WP/20, ICAO Archival Documents.

Working Paper, Request of the Republic of Belarus to the ICAO Council for its Consideration under Article 54 (j) of the Chicago Convention. December 26, 2021. C-WP/15285. ICAO Archival Documents.

Working Paper, Request of the Republic of Belarus to the ICAO Council for Its Consideration under Article 45 (j) of the Chicago Convention. May 25, 2022. C-WP/15418. ICAO Archival Documents.

Working Paper, The Incompatibility of Unilateral Restrictive Measures Impacting International Civil Aviation Activities with the Provisions of the Convention of International Aviation, Assembly – 41st Session. August 1, 2022. A41-WP/456, EX/210. ICAO Archival Documents.

2476th Meeting, United Nations Security Council Official Records. September 12, 1983. S/PV.2476. Available from https://documents.un.org/doc/undoc/gen/nl8/300/36/pdf/nl830036.pdf?token=YgmcyhrGsTSd0i3yEW&fe=true. Accessed April 18, 2024.

Datasets

Moyer, Jonathan D., Markle, Alanna., Meisel, Collin J., Szymanski-Burgos, Adam. "Relative National Power Codebook." *Diplometrics*. Denver: Frederick S. Pardee Institute for International Futures, Josef Korbel School of International Studies, University of Denver, 2024.

Pardee Centre for International Futures, UNGA Coincidence Score, February 20, 2024. Available from https://public.tableau.com/app/profile/pardeecenterifs/viz/VotesterTableauDashboard_16529835337750/UNGACoincidenceScores?publish=yes. Accessed April 17, 2024.

International treaties and conventions

"Convention on International Civil Aviation." Signed at Chicago on 7 December 1944.

"United Nations Interim Agreement on International Civil Aviation." Effective June 6, 1945. The American Journal of International Law 40, no. 2 (April 1946). Supplement: Official Documents (April 1946): 63–85.

Social media posts

International Civil Aviation Organization. Facebook post from May 23, 2021. www.facebook.com/InternationalCivilAviationOrganization/posts/pfbid02RS9j9LY6JhR4KSp3peSgne213LD9zfMdtpcf3zvebPmaunqNsqDL4DGe2dH2Hyv1l. Accessed February 2, 2024.

UN Resolutions

UN General Assembly Resolution 45/37 of 28 November 1990: Observer status of national liberation movements recognized by the Organization of African Unity and/or by the League of Arab States. Available from www.un.org/unispal/document/auto-insert-186275/. Accessed June 5, 2024.

UN Security Council Resolution 262 (1968) of 31 December 1968. Available from https://digitallibrary.un.org/record/90758. Accessed February 7, 2024.

UN Security Council Resolution 478 (1980) of 20 August 1980. Available from https://digitallibrary.un.org/record/25618. Accessed February 7, 2024.

UN Security Council Resolution 616 (1988) of 20 July 1988. Available from https://digitallibrary.un.org/record/42913. Accessed February 5, 2024.

UN Security Council Resolution 337 (1973) of 15 August 1973. Available from https://digitallibrary.un.org/record/93465?v=pdf. Accessed April 17, 2024.

Websites

Deutsche Welle. "Russia Recognizes Independence of Ukraine Separatist Regions." Accessed March 1, 2022. www.dw.com/en/russia-recognizes-independence-of-ukraine-separatist-regions/a-60861963

ICAO. "About ICAO." Accessed November 20, 2023. www.icao.int/about-icao/Pages/default.aspx

ICAO. "Air Navigation Commission." Accessed November 20, 2023. www.icao.int/about-icao/AirNavigationCommission/Pages/default.aspx

ICAO. "All Assembly Sessions." Accessed October 20, 2023. www.icao.int/publications/Pages/assembly-archive.aspx

ICAO. "Council President Presents Briefing to UN Security Council on the Forced Landing of Ryanair Flight FR4978 by Belarus." Accessed January 16, 2024, www.icao.int/Newsroom/Pages/Council-President-presents-briefing-to-UN-Security-Council-on-the-forced-landing-of-Ryanair-Flight-FR4978-by-Belarus.aspx

ICAO. "Council President." Accessed November 20, 2023. www.icao.int/about-icao/Council/Pages/President.aspx

ICAO. "Environmental Protection." Accessed December 17, 2021. www.icao.int/environmental-protection/Pages/default.aspx

ICAO. "ICAO and the United Nations." Accessed November 1, 2021. www.icao.int/about-icao/History/Pages/icao-and-the-united-nations.aspx

ICAO. "Organizations Able to be Invited to ICAO Meetings." Accessed November 2, 2021. www.icao.int/about-icao/pages/invited-organizations.aspx

ICAO. "The History of ICAO and the Chicago Convention." Accessed September 10, 2020. www.icao.int/about-icao/History/Pages/default.aspx

ICAO. "The ICAO Assembly." Accessed November 20, 2023. www.icao.int/about-icao/assembly/Pages/default.aspx

ICAO. "The ICAO Council." Accessed November 20, 2023. www.icao.int/about-icao/Council/Pages/Council.aspx

ICAO. "The Postal History of ICAO: Organization Promoting Technological Advancements in Civil Aviation." ICAO. Accessed February 6, 2024. https://applications.icao.int/postalhistory/iccaia_international_coordinating_council_of_aerospace_industries_associations.htm

ICAO. "Vision and Mission." Accessed November 20, 2023. www.icao.int/about-icao/Council/Pages/vision-and-mission.aspx

Jewish Telegraphic Agency. "PLO Gets Observer Status in the Icao." Accessed October 30, 2023. www.jta.org/archive/plo-gets-observer-status-in-the-icao

Kirby, Paul. "Why Has Russia Invaded Ukraine and What Does Putin Want?" *BBC News*. Accessed March 12, 2022. www.bbc.com/news/world-europe-56720589

Our World in Data. "Global Aviation Fatalities per Million Passengers, 2023." Accessed December 20, 2023. https://ourworldindata.org/grapher/aviation-fatalities-per-million-passengers

President of Russia. "Address by the President of the Russian Federation." Accessed December 1, 2022. http://en.kremlin.ru/events/president/news/67843

United Nations. "The UN and Ukraine: Year-Long War Spreads Global Fallout." Accessed January 15, 2024. https://news.un.org/en/story/2023/03/1134122

Secondary sources

Abbott, Kenneth W., and Duncan Snidal. "Why States Act through Formal International Organizations." In *The Politics of Global Governance: International Organizations in an Interdependent World*, edited by Paul F. Diehl, 9–43. Boulder: Lynne Rienner Publishers, 2001.

Agustini, Elfita, Kareng Yaya, and Victoria Ong Argo. "The Role of ICAO (International Civil Aviation Organization) in Implementing International Flight Safety Standards." *IWPOSPA* (2020): 100–114. https://doi.org/10.18502/kss.v5i1.8273

Angevine, Robert G., John K. Warden, Russell Keller, and Clark Frye. *Learning Lessons from the Ukraine Conflict*. Alexandria: Institute for Defense Analyses, 2019.

Archer, Clive. *International Organizations*. London: Routledge, 2001.

Bachmann, Sascha-Dominik. "Malaysia Airlines Flight MH17: The Day Russia Became a State Sponsor of Terrorism." *Amicus Curiae* 97 (2014): 14–28.

Barnett, Michael N., and Martha Finnemore. "The Politics, Power, and Pathologies of International Organizations." *International Organization* 53, no. 4 (1999): 699–732.

Bates, Stephen, Laura Jenkins, and Fran Amery. "(De)politicisation and the Father's Clause Parliamentary Debates." *Policy & Politics* 42, no. 2 (2014): 243–258. https://doi.org/10.1332/030557312X656007

Berridge, G. R. *Diplomacy: Theory and Practice*. Basingstoke: Palgrave Macmillan, 2010.

Blight, James G., Janet M. Lang, Hussein Banai, Malcolm Byrne, and John Tirman. *Becoming Enemies: U.S.-Iran Relations and the Iran-Iraq War, 1979–1988*. Lanham, MD: Rowman & Littlefield, 2012.

Booth, Douglas. "Hitting Apartheid for Six?: The Politics of the South African Sports Boycott." *Journal of Contemporary History* 38, no. 3 (2003): 477–493.

Broekema, Wout. "Crisis-Induced Learning and Issue Politicization in the EU: The Braer, Sea Empress, Erika, and Prestige Oil Spill Disasters." *Public Administration* 94, no. 2 (2016): 381–398. https://doi.org/10.1111/padm.12170

Burnham, Peter. "Globalization, Depoliticization and 'Modern' Economic Management." In *The Politics of Change*, edited by Werner Bonefeld and Kosmas Psychopedis, 9–30. London: Palgrave Macmillan, 2002. https://doi.org/10.1057/9780333993798_2
Burnham, Peter. "New Labour and the Politics of Depoliticisation." *British Journal of Politics and International Relations* 3, no. 2 (2001): 127–149. https://doi.org/10.1111/1467-856X.00054
Buzan, Barry, Ole Wæver, and Jaap de Wilde. *Security: A New Framework for Analysis*. Boulder: Lynne Rienner Publishers, 1998.
Cech, Erin A., and Heidi M. Sherick. "Depoliticization and the Structure of Engineering Education." In *International Perspectives on Engineering Education: Philosophy of Engineering and Technology*, vol. 20, edited by Steen Hyldgaard Christensen, Christelle Didier, Andrew Jamison, Martin Meganck, Carl Mitcham, and Byron Newberry, 203–216. Cham: Springer, 2015. https://doi.org/10.1007/978-3-319-16169-3_10
Checkel, Jeffrey T. and Peter J. Katzenstein. "The Politicization of European Identities." In *European Identity*, edited by Jeffrey T. Checkel and Peter J. Katzenstein, 1–26. Cambridge: Cambridge University Press, 2012.
Cichocki, Bartosz. "Poland." In *National Perspectives on Russia: European Foreign Policy in the Making?*, edited by Maxine David, Jackie Gower, and Hiski Haukkala, 86–100. Abingdon: Routledge, 2013.
Claude, Inis L. Jr. "Multilateralism – Diplomatic and Otherwise." In *Diplomacy*, vol. I, edited by Christer Jönsson and Richard Langhorne, 367–377. London: Sage, 2004.
Cooper, John Cobb. "The International Air Navigation Conference, Paris 1910." *The Journal of Air Law and Commerce* 19, no. 2 (1952): 127–143.
Corcoran, Farrel. "KAL 007 and the evil empire: Mediated disaster and forms of rationalization." *Critical Studies in Mass Communication* 3, no. 3 (1986): 297–316. https://doi.org/10.1080/15295038609366656
Cottey, Andrew. "The West, Russia and European Security: Still the Long Peace?." *The British Journal of Politics and International Relations* 24, no. 2 (2022): 207–223. https://doi.org/10.1177/13691481211036381
Dobson, Alan. *A History of International Aviation: From Its Origins through Transformative Evolution*. London: Routledge, 2017.
Eban, Abba. "Multilateral Diplomacy in the Arab-Israeli Conflict." In *Multilateral Negotiation and Mediation: Instruments and Methods*, edited by Arthur S. Lall, 41–48. New York: Pergamon Press, 1985.
Eckert-Ehrhardt, Matthias, "Self-Legitimation in the Face of Politicization: Why International Organizations Centralized Public Communication." *The Review of International Organizations* 13, no. 4 (2018): 519–546. https://doi.org/10.1007/s11558-017-9287-y
Emery, Christian. *US Foreign Policy and the Iranian Revolution: The Cold War Dynamics of Engagement and Strategic Alliance*. Basingstoke: Palgrave Macmillan, 2013.
Falk, Richard A. "The Beirut Raid and the International Law of Retaliation." *The American Journal of International Law* 63, no. 3 (July 1969): 415–443. https://doi.org/10.2307/2198865
Fawcett, Paul, Matthew Flinders, Colin Hay, and Matthew Wood. "Anti-Politics, Depoliticization, and Governance." In *Anti-Politics, Depoliticization, & Governance*, edited by Paul Fawcett, Matthew Flinders, Colin Hay, and Matthew Wood, 3–27. Oxford: Oxford University Press, 2017.
Feindt, Peter H., Sandra Schwindenhammer, and Jale Tosun. "Politicization, Depoliticization and Policy Change: A Comparative Theoretical Perspective on Agri-food Policy." *Journal*

of Comparative Policy Analysis: Research and Practice (2020): 509–525. https://doi.org/10.1080/13876988.2020.1785875

FitzGerald, Gerald F. "The Use of Force against Civil Aircraft: The Aftermath of the KAL Flight 007 Incident." *Canadian Yearbook of International Law* 22 (1984): 291–311. https://doi.org/10.1017/S0069005800002733

Flinders, Matthew, and Jim Buller. "Depoliticisation: Principles, Tactics and Tools." *British Politics* 1 (2006): 293–318. https://doi.org/10.1057/palgrave.bp.4200016

Flinders, Matthew, and Matt Wood, "Discursive Depoliticization and Political Disengagement." In *The Routledge Handbook of Language and Politics*, edited by Ruth Wodak and Bernhard Forchtner, 603–617. London: Routledge, 2017.

Flinders, Matthew, and Matt Wood. "When Politics Fails: Hyper-Democracy and Hyper-Depoliticization." *New Political Science* 37, no. 3 (2015): 363–381. https://doi.org/10.1080/07393148.2015.1056431

Foont, Brian E. "Shooting Down Civilian Aircraft: Is There an International Law." *Journal of Air Law and Commerce* 72 (2007): 695–725.

Forsythe, David P. "The UN and the Arab-Israeli Conflict: What Has Been Learned in 25 Years." *International Organization* 26, no. 4 (1972): 705–717.

Fraser, T. G. *The Arab-Israeli Conflict*. Basingstoke: Palgrave Macmillan, 2004.

Gidwitz, Betsy. *The Politics of International Air Transport*. Lexington: Lexington Books, 1980.

Haas, Ernst. *Beyond the Nation State. Functionalism and International Organization*. Stanford: Stanford University Press, 1964.

Habib, Benjamin. "The Enforcement Problem in Resolution 2094 and the United Nations Security Council Sanctions Regime: Sanctioning North Korea." *Australian Journal of International Affairs* 70, no. 1 (2016): 50–68. https://doi.org/10.1080/10357718.2015.1095278

Hadjipavlou-Trigeorgis, Maria, and Lenos Trigeorgis. "Cyprus: An Evolutionary Approach to Conflict Resolution." *Journal of Conflict Resolution* 37, no. 2 (1993): 340–360.

Harel, Isser. *The House on Garibaldi Street*. New York: Routledge, 2013.

Hay, Colin. *Why We Hate Politics*. Cambridge: Polity, 2007.

Hocking, Brian, Jan Melissen, Shaun Riordan, and Paul Sharp. *Futures for Diplomacy: Integrative Diplomacy in the 21st Century, Report no. 1*. The Hague: Clingendael, 2012.

Hooghe, Liesbet, and Gary Marks. "Politicization." In *The Oxford Handbook of the European Union*, edited by Erik Jones, Anand Menon, and Stephen Weatheril, 840–854. Oxford: Oxford University Press, 2012.

Houston, John A. "The United Nations and Spain." *The Journal of Politics* 14, no. 4 (1952): 683–709.

Hudson, Michael C. "The United States and the Middle East." In *International relations of the Middle East*, edited by Louise Fawcett, 283–306. Oxford: Oxford University Press, 2005.

Hurd, Ian. *International Organizations: Politics, Law, Practice*. Cambridge: Cambridge University Press, 2013.

Hussain, Nazir. "US-Iran Relations: Issues, Challenges and Prospects." *Policy Perspectives* 12, no. 2 (2015): 29–47. https://doi.org/10.13169/polipers.12.2.0029

Hutter, Swen, and Hanspeter Kriesi. "Politicizing Europe in Times of Crisis." *Journal of European Public Policy* 26, no. 7 (2019): 996–1017. https://doi.org/10.1080/13501763.2019.1619801

Jarvis, D. S. L. "Integration Theory Revisited: Haas, Neo-Functionalism, and the Problematics of European Integration, Policy." *Organisation and Society* 7, no. 1 (1994): 17–33. https://doi.org/10.1080/10349952.1994.11876793

Jenkins, Laura. "The Difference Genealogy Makes: Makes: Strategies for Politicisation or How to Extend Capacities for Autonomy." *Political Studies* 59, no. 1 (2011): 156–174. https://doi.org/10.1111/j.1467-9248.2010.00844.x

Kaelble, Hartmut. "Identification with Europe and Politicization of the EU since the 1980s." In *European Identity*, edited by Jeffrey T. Checkel and Peter J. Katzenstein, 193–212. Cambridge: Cambridge University Press, 2012.

Kania, Dinar Dewi, Dian Artanti Arubusman, Mustika Sari, Ridho Bramulya Ikhsan, and Safathira Zaldin. "Does ICAO's Climate Change Mitigation Policy based on International Agreements Reflect Global Environmental Justice?" *International Environmental Agreements: Politics, Law and Economics* 23, no. 4 (2023): 449–466. https://doi.org/10.1007/s10784-023-09619-5

Karlheinz, Haag. "International Action and the Role of ICAO." In *Aviation and Climate Change*, edited by Frank Fichert, Peter Forsyth, and Hans-Martin Niemeier, 104–116. Abingdon: Routledge, 2020.

Karns, Margaret P., and Karen A. Mingst. "International Organizations and Diplomacy." In *The Oxford Handbook of Modern Diplomacy*, edited by Andrew F. Cooper, Jorge Heine and Ramesh Thakur, 142–159. Oxford: Oxford University Press, 2013.

Karns, Margaret P., and Karen A. Mingst. *International Organizations: The Politics and Processes of Global Governance*. Boulder: Lynne Rienner Publishers, 2010.

Kent, Ann. "China's International Socialization: The Role of International Organizations." *Global Governance* 8, no. 3 (July–September 2002): 343–364.

Kent, Ann E. *Beyond Compliance: China, International Organizations, and Global Security*. Stanford: Stanford University Press, 2007.

Ker-Lindsay, James. "Great Powers, Counter Secession, and Non-Recognition: Britain and the 1983 Unilateral Declaration of Independence of the "Turkish Republic of Northern Cyprus"." *Diplomacy & Statecraft* 28, no. 3 (2017): 431–453. https://doi.org/10.1080/09592296.2017.1347445

Kidd, Bruce. "The Campaign against Sport in South Africa." *International Journal: Canada's Journal of Global Policy Analysis* 43, no. 4 (1988): 643–664. https://doi.org/10.1177/002070208804300406

Kleiner, Juergen. "The Inertia of Diplomacy." *Diplomacy and Statecraft* 19, no. 2 (2008): 321–349. https://doi.org/10.1080/09592290802096380

Klotz, Audie. *Norms in International Relations: The Struggle against Apartheid*. Ithaca: Cornell University Press, 1995.

Kobierecki, Michał Marcin. *Sports Diplomacy: Sports in the Diplomatic Activities of States and Non-State Actors*. Lanham: Lexington Books, 2020.

Krause, Lawrence B., and Joseph S. Nye. "Refections on the Economics and Politics of International Economic Organizations." *International Organization* 29 (1975): 323–342. https://doi.org/10.1017/S0020818300017975

Kriesi, Hanspeter. "The Politicization of European Integration." *Journal of Common Market Studies* 54 (2016): 32–47. https://doi.org/10.1111/jcms.12406

Kulski, W. W. "Soviet Diplomatic Techniques." *The Russian Review* 19, no. 3 (1960): 217–226.

Leukavets, Alla. "Russia's Game in Belarus: 2020 Presidential Elections as a Checkmate for Lukashenka?." *New Perspectives* 21, no. 9 (2021): 90–101.

Louis, Marieke, and Lucile Maertens. *Why International Organizations Hate Politics: Depoliticizing the World.* London: Routledge, 2021.

Lyne, Mona M., Daniel L. Nielson, and Michael J. Tierney. "Who Delegates? Alternative Models of Principals in Development Aid." In *Delegation and Agency in International Organization*, edited by Darren G. Hawkins, David A. Lake, Daniel L. Nielson, and Michael J. Tierney, 41–76. Cambridge: Cambridge University Press, 2009.

Lyons, Gene M., David A. Baldwin, and Donald W. McNemar. "The "Politicization" Issue in the UN Specialized Agencies." *Proceedings of the Academy of Political Science* 32, no. 4 (1977): 81–92.

MacKenzie, David. *ICAO: A History of the International Civil Aviation Organization.* Toronto: University of Toronto Press, 2010.

Malyarenko, Tatyana, and Stefan Wolff. "The Logic of Competitive Influence-Seeking: Russia, Ukraine, and the Conflict in Donbas." *Post-Soviet Affairs* 34, no. 4 (2018): 191–212. https://doi.org/10.1080/1060586X.2018.1425083

Manaev, Oleg, Natalie Rice, and Maureen Taylor. "The Evolution and Influence of Russian and Belarusian Propaganda during the Belarus Presidential Election and Ensuing Protests in 2020." *Canadian Slavonic Papers* 63, no. 3–4 (2021): 371–402. https://doi.org/10.1080/00085006.2021.1997285

Marquina, Antonio. "The Spanish Neutrality during the Second World War." *American University International Law Review* 14, no. 1 (1998): 171–184.

Di Mauro, Danilo. *The UN and the Arab-Israeli Conflict: American Hegemony and the UN Intervention Since 1947.* London: Routledge, 2012.

Mayring, Philipp. "Qualitative Content Analysis." In *A Companion to Qualitative Research*, edited by Uew Flick, Ernst von Kardorff, and Ines Steinke, 266–269. Sage: London, 2004.

Milde, Michael. *International Air Law and ICAO.* Utrecht: Eleven International Publishing, 2008.

Mitrany, David. *A Working Peace System: An Argument for the Functional Development of International Organization.* Chicago: Quadrangle Book, 1966.

Morgan, Craig A. "The Downing of Korean Air Lines Flight 007." *Yale Journal of International Law* 11, no. 1 (Fall 1985): 231–257.

Muldoon, James P. Jr. "Introduction." In *Multilateral Diplomacy and the United Nations Today*, edited by James P. Muldoon Jr., Joann Fagot Aviel, Richard Reitano, and Earl Sullivan, 1–12. New York: Routledge, 2005.

Muldoon, James P. Jr. "Multilateralism's New Mix: Implications for Diplomacy, International Organizations, and Global Governance." In *The New Dynamics of Multilateralism. Diplomacy, International Organizations, and Global Governance*, edited by James Muldoon, Jr., JoAnn Fagot Aviel, Richard Reitano, and Earl Sullivan, 333–343. Boulder: Westview, 2011.

Osiecki, Mateusz. "Shooting Down Civil Aircraft in the Light of Sovereignty in the Airspace." *Sociology Study* 6, no. 6 (June 2016): 392–401. https://doi.org/10.17265/2159-5526/2016.06.005

Palonen, Kari. "Four Times of Politics: Policy, Polity, Politicking, and Politicization." *Alternatives* 28 (2003): 171–186.

Parizek, Michal. "Control, Soft Information, and the Politics of International Organizations Staffing." *The Review of International Organizations* 12 (2017): 559–583. https://doi.org/10.1007/s11558-016-9252-1

Parizek, Michal, and Matthew D. Stephen. "The Increasing Representativeness of International Organizations' Secretariats: Evidence from the United Nations System, 1997–2015." *International Studies Quarterly* 65, no. 1 (March 2021): 197–209.

Pepermans, Yves, and Pieter Maeseele. "The Politicization of Climate Change: Problem or Solution?" *WIREs Climate Change* 7 (July/August 2016): 478–485. https://doi.org/10.1002/wcc.405

Petiteville, Franck. "International Organizations beyond Depoliticized Governance," *Globalizations* 15, no. 3 (2018): 301–313. https://doi.org/10.1080/14747731.2017.1370850

Pigman, Geoffrey Allen. *Contemporary Diplomacy: Representation and Communication in a Globalized World*. Cambridge: Polity, 2011.

Rauh, Christian, and Michael Zürn. "Authority, Politicization, and Alternative Justifications: Endogenous Legitimation Dynamics in Global Economic Governance." *Review of International Political Economy* 27, no.3 (2020): 583–611. https://doi.org/10.1080/09692290.2019.1650796

Rhodes, R. A. W. "From Marketisation To Diplomacy: It's the Mix that Matters." *Australian Journal of Public Administration* 56, no. 2 (1997): 40–53. https://doi.org/10.1111/j.1467-8500.1997.tb01545.x

Richards, John E. "Toward a Positive Theory of International Institutions: Regulating International Aviation Markets." *International Organization* 53, no. 1 (Winter 1999): 1–37.

Rietjens, Sebastiaan. "Unraveling Disinformation: The Case of Malaysia Airlines Flight MH17." *The International Journal of Intelligence, Security, and Public Affairs* 21, no. 3 (2019): 195–218. https://doi.org/10.1080/23800992.2019.1695666

Roberts, Alasdair. *The Logic of Discipline: Global Capitalism and the Architecture of Government*. Oxford: Oxford University Press, 2010.

Rose, Cecily. "Appeal Relating to the Jurisdiction of the ICAO Council." *American Journal of International Law* 115, no. 2 (2021): 301–308. https://doi.org/10.1017/ajil.2021.8

Scotto di Carlo, Giuseppina. "Analysis of UN Resolutions Relating to North Korea: A Comparison with Resolutions Relating to the Second Gulf War." *International Journal for the Semiotics of Law* 27, no. 4 (2013): 1–21.

Searle, John R. *Speech Acts: An Essay in the Philosophy of Language*. Cambridge: Cambridge University Press, 1969.

Shane, Jeffrey N. "Diplomacy and Drama: The Making of the Chicago Convention," *The Air and Space Lawyer* 32, no. 4 (special issue) (2019): 1–22.

Sharp, Edward. "Soviet Security Council Boycott." In *The Encyclopedia of the Korean War*, edited by Spencer C. Tucker and Paul G. Pierpaoli Jr., 797–798. New York: Bloomsbury, 2002.

Smith, Charles. "The Arab-Israeli Conflict." In International Relations of the Middle East, edited by Louise Fawcett, 217–240. Oxford: Oxford University Press, 2005.

Sochor, Eugene. *The Politics of International Aviation*. Basingstoke: Macmillan, 1991.

Soltani, Fakhreddin, and Reza Ekhtiari Amiri. "Foreign Policy of Iran after Islamic Revolution." *Journal of Politics and Law* 3, no. 2 (September 2010): 199–206.

Sterner, Michael. "The Iran-Iraq War." *Foreign Affairs* 63, no. 1 (Fall 1984): 128–143.

Stone, Diane. "Global Governance Depoliticized: Knowledge Networks, Scientization, and Anti-Policy." In *Anti-Politics, Depoliticization, & Governance*, edited by Paul Fawcett, Matthew Flinders, Colin Hay and Matthew Wood, 91–111. Oxford: Oxford University Press, 2017.

Stone, Randall W. *Controlling Institutions: International Organizations and the Global Economy*. Cambridge: Cambridge University Press, 2011.

Stultz, Newell M. "Evolution of the United Nations Anti-Apartheid Regime." *Human Rights Quarterly* 13, no. 1 (1991): 1–23.

Svik, Peter. *Civil Aviation and the Globalization of the Cold War*. Cham: Palgrave Macmillan, 2020.

Tarock, Adam. *The Superpowers' Involvement in the Iran-Iraq War.* Commack: Nova Science Publishers, 1998.

Tourtellot, Christopher T. "Membership Criteria for the ICAO Council: A Proposal for Reform." *Denver Journal of International Law and Policy* 11 (1981): 51–80.

Vincze, Viola. "The USS Vincennes Incident: A Case Study Involving Autonomous Weapon Systems." *HDR* 2 (2020): 92–101.

Weber, Ludwig. *International Civil Aviation Organization (ICAO).* Alphen aan den Rijn: Wolters Kluwer, 2023.

Wildavsky, Aaron B. "Budgeting as a Political Process." In *The International Encyclopedia of the Social Sciences*, edited by David L. Sills, 192–199. New York: Crowell, Collier, and Macmillan, 1968.

de Wilde, Pieter. "No Polity for Old Politics? A Framework for Analyzing the Politicization of European Integration." *Journal of European Integration* 33, no. 5 (2011): 559–575. https://doi.org/10.1080/07036337.2010.546849

de Wilde, Pieter, Anna Leupold, and Henning Schmidtke. "Introduction: The Differentiated Politicisation of European Governance." *West European Politics* 39, no. 1 (2016): 3–22. https://doi.org/10.1080/01402382.2015.1081505

de Wilde, Pieter, and Michael Zürn. "Can the Politicization of European Integration be Reversed?" *Journal of Common Market Studies* 50, no. 1 (2012): 137–153. https://doi.org/10.1111/j.1468-5965.2011.02232.x

Wolf, Peter. "International Organization and Attitude Change: A Re–examination of the Functionalist Approach." *International Organization* 27 (1973): 347–371. https://doi.org/10.1017/S0020818300003544

Wood, Matt, and Matthew Flinders. "Rethinking Depoliticisation: Beyond the Governmental." *Policy & Politics* 42, no. 2 (2014): 151–170. https://doi.org/10.1332/030557312X655909

Wood, Matthew. "Politicisation, Depoliticisation and Anti-Politics: Towards a Multilevel Research Agenda." *Political Studies Review* 14, no. 4 (2016): 521–533. https://doi.org/10.1111/1478-9302.12074

Young, Juliette Claire, John Robertson Young, and Béatrice Agathe Aubert. "Insights from Diplomacy for the Prevention and Resolution of Conservation Conflicts." *Conservation Letters* 15, no. 5 (2022): 1–9. https://doi.org/10.1111/conl.12891

Young, Marilyn J., and Michael K. Launer, "Kal 007 and the Superpowers: An International Argument." *Quarterly Journal of Speech* 74, no. 3 (1988): 271–295. https://doi.org/10.1080/00335638809383842

Zürn, Michael. *A Theory of Global Governance: Authority, Legitimacy, and Contestation.* Oxford: Oxford University Press, 2018.

Zürn, Michael. "Politicization Compared: At national, European, and Global Levels." *Journal of European Public Policy* 26, no. 7 (2019): 977–995. https://doi.org/10.1080/13501763.2019.1619188

Zürn, Michael. "The Politicization of World Politics and Its Effects: Eight Propositions." *European Political Science Review* 6, no. 1 (2014): 47–71. https://doi.org/10.1017/S1755773912000276

Zürn, Michael, Martin Binder, and Matthias Ecker-Ehrhardt. "International Authority and Its Politicization." *International Theory* 4, no. 1 (2012): 69–106. https://doi.org/10.1017/S1752971912000012

Index

Note: Figures are indicated by *italics*. Tables are indicated by **bold**. Endnotes are indicated by the page number followed by 'n' and the endnote number e.g., 20n1 refers to endnote 1 on page 20.

For Product Safety Concerns and Information please contact our EU
representative GPSR@taylorandfrancis.com
Taylor & Francis Verlag GmbH, Kaufingerstraße 24, 80331 München, Germany

www.ingramcontent.com/pod-product-compliance
Ingram Content Group UK Ltd.
Pitfield, Milton Keynes, MK11 3LW, UK
UKHW020007200926
475702UK00015B/2527
* 9 7 8 1 0 3 2 6 9 5 3 8 9 *